Read or better yet, reread this book! L[...] [...]d style compels the readers to see their [...] [...]d with stinging Law, glorious Gospel, and imaginative application, *Deliver Us* informs, instructs, and inspires all who desire to better understand Exodus, the most important book of the Old Testament. Like few others can, Lessing mines the depth and breadth of the text and delivers caches of precious gems for scholarly and "average" Christ-followers alike. Ultimately and most importantly, *Deliver Us* delves into the depth of Yahweh's story and points us precisely to Jesus' story, becoming a prayer of mercy for all whom our gracious God calls to "walk by faith, not by sight" (2 Corinthians 5:7).
—**Rev. Dr. Brian L. Friedrich, president, Concordia University, St. Paul, Minnesota**

In *Deliver Us*, Reed Lessing takes the reader on a compelling journey through the Book of Exodus. With remarkable skill in handling God's Word, Dr. Lessing relates the Exodus events to the backstory of Genesis, highlights psalms that recall God's saving acts in Exodus, and most importantly, reveals how Exodus anticipates Christ. Whether he's explaining the ten plagues or the Ten Commandments, Dr. Lessing holds the reader's attention throughout with dynamic prose. Like a pastor preaching to his congregation, Dr. Lessing uses life applications to hit the bullseye. With *Deliver Us*, Dr. Lessing expertly bears witness to the God who delivers us!
—**Rev. Dr. Christopher Kennedy, senior pastor, Shepherd of the Hills Lutheran Church, School, and Child Care, San Antonio, Texas**

With *Deliver Us: God's Rescue Story in Exodus*, Dr. Lessing gifts the Church with a refreshing review of Exodus that is creative and intensely interesting. He handles this second book of Scripture with a pastor's heart and a biblical scholar's expertise. With abundant illustrations, he again and again effectively applies Exodus to the Church and to individual believers of the twenty-first century. Those who read his book will gain new insights into and have a greater familiarity with Exodus.
—**Dr. Walter A. Maier III, professor of exegetical theology, Concordia Theological Seminary, Fort Wayne, Indiana**

DELIVER US

GOD'S RESCUE
STORY IN EXODUS

R. REED LESSING

CONCORDIA PUBLISHING HOUSE • SAINT LOUIS

Published by Concordia Publishing House
3558 S. Jefferson Avenue, St. Louis, MO 63118-3968
1-800-325-3040 • cph.org

Manufactured in the United States of America

1 2 3 4 5 6 7 8 9 10   31 30 29 28 27 26 25 24 23 22

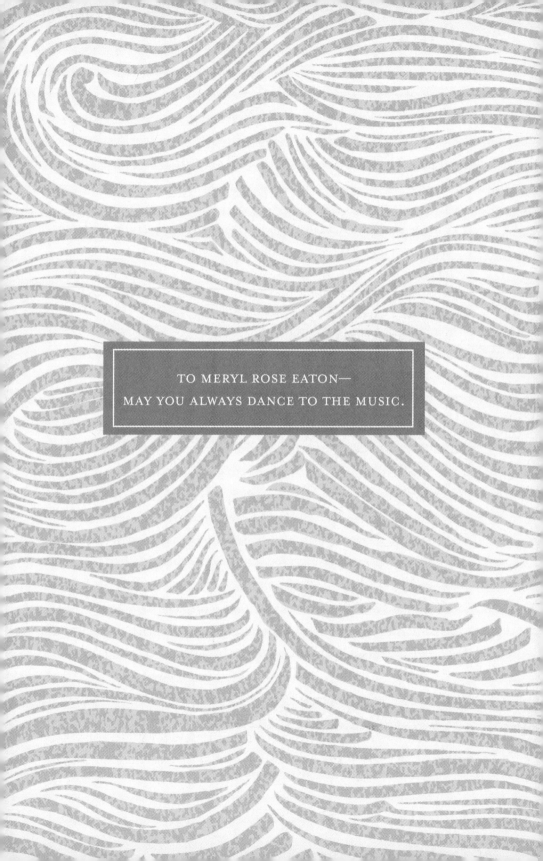

TO MERYL ROSE EATON—
MAY YOU ALWAYS DANCE TO THE MUSIC.

Introduction

I'm a lead-footed man in his sixties who can't carry a tune in a bucket. Although I took a mandatory music appreciation class in college and even played in a handbell choir, I've never known a lot about acoustics, notes, or singing in harmony. I do, however, recognize a good cadence when I hear it. And there's one in the Book of Exodus.

We need some background.

Moses writes, "There arose a new king over Egypt, who did not know Joseph" (Exodus 1:8 ESV). This king's name doesn't appear in the Book of Exodus. In fact, Moses never records the names of any Egyptian kings—also called pharaohs. Moses does, however, document the names of two women who begin the beat.

Down in the slave huts in Goshen we meet them—Shiphrah and Puah (Exodus 1:15). In his madness, the pharaoh wants these midwives to become his partners in killing Hebrew baby boys. The wave of Pharaoh's hand could mean life or death. But Shiphrah and Puah defy Pharaoh and resist his murderous rage. And just like that, they begin Israel's defiant dance of deliverance.

Soon the land of Goshen—the home of Israel in Egypt—starts swaying to the beat. The song picks up momentum when, with the second plague, Pharaoh is so distressed he tells Moses to remove countless frogs tomorrow (Exodus 8:10). Tomorrow? By the third plague (gnats), Egypt's magicians can't duplicate what God did through Moses and Aaron (Exodus 8:16–19). As divine afflictions become more intense, the tempo becomes more emphatic—reaching a summit with the Passover and death of every firstborn in Egypt. God saves Israel through lamb's blood along with a mighty hand and outstretched arm. He parts the Red Sea and crushes Pharaoh's army, along with his horses and chariots.

Who would have thought?

When the Israelites reach the other side of the Red Sea, Miriam and all the women—with tambourines in hand—dance to the music. Their song? "Sing to the LORD, for He has triumphed gloriously; the horse and his rider He has thrown into the sea" (Exodus 15:21 ESV).

We have a name for this song that keeps moving, keeps surprising, and keeps delivering. It's called the Gospel.

God reveals His symphony of celebration most magnificently in Jesus Christ our Lord. Another regime—this time Rome—did everything it could to pull the plug on our Savior's merciful melody. Pontius Pilate enlisted slappers, beaters, spitters, whippers, and mockers. And don't forget the nailers. But on the third day, the swing of salvation was amped up for the entire world to hear. Jesus is alive. Death has no more dominion over Him!

Have you lost the beat? forgotten the rhythm? misplaced the lyrics? Don't remember the tune? Do you feel like you're stuck in the slavery of anxiety, fear, worry, regret, and despair—with no way out? Have you had enough of bricks, whips, and the enemy's countless bag of tricks? Does your Red Sea look insurmountable and impassable?

I invite you to walk through the pages of Exodus with me. Grab your Bible. Take notes. Highlight. Underline. Pray. You will meet Shiphrah and Puah, Moses and Miriam, Aaron and Jethro—and best of all, you will meet Jesus, our Lord. Christ will move you from bondage to breaking free, from hopeless dirges to endless hallelujahs. *What Jesus did for Israel in the past, He will do for you today.* The Book of Exodus will have you swaying to the beat and dancing to the music. Why?

This is *our* story. This is *our* song.

TABLE OF CONTENTS

Introduction

CHAPTER 1

This Is Our Story:
An Introduction to Exodus

He turned the sea into dry land; they passed through the
river on foot. There did we rejoice in Him.
(Psalm 66:6 ESV)

The Book of Exodus has everything Hollywood would ever want. It's a gasp-and-gulp story with twists and turns that constantly shock and surprise. Cecil B. DeMille knew this. That's why he produced, directed, and narrated the 1956 blockbuster movie *The Ten Commandments*. Remember? It starred Charlton Heston as Moses and Yul Brynner as Pharaoh. Over a generation later—in 1998—Jeffrey Katzenberg, Steven Spielberg, and David Geffen of DreamWorks also realized that Exodus was a sure bet. That's why they created the animated movie *The Prince of Egypt*.

Without a doubt, Exodus is one of the world's greatest books ever written. Think about the burning bush, the ten plagues, the Passover, the Red Sea, the manna, the Ten Commandments, the golden calf, and the tabernacle. And then there's Moses!

More importantly, there's Yahweh.

In the Book of Exodus, we meet Yahweh—translated as "Lord" in most English Bibles—the God who wields all power in heaven and on earth. Yahweh is the God of Abraham, Isaac, and Jacob. He is devoted to their descendants, the Israelites, through thick and thin. Throughout Exodus, Yahweh is sovereign and saving, tough and tender, mighty and merciful. Yahweh is all of this—and so much more. He leads Israel from a known evil (Egypt) to an elusive good (the Promised Land). *This is our story as well.*

That's why the Book of Exodus invites us to enter its story—to get out of the stands, march onto the field, and get in the game. Moses writes the book so we can imagine ourselves in the drama—to strain under bricks, feel the east wind as it divides the Red Sea, and taste the manna on our lips and in our mouths. By firing our imaginations, the exodus narrative changes our identity, reshapes our desires, and forever redirects our future.

That's quite a story!

OUR STORY

Who said this? "Four score and seven years ago." Abraham Lincoln, in the *Gettysburg Address*. Who wrote this? "It was the best of times, it was the worst of times." Charles Dickens, in *A Tale of Two Cities*. Who made this line famous? "A long time ago in a galaxy far, far away." George Lucas in *Star Wars*. Who announced this on the steps of the Lincoln Memorial in Washington DC? "I have a dream." That's right, Martin Luther King Jr. What's my point? Everyone has a story.

Including you.

We begin telling stories when we're small children. Parents and teachers help us begin learning the skill of organizing experiences sequentially in time. "This happened. Then—by golly—that happened!" We revise our stories as we grow and get new information. "I didn't know we moved when I was just two years old." "So that's what happened to Uncle Bob? He died in an auto accident?" Telling our story and reinterpreting it along the way is how we adjust to life's joys and sorrows, highs and lows, ups and downs.

A parent's first words to a crying child who comes running to her are often, "What happened?" We know it's healthy to put terrifying experiences into stories as a way to process. Conversely, it's catastrophic when we can't verbalize our story. A wordless past implies a hopeless future.

How do we come up with our story? We collect experiences and order them into days and months, years and decades. We include heroes and villains; celebrations and humiliations; fire, tempest, darkness, and rain. Before we know it, we have our story. Every so often, though, we add to, delete, and edit it—especially when we experience major turning points in life.

THE DOMINANT STORY OF OUR DAY

Having just witnessed the birth of their first child, the new parents are ecstatic. The next day an attorney steps into the maternity room, puts down his briefcase, takes out a document, and begins reading it to the newborn child. Clearing his throat, the attorney warns, "Be advised that human life is difficult and, in all cases, ends in death. Some people have reported experiences with lethal viruses, esophageal cancer, and jihadist terrorists. Birth can also result in fatal encounters with tsunamis, drunk drivers, and nuclear disasters. Side effects of living include dental cavities, migraine headaches, and backed-up traffic on interstate highways. Welcome to the post-umbilical-cord world!"

Is this all there is to our story? Is it all just a series of setbacks that begin at the cradle and end in a casket? Many would say, "Yep. That's it. You've got it right. Life is a cosmic accident. We're here by chance. So have fun. Do it soon. When you die that's it—forever." The somber scenario continues. "When you die, you'll lose everything to the next generation. Your children will rent out your house, purge your possessions, and spend their inheritance wining and dining on the French Riviera. You'll become a distant memory at Thanksgiving meals and then be forgotten altogether."

What a sad story! Can this be true? Is this all there is?

THE EXODUS STORY

You're not stuck. Your feet aren't glued to the floor. The opportunity to live hasn't slipped through your hands. You're not bound to reliving stories that ricochet like bullets inside your head. The past need not hold sway. The walls can come tumbling down. Your story—no matter how painful—isn't set in stone.

Improvisational actors and actresses employ the phrase, "Yes, and." The goal is to keep the story going, which means neither negating nor agreeing with past statements, but adding something new that moves the story forward.

This is the Book of Exodus.

Moses invites us to emend, correct, and add to our story through his story—the Exodus story. The genius of Exodus is that God places us into its grand narrative. He wants us to say, "Yes, and." "Yes, I experienced a traumatic childhood. Yes, I have deep insecurity. Yes, I wrestle with a lack of self-worth and the fear of failure . . . *and* God has rescued me from my past, brought me out of bondage to sin through Holy Baptism, and now leads me to the promised land, even as He daily provides everything I need in Christ Jesus."

Our story doesn't need to stay stuck in perpetual pain. It doesn't have to be circular and marked with misery and despair. And we certainly don't have to keep letting others write our story—accenting our worst moments and greatest failures. As baptized believers in Jesus, we're part of a bigger story—the exodus story. God invites us to rewrite our well-rehearsed stories, adding to them His gifts of redemption and new life.

However, I must warn you. It takes spine to tamper with and edit our story. It's so much easier to let sleeping dogs lie. Would you like an example? Meet an invalid who became stuck in the same sorry story for thirty-eight years.

APATHY

Perpetual student Johnny Lechner finally moved on from the University of Wisconsin-Whitewater. We all probably know someone who extended a four-year college program into six or seven years. Lechner went well beyond that. He had been working on a four-year degree for twelve years. Lechner liked sleeping in late, listening to music, going to a class or two, and then hanging out with friends. What a life!

This sounds ridiculous on a college level—twelve years to get a four-year degree. But don't we all struggle with this on a personal level? Don't we all get comfortable and settle in? Don't we all become mired in the malaise of apathy?

Apathy is an English word made up of two Greek words—*a*, which means "no" and *pathos*, which means "passion." Apathy means I have no passion, no enthusiasm, no vim, no vigor. Apathy means my-get-up-and-go got up and went. And apathy's favorite word is what? "Whatever!" In John chapter 5, Jesus launches a frontal attack against apathy. Why? Jesus doesn't want our story to become encased in cement.

One day, while in Jerusalem on the Sabbath, Jesus comes to the Pool of Bethesda—an Aramaic word meaning "House of Mercy." Two thousand years ago, an underwater spring occasionally caused Bethesda to bubble. Some believed it meant an angel was dipping his wings into the water. They also believed that the first person to touch the water after the angelic presence would be healed. Did healing happen? I don't know. But I do know that a crowd of invalids was willing to give it a try. What did they have to lose?

Picture a World War I battleground in northern France strewn with bloodied bodies—and you see Bethesda. Imagine a senior care facility overcrowded and understaffed—and you see Bethesda. Call to mind the orphans in Bangladesh or the abandoned in Haiti—and you see Bethesda. Most people walked by, as quickly as possible. *But not Jesus.*

Remember the movie *Groundhog Day*? A television weatherman on location in Punxsutawney, Pennsylvania relives Groundhog Day, day after day. His story never changed. Sound familiar? It did to the invalid at Bethesda. Jesus asks him, "Do you want to be healed?" (John 5:6 ESV).

One pastor was showing a neighboring pastor around his new church and, referring to the sound system, he said, "We still have a number of dead spots." His pastor friend said, "Brother, every church has a number of dead spots!"

Oh, we get by, don't we? We show up and yawn our way through the ordeal. Like the muddy Mississippi, we roll along. We shrug our shoulders, make excuses, and keep living half-baked, half-hearted Christian lives.

Apathy is killing us.

It was one of those high school classes where you arrived early to get a *back*-row seat. One day, two students got there late, so they had to sit in front-row seats. Let's just say that they were less than enthusiastic when it came to trigonometry. The teacher finally got fed up. He grabbed a piece of chalk, turned around to the chalkboard, and began slashing away in big letters: A-P-A-T-H-Y. The trig teacher underlined it twice, then slammed an exclamation point that broke the chalk. One of the students in the front row struggled to read the word. He slowly said, "A-pay-thee." Then he leaned over and asked his friend, "What is a-pay-thee?" His friend's response? "Who cares?"

What is a-pay-thee—*apathy*—doing in your life? How is it eroding your faith? Hurting your health? Damaging your work? Harming your children? How long have you had that bad attitude? That bad habit? That bad excuse? That bad addiction? Has it been thirty-eight years? And what's that look like in your story?

John's Gospel begins with this statement, "In the beginning was the Word" (John 1:1 ESV). Christ is the Word. Christ has the Word. Christ gives the Word. Christ speaks the Word. *Christ writes new stories through His almighty Word.*

It reminds me of a private who one day caught Napoleon's runaway horse. When he brought it back, Napoleon said, "Thank you, *Captain*." With one word, the private was promoted to captain. The soldier went to the quartermaster and asked for a captain's uniform. He went to the officer's quarters and chose a captain's bunk. He went to the officer's hall and ate a meal with all the captains. Napoleon said it. That settled it. The soldier believed it. He went from a private to a captain with just a word.

Through His Word, Christ turns our place of pain into Bethesda—a house full of mercy. "Jesus said to him, 'Get up, take up your bed, and walk.' And at once the man was healed, and he took up his bed and walked" (John 5:8–9 ESV). That's what I call a new story. Apathy is undone!

THIS IS MY STORY

"Blessed Assurance" is a well-known Christian hymn. Fanny Crosby—who was blind from infancy—wrote the lyrics in 1873. They include these words: "This is my story, this is my song."

Paul's teacher Rabbi Gamaliel would resonate with these lyrics. As quoted in the *Mishnah Pesachim,* an early Jewish writing, Gamaliel said, "In every generation a person must so regard themselves as if they themselves came forth out of Egypt." The Mishnah continues with these mandates:

> Therefore we are obligated to thank, praise, glorify, extol, exalt, honor, bless, revere, and laud the One who performed for our forefathers and for us all these miracles: He took us out from slavery to freedom, from sorrow to joy, from mourning to a festival, from darkness to a great light, and from enslavement to redemption.

What God did for Israel He does for all who call on His name. That's what Gamaliel teaches. So does Paul. And so does Moses.

How can we make the exodus story our story?

We can use our imagination. There's a big difference between imagination and fantasy. Fantasy sees what isn't real. Fantasy lives in the land of make-believe. Fantasy fixates on a Never Never Land.

God, on the other hand, invites us to use our spiritual imagination. His Word engages us not only on a cognitive or knowledge level but also on an experiential level. Propositional truth is very important—but God wants to do more than correct our faulty thinking. God also wants to change our affections and emotions. He wants to change our stories, and He does it through our sanctified imagination.

Here's the bad news. According to Genesis 6:5, our imagination has been twisted and broken by sin—it's only evil all the time. Here's the good news. God reshapes and restores our imagination. God enables us as new creations in Christ to envision what is real. Here, Hebrews 11:27 comes up huge. It says of Moses, "He endured as seeing Him who is invisible" (ESV). Moses used his God-given imagination to become part of a greater story—God's exodus story. Paul, for his part, summons us to visualize great things from God—who can do far more than we ask or imagine (Ephesians 3:20).

EXODUS IN THE OLD TESTAMENT

Several Old Testament authors employ the exodus motif to spark their readers' imagination, inviting believers to see themselves in the story. That is to say, after the books of the Pentateuch, Moses doesn't do the saving. Joshua, David, or someone like Elijah functions as God's deliverer. Pharaoh isn't the enemy. Eglon, Sennacherib, or Nebuchadnezzar wears the black hat. And the Israelites aren't leaving Egypt and going to the Promised Land. They are, however, leaving sin and death and heading toward heaven. God's action in the past creates confidence that in current Egyptlike pain, He will come through. Old Testament writers assert that if Yahweh did it once—even twice—He can do it again.

Let us count the ways!

King David was under the gun. The superscription for Psalm 18 states, "The LORD delivered him from the hand of all his enemies, and from the hand of Saul." How did God deliver David? Through Exodus power and might. "Then the channels of the sea were seen, and the foundations of the world were laid bare at Your rebuke, O LORD, at *the blast of the breath of Your nostrils*. He sent from on high, He took me; *He drew me* out of many waters" (Psalm 18:15–16 ESV, emphasis added). The expression, "the blast of Your nostrils" comes directly from Exodus 15:8 (ESV)—Israel's song at the Red Sea. Additionally, David's statement, "He drew me out" comports with Exodus 2:10, where God saves Moses from death by drowning in the Nile River. In fact, *Moses* is a Hebrew word that means "draw out of water." Both Israel's rescue at the sea and Moses' rescue from the river become David's rescue from his enemies—especially King Saul. *The Book of Exodus gives David his story and his song.*

Other psalms appropriate Israel's salvation at the Red Sea—along with Moses' experience at the Nile—to describe divine deliverance from adversaries. Mimicking David, these psalmists use water imagery to depict their foes, as David does when he praises Yahweh for salvation from "many waters" (Psalm 144:7 ESV) or "flood [that] would have swept us away" (Psalm 124:4 ESV). Motifs from Exodus are reworked and applied to the author's current crisis.

Psalm 66:6 is more pointed. It envisions *us*—yes, you and me—as going through the Red Sea. "He turned the sea into dry land; they passed through the river on foot. There did *we* rejoice in Him" (ESV). What God does for Moses and Israel, He does for all His people. When we're faced with an overwhelming flood of pain, problems, and perplexities, God shows up for us—just like He did in the Book of Exodus.

That's what Moses teaches us to imagine. "The Egyptians mistreated *us* and made *us* suffer, putting *us* to hard labor. Then *we* cried out to Yahweh, the God of our fathers, and Yahweh heard *our* voice and saw *our* misery, toil and oppression. So Yahweh brought *us* out of Egypt"

(Deuteronomy 26:6–8, emphasis added). What God did in the past, God still does today.

This story is our story! This is our song!

Isaiah knows. He uses Israel's exodus from Egypt to announce God's saving power for sixth-century Judean exiles in Babylon. We can compare Isaiah's adoption of the story to a musical shift to a higher key. In Isaiah 40–55, the prophet portrays God's rescue of Israel from Babylonian captivity as a new exodus—only bigger and better. Consider this prophetic oracle and watch how the prophet composes it in the present tense: "Thus *says* the LORD, who *makes* a way in the sea, a path in the mighty waters, who *brings* forth chariot and horse, army and warrior; they lie down, they cannot rise, they *are* extinguished, quenched like a wick" (Isaiah 43:16–17 ESV, emphasis added). God renews exodus mercy and might for forlorn Babylonian refugees. Every nation that comes after Israel with chariots and horses—or any weapon of war—is bound to fail.

Staring down the same evil empire in late seventh century BC, Habakkuk prays, "O LORD, I have heard the report of You, and Your work, O LORD, do I fear. In the midst of the years revive it; in the midst of the years make it known" (Habakkuk 3:2 ESV). To paraphrase the prophet, "God, make the exodus story our story!"

CHRIST'S EXODUS

The full meaning of Israel's deliverance at the Red Sea—frequently rehearsed and reiterated in the Old Testament—comes to fruition in Christ. When speaking with Moses and Elijah on the Mount of Transfiguration, Jesus refers to His death and resurrection. Importantly, He uses the Greek word *exodus* (Luke 9:31). Just as Israel miraculously passed through the water and into the Promised Land, so Jesus promises He will pass from death to life.

Christ's Easter exodus from the grave on the third day is how He leads us—the new Israel—out of the bondage of our Egypt. In 1 Corinthians 10:16, Paul underscores our participation with Jesus where he teaches that in the Holy Supper we receive Christ's true body and blood. Likewise, through the sacrament of Holy Baptism, the apostle announces that we share in Christ's exodus story (1 Corinthians 10:2).

EXODIZED

Several years ago, I was talking with my older sister about our childhood home in Denver, Colorado. Luann insisted we had a slide and a swing set in our backyard. I said we didn't. The conversation went back and forth until Luann began digging through some old pictures and—sure enough—she found several black-and-white photos with both of us on the slide and in the swings.

Just because I didn't remember our slide and swing set doesn't mean they weren't in our backyard. And—infinitely more important—just because we may not remember our baptismal salvation doesn't mean it didn't save us. We might have a certificate, perhaps a candle, and probably beautiful pictures—in color!

In Holy Baptism, we experience a personal exodus. Like Pharaoh long ago, our old self drowns and dies. And, baptized into Christ, like Israel long ago, we are freed from bondage and are now heading for our heavenly promised land. We joyfully confess with Martin Luther, who clung to these words when tempted by Satan, "I *am* baptized!" Exodus grace and goodness are ours—*now*. To coin a word, Baptism exodizes us.

Do you see the progression? Holy Baptism connects us to Jesus, who, in turn, connects us to Israel's exodus story.

That's what Paul tells believers in Rome. He writes, "All of us who have been baptized into Christ Jesus were baptized into His death" (Romans 6:3 ESV). Where does Paul get the idea that what happened to Jesus happened to us too? From the Book of Exodus! When Jesus was crucified, so was our old Adam and ancient Eve. The apostle affirms, "Our old self was crucified with Him" (Romans 6:6 ESV). Our sinful past is past—it's crucified, dead, and buried.

Baptism not only forgives the past. Baptism empowers life today. "We were buried therefore with Him by baptism into death, in order that, just as Christ was raised from the dead by the glory of the Father, we too might walk in newness of life" (Romans 6:4 ESV). Our walk is new. We have new hope and a new attitude.

The past? Forgiven. The present? Empowered. What about the future? It's most glorious! "For if we have been united with Him in a death like His, we shall certainly be united with Him in a resurrection like His" (Romans 6:5 ESV). Can you imagine that?

When we put Romans 6:3–5 together, what do we see? Christ's story is our story. We were dead. Now we're alive. We were sinking in sand. Now we're standing on the Rock. We lived like victims. Now we live in victory—Christ's resurrection victory. God brought us out of bondage to sin. Today we're living in God's wonderful promises in Jesus Christ. This is our story and we're sticking to it!

NEW TESTAMENT ECHOES OF THE EXODUS

The Holy Spirit inspired the Bible so that earlier parts correspond with later parts. Old Testament exodus patterns provide a grid that New Testament authors build upon. These writers, though, do more than consent to the truth of Israel's exodus. For them it's a lived reality. Israel's exodus informed *and* transformed them.

Peter, for example, envisions the baptized as having left bondage in Egypt and currently pressing on toward their inheritance in heaven (1 Peter 1:4). Like Israel, believers have been purchased with the Passover Lamb's blood—the blood of Jesus (1 Peter 1:19). Moreover, Peter's phrase, "girding your loins" (1 Peter 1:13), is an exodus image meaning that it's time to leave Egypt (cf. Exodus 12:11)—our old life of slavery to sin. Using the words of Exodus 19:5–6, 1 Peter 2:9 affirms, "You are a chosen race, a royal priesthood, a holy nation, a people for His own possession" (ESV). *Exodus history is our history.*

Take the Book of Revelation. John follows Peter, Paul, and others by employing the Book of Exodus to describe what God is doing now. In Revelation 1:4—a reflection of Exodus 3:14—John signals for us to read his book through the lens of Israel's exodus from Egypt. After all, we're the new Israel, for Christ has "made us a kingdom, priests to His God" (Revelation 1:6 ESV)—a clear echo of Exodus 19:6.

Twenty-eight times in Revelation, John calls Jesus the Lamb. Christ is not only the slaughtered Passover Lamb. Christ is the victorious Lamb (Revelation 17:14) who will reign as King forever and ever (Revelation 11:15)—a direct quote from Exodus 15:18.

Cementing these links between Exodus and Revelation, John asserts that in the new heavens and new earth, "the sea was no more" (Revelation 21:1 ESV). Here, the term *sea* connotes universal evil. And, just as God dried up the sea for Israel to escape from Egypt, so He will remove every form of evil from the new Jerusalem. As a matter of fact, the movement in both Exodus and Revelation 21–22 is through threatening waters, to the mountain (Exodus 19:1; Revelation 21:10), for worship (Exodus 24–40; Revelation 21:22). Revelation's final exodus is the first exodus in a much greater way.

Here's my main point: Israel's exodus from Egypt is the central storyline of the Bible and God's plan for the world. Through the Book of Exodus, God established a pattern for the rest of Holy Scripture as well as for our own stories. Divine salvation and God's unrivaled rule form the backbone of the biblical narrative, fire the imagination of Israel's poets, and shape the New Testament understanding of the Gospel. *The Book of Exodus provides the fundamental message of Holy Scripture.*

THE BACKSTORY

I hope you're seeing that the exodus story isn't a one-off, an outlier, or just one part of the Bible. The exodus story is *the* story. The exodus story is *our* story. It's a story, though, with a backstory.

How do backstories work? Good question!

Backstories create a network of words, characters, and events to give insight and depth to the main story. Expressed differently, backstories take place on a side stage to illumine action on the center stage.

In the original Hebrew, the Book of Exodus begins with the word *and*. Exodus 1:1 literally states, "*And* these are the names." The conjunction *and* implies continuity. It connects Exodus with its backstory—the Book of Genesis. *Exodus takes Genesis forward.*

The next six words in the Hebrew of Exodus 1:1 repeat the words of Genesis 46:8. Both list a genealogy. Additionally, Exodus 1:7 comes very close to the creational ideas expressed in Genesis 1:28 and 9:1.

Just like peas and carrots, Laurel and Hardy, and Batman and Robin, Genesis and Exodus are meant for each other. What God does for Abraham's family in Genesis, He repeats for the entire nation of Israel in Exodus.

Would you like to see more connections between the two books? I hope so! First, Pharaoh's building program (Exodus 1:10–11) mirrors the Tower of Babel account in Genesis 11:1–9. Both display pride and pretense. Both fall under divine judgment. Second, Moses' "ark" (Exodus 2:3) is a Means of Grace, just like Noah's ark. In fact, the Hebrew word rendered ark, *tebat*, only appears in the Old Testament in these two places—inviting us to expect that Moses, like Noah, will accomplish great things for God. Third, Exodus 13:21 describes light in the darkness, an echo of Genesis 1:3, while the division of the Red Sea (Exodus 14:21) equates with Genesis 1:7 when God divides the water above from the water below. Fourth, the emergence of dry land (Exodus 14:29) also comports with Genesis 1:9 where God says, "Let the dry land appear" (ESV).

These comparisons, however, are secondary to the primary backstory in Genesis for Exodus—Abram's departure out of Egypt. Note these events that connect the two books:

- God poured out plagues against Egypt both when a pharaoh tried to take Sarai as his wife as well as when another pharaoh refused to let Israel go (Genesis 12:17; Exodus 7–12).
- The pharaohs command people to leave Egypt (Genesis 12:19; Exodus 12:30–33).

- God's people depart from the land of the Nile (Genesis 13:1; Exodus 13:18), leaving with great possessions (Genesis 12:20; Exodus 12:35–36).

Moses confirms these parallels by using the same words in both books. For instance, the noun *plague* occurs in the Old Testament in Genesis 12:17 and then again in Exodus 11:1—the first two uses of the word in the Bible. Moreover, the words for "severe famine" and "descend" to Egypt come in Genesis 12:10; 43:15; and 47:4—setting up both departures from the land of the Nile in Exodus.

What are we to make of these thematic and verbal associations? Because God delivered Abram from Egypt, He will do the same for Moses and Israel.

Add Genesis 15 to our growing list. It's a pivotal backstory for the Book of Exodus. Let's consider a few links. First, Moses writes, "Then the LORD said to Abram, 'Know for certain that your offspring will be sojourners in a land that is not theirs and will be servants there, and they will be *afflicted* for four hundred years. But I will bring judgment on the nation that they serve, and afterward they shall come out with great possessions" (Genesis 15:13–14 ESV, emphasis added). In addition to providentially predicting plagues and possessions, the word *afflict* (Genesis 15:13) functions like a drumbeat in the early chapters of Exodus (e.g., Exodus 1:11, 12; 3:7; 4:31). Second, in Genesis 15:17, God appears in, with, and under a billow of smoke and flaming torch—previewing His leading Israel out of Egypt through cloud and fire (Exodus 13:21). Moses seals these Genesis/Exodus connections with these words, spoken by Yahweh to Abram: "I am the LORD who brought you out from Ur of the Chaldeans" (Genesis 15:7 ESV). Note the parallel in Exodus 20:2: "I am the LORD your God, who brought you out of the land of Egypt" (ESV). Abram's escape from Ur and its idolatry (see Joshua 24:2) prefigures Israel's escape from Egypt with its false gods (see Exodus 12:12). Genesis 15 has exodus written all over it.

When we arrive at the Sodom and Gomorrah narrative in Genesis 18–19, exodus connections again pick up their pace. Abraham (God changed his name in Genesis 17:5) and Sarah serve their divine guests "cakes" and "unleavened bread" (Genesis 18:6). In Genesis 19:3, Lot serves his angelic guests "unleavened bread." These terms don't appear again until the Passover narrative (Exodus 12:8, 15, 17, 18, 20, 39; 13:6, 7). Additionally, both stories share these motifs:

- They're the only two places in the Old Testament that have human "crying" along with God's "descent" to "see" and "know" about the problem (Genesis 18:20–21; Exodus 3:7–9).

- Lot's departure from Sodom includes the exodus terms "passing," "destroying," "making haste," and "rising up to go" (Genesis 18:3, 5; 19:14; Exodus 12:23, 31).

- Both stories highlight safety behind a door (Genesis 19:6–11; Exodus 12:7–14).

- Just as Lot's wife hesitated to leave Sodom (Genesis 19:16, 26), which was "like the land of Egypt" (Genesis 13:10 ESV), so Israel continually looked back to Egypt (e.g., Exodus 14:12; 16:3; 17:3). At one point, they even call Egypt "a land flowing with milk and honey" (Numbers 16:13 ESV).

During our journey through Exodus, we'll discover many more places, plots, and people that first appear in Genesis. Knowing the backstory is critical to knowing the Exodus story—and hence our story.

INTERNAL CONNECTIONS

The Book of Exodus is a long story. My! It has forty chapters! How can we keep track of it all?

Moses helps us. He composed the Bible's second book with internal links to provide overall structure and coherence. A few examples are in order. Moses' salvation from the Nile River (Exodus 2:5) prefigures Israel's deliverance at the Red Sea (Exodus 14). His killing one Egyptian (Exodus 2:11–12) foreshadows divine retribution against many Egyptians. Moses' ability to provide water for Zipporah and her sisters (Exodus 2:17) foreshadows his water miracles both at Marah (Exodus

15:23–27) and at Rephidim (Exodus 17:1–7). The divine visitation in the burning bush (Exodus 3) presages God's presence upon Mount Sinai (Exodus 19). Moses' encounter with God with deadly intent (Exodus 4:24–26) points to the Passover and Egypt's similar experience when God passes through Egypt and strikes down every firstborn person and animal (Exodus 12:1–13).

Additionally, many plagues point to greater Egyptian disasters at the Red Sea. For example, Aaron's rod swallows the magicians' rods (Exodus 7:12) thus foreshadowing the Egyptian army getting swallowed in judgment and death (Exodus 15:12). These are the only verses in the book where Moses employs the verb *swallow*—binding the two events together.

Exodus has many more early events that preview later ones. Be on the lookout. I'll help along the way!

OUTLINING EXODUS

There are at least four different ways we can outline the Book of Exodus. The first is based upon locations:

- Israel in Egypt (Exodus 1:1–13:16)
- Israel in the wilderness (Exodus 13:17–18:27)
- Israel at Sinai (Exodus 19:1–40:38)

The second highlights divine benefits:

- God's gift of salvation (Exodus 1:1–18:27)
- God's gift of His Word (Exodus 19:1–24:18)
- God's gift of the tabernacle (Exodus 25:1–40:38)

Both outlines accent movement—Israel's and Yahweh's. Israel goes from bondage to freedom, from despair to praise, from Egypt to Sinai, and from serving Pharaoh by building store cities to serving Yahweh by building a tabernacle. Yahweh is also on the move. He's almost completely absent in Exodus 1 when a pharaoh's genocidal policies make life a living hell for Israel. Yet, by chapter 3, Yahweh comes down into the burning bush—foreshadowing His descent upon Mount Sinai in Exodus 19. By the end of the book, Yahweh has moved into the tabernacle, filling it with glory.

A third way to outline Exodus is through the Hebrew word for "serve." Appearing ninety-seven times in the book, *serve* may denote slave labor (e.g., Exodus 1:14; 2:23; 6:6). However, when applied to Israel after the exodus, it means service to Yahweh (e.g., Exodus 27:19; 36:1, 3, 5; 39:32, 42). From this viewpoint, the Book of Exodus describes Israel's progress from serving one master to another. One kills and destroys. The other liberates and loves. This question, then, drives one of the book's major plot lines. Whom will Israel serve? A cruel ruler who knows no mercy or their rightful King whose mercy never ends?

A fourth way to understand Exodus is through its two main features—deliverance from Egypt and a divine encounter on Mount Sinai. That is, rescue from Pharaoh and a relationship with Yahweh. Exodus 6:6–7 describes this two-part structure. After initial resistance from Pharaoh in chapter 5, Yahweh reassures Moses: "I will bring you out from under the burdens of the Egyptians, and I will deliver you from slavery to them, and I will redeem you with an outstretched arm and with great acts of judgment" (Exodus 6:6 ESV) and "I will take you to be My people, and I will be your God" (Exodus 6:7 ESV). Exodus 6:6 refers to Yahweh's actions in Exodus 1–18, while Exodus 6:7 refers to Yahweh's covenant-making and dwelling with Israel in the rest of Exodus—the part of the book where Israel frequently rebels against God. The prophet Hosea likewise envisions the story as having two parts. "When Israel was a child, I loved him, and out of Egypt I called My son [Exodus 1–18]. The more they were called, the more they went away [Exodus 19–40]" (Hosea 11:1–2 ESV).

THE HISTORICAL SETTING

The Book of Exodus is a story of two kingdoms in conflict—God's and Egypt's. Hell will freeze over before they settle on a truce. And there's no demilitarized zone where people can live peacefully, claiming to be neutral. Both kingdoms demand unbending loyalty. There can be no compromise. Pharaoh's kingdom is deceptive and dark. Yahweh's is full of grace and truth. When did this battle for the ages take place?

Joseph came to power (see Genesis 41:37–46) when the Hyksos pharaohs ruled the land of the Nile. *Hyksos* means "rulers of foreign lands" and refers to outsiders from modern-day Syria and Iraq. Pharaoh Ahmose I (1539–1515 BC)—an indigenous Egyptian king—defeated the Hyksos and thus reunified Lower Egypt with Upper Egypt. This makes Ahmose I the pharaoh "who did not know Joseph" (Exodus 1:8 ESV). He refused to honor prior arrangements with the Hebrews because they were made by a former Hyksos pharaoh—a despised foreigner. Why help Joseph's descendants? He became prime minister during enemy occupation!

The result? With Exodus 1:8, Egypt deemed the Israelites foreigners in a land that now despised foreigners. The events of Exodus 1–2 occur right after this changing of the guard.

During this time, the Hebrews labored under Ahmose I to build the store cities of Pithom and Raamses (Exodus 1:11). The only time when Hebrews could have worked at Pithom was during the fifteenth century BC. This means that Raamses in Exodus 1:11 is a scribal update—at the time the city was called Goshen (cf. Genesis 47:11). Understood this way, Raamses in Exodus 1:11 is like Dan in Genesis 14:14—a later updating of the text. Such clarifications appear in other places in the Pentateuch (e.g., Genesis 13:18; 14:14; 23:19; 37:14; Numbers 13:22; 14:45; 21:3; Deuteronomy 1:44).

Therefore, putting the relevant data together, Moses was born into Israel's cauldron of pain in 1526 BC. When he was forty years old and wanted for murder, Moses high-tailed it out of Egypt and remained exiled in Midian for forty years (Acts 7:29; cf. Exodus 2:23). Thus, counting back eighty years (Exodus 7:7) from the time Moses spoke to Pharaoh immediately preceding the plagues (Exodus 7:14–25), the exodus happened in 1446 BC. The pharaoh of the exodus, therefore, was Thutmose III (1479–1425 BC).

Under Thutmose III, Egypt reached one of its military zeniths, sending forth seventeen campaigns into the Fertile Crescent. Back at home, Thutmose added to Egypt's monumental architecture by enslaving foreigners, some of whom were Hebrews. One piece of artwork — created in Egypt in about 1460 BC—depicts outsiders making bricks for a temple in Thebes.

The year of Israel's departure from slavery is confirmed by 1 Kings 6:1—a verse indicating that the exodus occurred 480 years before the fourth year of Solomon's reign. Solomon's fourth year was 967 BC, supporting the Exodus date in 1446 BC.

Judges 11:26 further affirms this chronology. Jephthah argues against the Ammonite's aggressive moves on the basis that Israel had a right to the land because they had occupied it for 300 years. If 1100 BC is taken as a proximate date for Jephthah's activities, this would place Israel's occupation of the Transjordan under Moses (Numbers 21) around 1400 BC—about forty years after the Hebrew slaves left Egypt.

It's common to assume that only one pharaoh appears in the Book of Exodus. Exodus 1–15, however, introduces us to three: (1) Exodus 1:1–7 implies that there was a Hyksos pharaoh who welcomed Joseph and his family; (2) Pharaoh Ahmose I, who enslaved the Hebrews (Exodus 1:8) and whose death is mentioned in Exodus 2:23 and 4:19; and (3) the pharaoh of the exodus, Thutmose III (Exodus 4:21–15:21). In later texts (e.g., 1 Kings 11:40; 2 Kings 19:9; 23:33–35), Old Testament authors name pharaohs. Why, then, doesn't Moses? By not giving pharaonic names, he employs the Egyptian custom of not naming an enemy so as to bring him shame and not glory.

CHRIST IN THE BOOK OF EXODUS

The Book of Exodus describes burning bushes that don't burn, plagues that are beyond normal, sea walls that stand still, a wilderness that miraculously waters and feeds people, and a mountain with a fire on its top. Yet, in all its shock and awe, this book of Moses does more than present a history lesson of Israel's past. More importantly, Exodus paints a beautiful portrait of Jesus.

How so?

Like Israel, Jesus was called out of Egypt (Matthew 2:15; cf. Hosea 11:1). And, like Israel, Jesus celebrates Passover (e.g., Mark 14:12–25)—yet He is also paradoxically the Passover Lamb (1 Corinthians 5:7). Jesus is like Moses when He gives divine instruction upon a mountainside (Matthew 5–7). And John compares Jesus to Israel's tabernacle as well as its divine glory (John 1:14).

Christ is also prefigured in the Book of Exodus because He shares many of Israel's traits. Like Israel (Exodus 4:22), Jesus is the Father's firstborn Son—both in creation and in redemption (Colossians 1:15, 18). Additionally, similar to Israel's forty-year wilderness journey (Deuteronomy 1:3), Christ was tempted in the wilderness for forty days (e.g., Matthew 4:1–11). He is the Rock that followed Israel in the desert (1 Corinthians 10:4; cf. Exodus 17:1–7) and He assumed the role of Moses as the world's greatest intercessor (e.g., Luke 23:34; Hebrews 7:25; cf. Exodus 32:11–14).

John—more than Matthew, Mark, and Luke—builds a large part of his Gospel upon the Book of Exodus. Consider these words of Jesus in John 5:46, "For if you believed Moses, you would believe Me; for he wrote of Me" (ESV). The most important link between Moses and Jesus, however, is the Passover—a festival that the fourth evangelist refers to in his Gospel in John 2:13, 23; 6:4; 11:55; 12:1; 13:1; 18:28, 39; and 19:14. John is emphatic. Jesus is the Passover Lamb (John 1:29, 36). That's why His crucifixion coincides with the Jewish Passover (John 19:14).

The Fourth Gospel also accents Yahweh's "I AM" statement in Exodus 3:14. John records Christ's seven "I am" statements (John 6:35; 8:12; 10:7, 11; 11:25; 14:6; 15:1). With his love of sevens, John also documents seven signs that comport with several of the signs/plagues in Exodus (John 2:1–11; 4:46–54; 5:1–15; 6:5–14, 16–21; 9; 11:1–45). God gives both sets so people may know Him (e.g., Exodus 9:29; John 20:30–31). Finally, John alludes to Israel's bondage and subsequent freedom from Egypt when he records these words of Jesus: "If the Son sets you free, you will be free indeed" (John 8:36 ESV).

You and I need freedom from slavery—from a modern-day Egypt.

OUR ADDRESS IS EGYPT

Israel's exodus is not an event bound to the past. God's deliverance is ongoing. One of the most important implications of this truth is that we're slaves. We're all slaves to selfishness, sin, and the spiritual reality behind our misery—the ancient serpent who is the devil and Satan.

Both Israel's and our story begin in captivity. What does that look like? It's heaven at the top but it's hell at the bottom. That's why we spend much of our lives scrambling to the top of pyramids. One way we do this is by seeking people's approval.

Our longing for acceptance and approval influences the kind of clothes we wear, the kind of car we drive, the kind of house we buy, even the kind of career we choose. Remember how as a teen you longed to be accepted—even to the degree that when someone from your group said, "I dare you," you did it because you wanted to be popular? Some of us have colorful high school stories that revolve around this idea—and we won't tell our children until they turn forty. Even then, some of the more embarrassing details will be edited out!

There's a part in all of us that wants to be accepted, validated, and affirmed by Egypt's movers and shakers. Think of "Egypt" as this world that enslaves us with promises it can't keep and with pleasures that will never endure.

This is why the Bible depicts Egypt as more than just a totalitarian state obsessed with money, machinery, and making profits. The land of the Nile is also likened to Rahab, a sea monster that wreaks spiritual death and destruction. Note that this Rahab is different from the Rahab in Joshua 2 where the name denotes the prostitute who hid Israel's twelve spies. Although spelled the same in English, each Rahab is spelled differently in Hebrew.

The association of Egypt with Rahab—a dragonlike sea monster—appears in Psalms 87:4 and 89:10, as well as in Isaiah 30:7. These verses explain why the "snake" representing Egypt in Exodus 4:3 becomes a "dragon" in Exodus 7:9–10. Who is the ultimate dragon in the Bible?

You probably know—Satan.

The God who sets people free from seeking approval from Egypt/Rahab is the same God who also frees us from captivity to another enemy, spelled M-O-R-E—more.

CRUSHED BY MORE

I don't know about you, but I could do without those stern warnings in the television pharmaceutical commercials. I understand why these ads issue such harsh warnings. By law, medical manufacturers must warn us about potential tragedies so that, when we take their pills and grow a third arm or a second head, we can't sue them. I get that. Still, there's something unsettling about merging happy faces with voice-over warnings about death.

Welcome to Egypt—the land of happy faces trying to conceal death's harsh reality. From one angle, everything looks good and grand. Happy people are financing, building, and profiting from all the pyramids. From another angle, people are dying—Hebrew slaves down in the land of Goshen. To fill their bank accounts and pad their savings, Egyptians enslaved the descendants of Abraham, Isaac, and Jacob to make bricks. This sick system was driven by one word, one idea, one concept: *more.*

Most buildings in Egypt were made from the alluvial mud supplied by the Nile. To get an idea of how organized the brick-making business was, consider that the pyramids of Pharaoh Sesostris III (1878–1839 BC) at Dahshur took 24.5 million bricks to build. That's a whole lot of mud! And there was always the need for more.

It's hardly surprising that Egyptians considered brick makers to be dirtier than pigs. Mud, dirt, dust, and sweat covered Hebrew slaves until their skin began to harden and crack. We think that occasionally we have a tough day at work! And get this. Egypt's slaves were rarely—if ever—allowed to bathe.

Historians believe that within two decades, brick makers' arms and legs were rendered useless because of their bone-crushing work. Soon after that, people died. Egypt was ruled by spiritual monsters—indeed, dragons—that chewed people up and spit them out, one brick, one building, one pyramid at a time.

Thutmose III wouldn't concede an inch: "He said, 'You are lazy, lazy; that is why you say, 'Let us go and sacrifice to Yahweh'" (Exodus 5:17). The pharaoh's foremen bark out these orders: "You shall by no means reduce your number of bricks, your daily task each day" (Exodus 5:19 ESV). The king cared for people only insofar as they were instruments to produce wealth for those who wielded all the power. And the slaves? They were dehumanized in a system that was reduced to a single pharaonic mandate: "More bricks!" There's that word again—*more*.

Wet clay and straw were poured into molds, then placed on slaves' heads, who carried bricks to be baked. Once hardened, bricks were hauled again—this time to the worksite. The expression "back-breaking work" took on a new definition.

Egypt's system was so successful that the regime needed *more* space to store *more* stuff. "They built for Pharaoh store cities, Pithom and Raamses" (Exodus 1:11 ESV).

EGYPT 2.0

Solomon famously writes, "There is nothing new under the sun" (Ecclesiastes 1:9 ESV). Egypt, in the days of Moses and Miriam, lives on. Take, for instance, our own "store cities." In America, storage units generate an annual profit of $39.5 billion. Want a few more numbers? In the United States, we have over 49,000 storage facilities that take up 1.9 billion square feet. That's more than the rest of the world's storage space combined. It's not enough. Americans need more space for more stuff. Welcome to "Egypt 2.0."

Americans measure success not only by the amount of stuff we have but also by the square footage of our home. In the 1940s, the average new American home was 1,200 square feet. By 1983, the average was 1,700 square feet. In 2016, the average new home had a square footage of 2,600 square feet. We have succumbed to the pharaonic mandate, "More bricks!" Need more convincing?

When Bernie Madoff wasn't flying his private jet or watching sunrises from the deck of one of his yachts, he was living a life of luxury inside his ten-thousand-square-foot apartment in New York City. One of his yachts put him back a measly seven million dollars. His jet cost twenty-four million dollars. He had homes in France, on Long Island, and in Palm Beach, Florida. To stand in his Manhattan office was to stand in the epicenter of financial success. *Or so it seemed.*

It was the morning of December 10, 2008. That's when it all ended. That's when he faced the music. That's when Bernie Madoff confessed that it was all one big, gigantic lie—a huge Ponzi scheme. Madoff swindled people out of 65 billion dollars—65 *billion* dollars!

What makes a person live a lie for years? For decades? For their entire lives? You know. It's easy to get addicted. One word—*more.*

Egypt lives on.

Bernie Madoff lost just about everything. At age 71, he was sentenced to life in prison, and he died behind bars at 82. In 2010, one of his sons committed suicide. In 2022, a sister and brother-in-law died in an apparent murder-suicide. Madoff's mistake? He became obsessed with bricks—more and more bricks.

So are we. Every month, one-third of American adults are behind on their bills while the average credit card debt in America is $16,883. Just listen to the radio. "You can make $100,000 a year in as little as two hours a week, working from your home." "You can earn millions from real estate without any money down." "You don't have to wait. You don't have to work. You can have everything you want right now!" People will do almost anything, just to get more.

On the night of November 16, 1930, Henrietta Garrett, an eighty-one-year-old widow, died in Philadelphia, starting the most famous case of inheritance litigation in American history. What happened? Garrett failed to leave a will for her $17-million estate.

At the time of her death, Henrietta had only one relative—a second cousin. Yet twenty-six thousand people from forty-seven states and twenty-nine foreign countries, represented by more than three thousand lawyers, tried to claim a part of her estate. In their efforts to get Henrietta's money, people committed perjury, faked family records, changed their names, altered data in family Bibles, and concocted absurd lies. Twenty-two were jailed, three were murdered, and two committed suicide. When will we ever learn?

A long time ago, I was at McDonald's with one of my daughters, Lori Beth. Lori was three at the time. She ordered McDonald's french fries. I didn't. Big mistake. McDonald's french fries have an aroma that overcomes me until I know I'll die if I don't have at least one! I reached over and grabbed one of Lori's french fries. Another big mistake! Lori grabbed my hand and blurted out, "Mine!"

Lori didn't realize that I spoke the order for french fries. I bought the french fries. I carried the french fries to the table. I even doused the french fries with loads of salt and ketchup. Lori had those delicious McDonald's french fries because of her kind and caring father (not to mention that he's good-looking and over-the-top athletic!). How dare Lori yell, "Mine!"?

Mine and *more*. What do they have in common? They're Egypt's two favorite words.

Jesus knows all about Egypt 2.0. "No servant can serve two masters, for either he will hate the one and love the other, or he will be devoted to the one and despise the other. You cannot serve both God and money" (Luke 16:13 ESV). Jesus doesn't say, "You shouldn't serve two masters."

Jesus doesn't say, "Don't serve two masters." Jesus says, "You *can't* serve two masters." It's impossible to serve both God and money. If I don't get my attitude about money right, everything else in life will go completely wrong. I'll become a slave to more and more bricks—running around like a fool claiming that everything I have is all mine.

The first person to reach the status of billionaire was a man who knew how to make bricks. He tailored every decision, attitude, and relationship to create power and wealth. At the age of twenty-three, he was a millionaire; by age fifty, a billionaire. But three years later, at the age of fifty-three, he became sick. His entire body became racked with pain. In complete agony, the world's only billionaire could digest just milk and crackers. An associate wrote, "He couldn't sleep, wouldn't smile, and nothing in life meant anything to him." His personal physicians predicted he would die within a year.

The billionaire awoke one morning and announced that he wanted to channel his assets to hospitals, research, and mission work. On that day, John D. Rockefeller established his foundation. This new direction eventually led to the discovery of penicillin, cures for malaria, tuberculosis, and diphtheria. But perhaps the most amazing part of Rockefeller's story is that the moment he began to renounce the "more and mine" mindset, his body's chemistry was altered so significantly that he got better. John D. Rockefeller lived to be ninety-seven. Another reason for Rockefeller's recovery is that he denounced *more* and *mine*'s first cousin—hurry.

HURRY UP!

If my goal is to make as many bricks as possible in the shortest amount of time as possible, then I find myself regularly on the treadmill called "hurry." The word *hurry* is related to "hurricane." The last time I checked, hurricanes bring ruin, upheaval, and devastation. The same can be said of hurry—so much to do and so little time to do it! Some of my best moments in life have actually happened because I was in a hurry. Not!

True confession. I'm a type-A, get-stuff-done kind of guy. Some people say I'm AAA, but that's how batteries are classified, not people. The last thing I want people to ever say about me is that I'm slow. To me, "slow" has negative connotations. Slow service. Slow movie. Slow runner. A friend once invited me to a tractor-pulling event. His last words were, "If you don't have anything to do." Me? Nothing to do? That would send shockwaves throughout the universe! *I must always have something to do.*

That's life in Egypt. Always in a hurry. Why? There are always more bricks to make. *Always.*

How did we get here? Something huge happened in AD 1370. That's when leaders in Cologne, Germany, installed the world's first public clock. Soon, other European cities followed suit. The result? People said goodbye to natural ways of ordering their lives. Instead of allowing the sun and moon to provide rhythm, they were now "on the clock." Fast-forward to 1879 and Thomas Edison's light bulb. Now people were able to work past sunset. Over the next hundred years, the average night's sleep went from eleven hours to seven.

All of this reached a breaking point in 2007—that's the year Steve Jobs introduced the iPhone, the year Facebook opened to anyone with an email address, the year Twitter became its own platform, and the year Intel changed from silicon to metal chips. Yes, it was the beginning of the digital age—algorithms, acceleration, and caffeination.

What's this nonstop activity doing to us? I think you know. Do you find yourself frantically searching for the shortest checkout lane at the grocery store? Do you drive as though you're in the Indy 500? Do you look for reprieve in the latest Netflix wham-bam along with a glass of cheap wine? Do you multitask to the point that sometimes you forget one of your tasks? Are you caught in the tyranny of the urgent, often forgetting what's important? What would happen if you took in less sugar, caffeine, processed carbs, and alcohol? Would your life crash and burn?

When I was ten years old, I was playing Monopoly with my sister and some cousins. My first time around the board, I landed on Illinois Avenue and Park Place. I bought them both. Then I added Indiana Avenue and Boardwalk to my portfolio. In the next hour, I increased my portfolio to all four railroads, and yes, by that time I owned eight hotels! While everyone else was counting their five- and ten-dollar bills, I was rolling in hundreds of dollars. Finally, at about 10:00 p.m., everyone else went bankrupt. I ruled the world! My sister and cousins got up from the table and went off to bed. They didn't even congratulate me. "Wait a minute!" I cried out. "Someone needs to pick up the game." "Reed," they said, "that's your reward for winning. Good night!" I sat there, all alone—with my property and hotels and money. Then it dawned on me. All this stuff doesn't amount to a hill of beans! When the game is over, it all goes back in the box.

When the game is over, it all goes back in the box.

Egypt will never say that.

The purveyors of American consumerism will never tell us what brick-making, hurrying, and scrambling for more will achieve, so let me remind you. Adopting a brick-quota mindset brings chronic anxiety, depression, burnout, and little long-term satisfaction. Why do you think there are so many deaths of despair in our country—that is, deaths by suicide, drug overdose, and alcoholism?

We're all trying to scratch an itch in the lower-middle part of our back. It's out of reach—just barely, but we keep reaching with all our might. Why is that? It's easy to think that if we can just slam-dunk our next quarterly report, sales commissions, Instagram post, sermon—you name it—then the itch will be scratched. "Surely for nothing they are in turmoil; man heaps up wealth and does not know who will gather!" (Psalm 39:6 ESV).

When Richard Nixon was president, social experts predicted that by the twenty-first century, Americans would work in the morning and have the rest of the day off. What happened? Let me answer that with some Q&A.

How much time does the average American spend on social media every year? That would be 912, hours or about thirty-eight days and nights. What about television? That would be 1,460 hours, or roughly sixty days and nights. And what is the constant message on social media and television? Be kind to your neighbor? Forgive those who wrong you? Be content with what you have? Ha! The message is singular. When in Egypt, do as the Egyptians do. Live by these watchwords: *more, mine,* and *hurry up.*

LET'S LEAVE!

The lights of Egypt, the sounds of Egypt, the glitz and glamour of Egypt—they all scream, "Stay in Egypt!" To do so is to be like a thirsty person choosing to drink raw sewage instead of water from a mountain stream. To remain in Egypt is to be like a bankrupt company rejecting a government bailout.

The prison is near-impossible to leave. Our bondage began with one more drink, one more lie, one more fling, one more glance. But one more always longs for one more, and then just one more. I know. Oh God, I know. With each passing day, it becomes easier to deny that I'm stuck on stuff that kills and steals and destroys. Egypt gives us a story with no salvation, a story with no deliverance, a story with no hope and no future. *It's time to leave.*

Leaving Egypt is a mutiny against materialism. It's a rebellion against the regime's worldview. It's an insurrection against a sick pharaonic system. It's a vow to never become a slave—or worse, a slave-driver—again. Most incredibly, leaving Egypt is an act empowered by God's transforming grace.

The system is skewed. Always has been. Always will be. Egypt is Egypt. Nothing more. Nothing less. If you're tired of bricks and want a new story, keep reading.

CHAPTER 2

The Salvation Story Begins:
Exodus 1–2

He sent from on high, He took me; He drew me out of
many waters. (Psalm 18:16 ESV)

The dominant story of our day is peddled by the young and beautiful who guarantee we can be young and beautiful—just like them—if we buy things we don't need, with money we don't have, to impress people we may not even like. This narrative is hammered into our heads at an alarming rate. On a typical day in America, from the time we open the morning paper (or, more likely, log on to Yahoo News) until we finally doze off in front of another rerun of *I Love Lucy*, digital marketing experts estimate that we see between 4,000 to 10,000 ads.

These images winsomely portray the dominant American story, "You can buy lasting happiness!"

We need a countercultural story. Thank God, He gives us one. It begins in Exodus 1–2. These chapters take us from a family to a nation, from bold women to an arrogant pharaoh, and from endangered children to the God of all compassion who comes to rescue His people.

NAMES

In William Shakespeare's *Romeo and Juliet*, Juliet wistfully wonders, "What's in a name? That which we call a rose by any other name would smell as sweet." The point? It doesn't matter that Romeo is from a rival family named Montague. Names mean nothing for Juliet. Names mean *everything* in the Book of Exodus.

Let's start with the name of the book itself. *Exodus* comes from two Greek words that, when placed together, mean "the way out." This is a major motif in the book. God provides Israel's way out of bondage and slavery from Egypt.

While "Exodus" is the Greek title for the second book in the Pentateuch, the Hebrew title—when translated—means "And These Are the Names." I know that sounds strange, but what we call "Exodus" is also a book about names. What names? Shiphrah and Puah, Moses and Miriam, Aaron and Jethro. But the book's greatest name is God's name—Yahweh. Old Testament authors use this name 6,828 times.

Yahweh is the Hebrew word behind the English "Lord." Unfortunately, "Lord" implies that the God of the Old Testament only has a title. How can we know someone without knowing that person's personal name?

"Lord" is a regrettable translation that began when pious Jews—after the Old Testament was completed—decided to stop using *Yahweh*. Why? They were afraid of breaking the Second Commandment by taking God's name in vain. In place of *Yahweh*, therefore, Jews read *Adonai*—a Hebrew word for "Lord." Those who translated the Hebrew Old Testament into Greek continued with the Greek word *Kyrios*, which also means "Lord."

There you have it. The result? We're stuck with "Lord," making it appear that the God of the Old Testament is distant, aloof, and ultimately unknowable. This is most certainly *not* true.

Names in the Bible frequently define a person's character or destiny. For instance, God changes Abram's name ("exalted father") to Abraham ("father of many"). He changes Jacob's name ("trickster, liar") to Israel ("God declares righteous"). Jesus famously changes Simon bar Jonah to Peter, meaning "Rock."

When we get to Exodus 3, Moses will teach us what God's name means. He'll do it again in chapters 6 and 34. Exodus defines *Yahweh* like no other book in the Old Testament.

JOSEPH

Joseph is another prominent name in Exodus, linking Genesis (the backstory) with Israel's deliverance (our story).

The Book of Genesis ends with these words: "Joseph died, being 110 years old. They embalmed him, and he was put in a coffin in Egypt" (Genesis 50:26 ESV). After opening with a list of names in Exodus, Moses says Egyptians conscripted the Israelites to be state slaves. God's people appear to be hopelessly stuck in a coffin, just like Joseph.

Yet Joseph said this on his deathbed: "God will surely visit [the Hebrew for "surely visit" is *paqod yipqod*] you and bring you up out of this land to the land that He swore to Abraham, to Isaac, and to Jacob" (Genesis 50:24). God tells Moses, "I have surely visited [*paqod paqadti*] you and seen what has been done to you in Egypt" (Exodus 3:16). Then these climactic words: "Moses took the bones of Joseph with him, for Joseph had made the sons of Israel solemnly swear, saying, 'God will surely visit [*paqod yipqod*] you, and you shall carry up my bones with you from here'" (Exodus 13:19). Do you see the same Hebrew words in all three verses? What do they spell? Hope!

Egypt wasn't the last word for Joseph. Egypt wasn't the last word for Israel. *Egypt will never be the last word for us.*

A TELEPHONE BOOK

Exodus 1:1–6 reads much like a telephone book. I know—people of a certain age have no idea what I'm talking about. Back in the dark ages, you'd actually have to look up someone's phone number in a book. That's what Exodus 1:1–6 sounds like—a big, fat, dull, telephone book. It's a lengthy and laborious list.

Long ago, I realized that it's best to avoid biblical lists. Shun lists. Never write about lists. Narratives? Yes. Parables, proverbs, and prayers? Yea! But lists? No way!

However, a pot of gold lies at the end of the list in Exodus 1:1–6. Two key words in Exodus 1:7 highlight Israel's extraordinary growth during the nation's time in Egypt. "But the people of Israel were *fruitful* and increased greatly; they *multiplied* and grew exceedingly strong, so that the land was filled with them" (ESV, emphasis added). The words *fruitful* and *multiplied* also appear in Genesis 1:28; 9:1, 7. These three verses—when placed together—indicate that what God did when He created the world (Genesis 1:28), He did again after Noah's flood (Genesis 9:1, 7). The thrust, therefore, is that the same creational power displayed in Genesis is now God's gift to Israel in Exodus—who, like Noah, will be Yahweh's new creation to restore all things. This brings us to another Genesis backstory associated with Exodus 1:7.

In Genesis 12:2–3, God tells Abram, "I will make of you a great nation, and I will *bless* you and make your name great, so that you will be a *blessing*. I will *bless* those who *bless* you, and him who dishonors you I will curse, and in you all the families of the earth shall be *blessed*" (ESV, emphasis added). The term *curse* appears five times in Genesis 1–11 (Genesis 3:14, 17; 4:11; 5:29; 9:25). God counters that with a five-fold promise of blessing to Abram in Genesis 12:2–3.

According to Exodus 1:7, therefore, God is fulfilling His promise to Abram. The Israelites are becoming a great nation. They will channel God's blessings to the nations—ultimately through Christ Jesus our Lord. *Curses must yield to blessings.*

Exodus 1:1–5 confirms this interpretation. Jacob's seventy descendants who went down to Egypt correspond to the seventy descendants of Noah in Genesis 10. Through Israel's seventy, God will bring His blessing to Noah's seventy—that is, to the entire world. God's promise to Abram, that he would become a great nation (Genesis 12:2), is now being realized. Yahweh will use Israel to bring abounding mercy and grace to the world.

Taken together, Exodus 1:1–7 announces God's plan to use Israel as His conduit to bless all the families of the earth. This sets the stage for Exodus 1:8–15:21. Two pharaohs will attempt to derail Yahweh's purposes. Egypt will suffer heartache and hell for it.

TROUBLE IN RIVER CITY

Because of a famine in 1847 BC, Jacob and his family traveled from Canaan to Egypt—that's what Exodus 1:1–7 implies. Fast forward three hundred years and we come to Exodus 1:8 where a new pharaoh comes to power who doesn't know Joseph. In the Hebrew language, the idea of knowing implies more than being acquainted with facts and figures. Instead, it denotes a relationship that has depth, commitment, and genuine concern. Putting it more colloquially, then, the new *Egyptian* (not Hyksos) pharaoh, is about to trash Joseph's descendants.

Beginning in Exodus 1:8, Egypt's regime begins to dishonor the Israelites. This will not end well for the land of the Nile. How come? Genesis 12:3 makes it clear that Yahweh will unleash the full weight of His curses upon every enemy of His people.

We're now in an era where the Israelites—by and large—are ignorant of God's name. While Hebrew midwives fear God (Exodus 1:17), no other Hebrews in Exodus 1–2 acknowledge Yahweh. True, they cry out, but not to God (Exodus 2:23). Yahweh, however, hears their lament—after all, they're still His people, even when they don't know how to pray. What grace!

Soon, not only Israel but all of Egypt will hear about Yahweh. The dark night sky will light up with brilliant fireworks—all from a burning bush on Mount Sinai. But first, there's trouble down by the Nile, in river city.

In Exodus 1–2, the nemesis isn't a snake in the grass, or an older brother named Cain, or a young nephew named Lot. Instead, Moses introduces us to an unbelieving, arrogant, and foolish pharaoh. It's 1539 BC, and his name is Ahmose I. We meet him in one of the most abrupt literary moves in the Bible. "Now there arose a new king over Egypt, who did not know Joseph" (Exodus 1:8).

The king may be new, but Joseph's rejection wasn't. Envision a seventeen-year-old teenager stuck in a waterless pit. His hands are bound. His ankles tied. His eyes are wet from tears. His voice is hoarse from crying. His brothers (*his brothers!*) sit down to eat and drink—all while the seventeen-year-old is screaming at the top of his lungs, "Let me out!"

It sounds like a cable TV show, but we know better. Joseph—the seventeen-year-old—is captured by his brothers while they're sixty miles away from home and their father Jacob's watchful eye. "They *stripped* him of his robe, the robe of many colors that he wore. And they *took* him and *threw* him into a pit" (Genesis 37:23–24 ESV, emphasis added). These are murderous verbs. Stripped. Took. Threw.

Joseph didn't see this coming. Joseph didn't get out of bed that morning and say, "I'd better pack some extra food and water and put on padded clothing and a helmet because today my brothers are going to throw me into a waterless pit." The attack comes as a complete surprise.

Joseph's brothers then sell him to some Ishmaelites coming from Gilead on their way to Egypt (Genesis 37:25–28). Twenty-four years later, a Hyksos pharaoh elevated Joseph to be second-in-charge in Egypt. God turned the evil perpetrated against Joseph for good, the saving of many lives (Genesis 50:20)—including Joseph's brothers. God vindicated Joseph.

And God will vindicate Joseph again. Only this time, He will vindicate Joseph's entire family—the people of Israel.

EGYPT ENSLAVES GOD'S PEOPLE

Here's my translation of Exodus 1:13–14: "The Egyptians ruthlessly forced the sons of Israel to *serve*. And they caused their lives to become bitter through harsh *service*, with mortar and with bricks and with every sort of *service* in the field. In all their *service* they ruthlessly made them *serve*" (emphasis added). Words connected to serving appear five times in Exodus 1:13–14 while the adverb *ruthlessly* comes twice—at the beginning and at the end. Egypt treated the Israelites like animals. It's hardly surprising that after the exodus, God forbids His people to ever deal with anyone "ruthlessly" (Leviticus 25:43, 46, 53).

I remember when my three children experienced the delight of driving. It was a sight to see—the look of ecstasy on their faces when they first got their driver's licenses. I gave them full use of a car with one condition. If I needed them to give one of the other children a ride or run an errand for the sake of the family, they were expected to do so. I can still hear each of them protesting, "Oh, come on Dad! That's not fair!"

You know what the issue was. It was ownership. I owned the car. Abi, Jonathan, and Lori didn't. Once they understood the idea of ownership, everyone got along great—well, most of the time, everyone got along great!

Ownership. That's the issue in Exodus 1. That's also the theme in the book's first fourteen chapters. Who owns Israel? Egyptian pharaohs or Yahweh? The story begins with Egyptians owning the Israelites. Who will dare take the first steps toward freedom by standing up to the rotten regime? Two women will—Shiphrah and Puah.

These are names to remember.

MIDWIVES TO THE RESCUE

"Then the king of Egypt said to the Hebrew midwives, one of whom was named Shiphrah and the other Puah" (Exodus 1:15). Pharaoh Ahmose I barks out orders. The midwives are to murder Hebrew baby boys. Time passes. Nothing happens. When the pharaoh asks why Shiphrah and Puah aren't obeying his demands, the midwives outmaneuver the king. Their answer? "The Hebrew women are not like the Egyptian women, for they are vigorous and give birth before the midwife comes to them" (Exodus 1:19 ESV). The pharaoh is befuddled. He's speechless. But not for long.

Ahmose I issues his second executive order. "Every son that is born to the Hebrews you shall cast into the Nile, but you shall let every daughter live" (Exodus 1:22 ESV). Do you see what's happened? The king moves from keeping the Israelites from escaping (Exodus 1:10) to the grisly business of genocide. Do you catch the irony? Egypt's leader wants to drown the Israelites in the water of the Nile. His successor will experience exactly that—his own drowning in water. Only it will be the water of the Red Sea (Exodus 14:26–28). What goes around comes around!

WHO ARE THE HEBREWS?

What can we say about *Hebrew*, a term that appears for the first time in this book in Exodus 1:15? This much is certain. *Hebrew* denotes ethnicity—specifically, descendants from Eber (Genesis 10:21–25) including Shem, Abraham, Isaac, Jacob, and Joseph.

Outside the Old Testament, *Hebrew* referred to people with low social status—soldiers, slaves, and blue-collar workers. Therefore, in the broader world of the ancient Middle East, a Hebrew was someone who lived on the margins, rejected by the cultural elite. To call someone a "Hebrew," then, was to mark them as socially marginalized—somewhat analogous to our term "Gypsy." Culturally, not all Hebrews were Israelites. Biblically, however, all Israelites were considered Hebrews—especially by the Egyptians. Recall that the empire treated them *ruthlessly*.

EGYPTIAN PHARAOHS

According to the Japanese constitution of 1889, the Japanese Emperor Hirohito, head of state during World War II, had divine power. The U.S. strategy of using overwhelming force at Hiroshima and Nagasaki in August 1945 was to bomb the emperor into submission by demonstrating he was not godlike. It worked. The war came to an end. One year later, Japan changed the emperor's title to "constitutional monarch."

Egyptian pharaohs were also considered divine. *Pharaoh*—a title, not a name—in Egyptian means "Great House," thus comporting with our use of terms like *City Hall* and *White House* to mean the leaders who occupy offices there. While these expressions imply leadership, *Pharaoh* implies deity. Kings in Egypt didn't represent a god. They were considered gods themselves. In state propaganda, a pharaoh was called "the perfect god." One text even describes him as "the great god." An inscription on the tomb of Rekhmire—an ancient Egyptian government official who lived at the time of Moses—states: "Pharaoh is a god by whose dealings one lives, the father and the mother of all men, alone by himself without an equal." The way pharaohs posture and preen in their monumental architecture reflects this belief.

Archaeologists have discovered Egyptian pharaohs buried with golden masks. The gold signified that the king was a son of Amon-Re—Egypt's sun god. In Egyptian mythology, when pharaohs die, they rise from their tombs, ascend to heaven, and become united with the golden sun. Each pharaoh was acclaimed a sovereign defender of his people and a warrior without equal.

It's shocking, therefore, that the second half of Exodus 1 mocks Pharaoh Ahmose I. He thinks he's dealing shrewdly with Joseph's descendants (Exodus 1:10). It's the Hebrews, though—and women at that—who deal shrewdly with Pharaoh. Shiphrah and Puah outsmart him in chapter 1, while Miriam and Jochebed bamboozle him in chapter 2. *The first become last and the last become first.*

While I'm including pharaonic names to help you better follow the history, we never learn their names in the Book of Exodus. In contrast to Moses' writings, other parts of the Old Testament give us "Shishak king of Egypt," who reigned during the life of Solomon (1 Kings 11:40), as well as "Pharaoh Neco," who killed the godly King Josiah (2 Kings 23:29). But in Exodus? The no-name pharaohs, with their godlike posing and pretending, can't even obtain compliance from Hebrew slaves. Ha! The Bible helps us remember the marginalized midwives—Shiphrah and Puah. The pharaohs? They aren't worth remembering!

HIDING IN A CAVE

I found us in a story about a Japanese soldier who lived on the island of Guam during World War II. His name? Shōichi Yukoi.

It was the end of 1944. American Marines landed on Guam and captured the island. Fearing for his life, Yukoi headed for the hills. And, even though the war between the United States and Japan ended ten months later, he spent the next twenty-eight years hiding in Guam's caves. For twenty-eight years, Yukoi hid in underground jungle caves, fearing to come out even after finding leaflets declaring World War II had ended (deeming them Allied propaganda). His diet consisted of jungle rats, snails, and frogs. Finally, on January 24, 1972, two men discovered Yukoi. Upon his return to Japan, Yukoi said, "It is with much joy that I have returned." I would think so!

We're much like Shōichi Yukoi. Although freedom has been won for us in Jesus Christ, the enemy has us hunkered down out of fear.

Fear. It pokes its ugly head into our lives and says, "What if?"—"What if the job doesn't last?" "What if the relationship doesn't last?" "What if the retirement income doesn't last?" Fear propels us to hide in the shadows, live on the edges, and stay cramped in caves.

If you want to make a counterfeit $20 bill, you don't use orange construction paper, cut it in the shape of a triangle, put Donald Duck's picture in the center, and rubber stamp "20" on the front and back. That deceives no one. Satan doesn't appear as a little red man with a tail and pitchfork in his left hand. He wears the garb of authenticity and whispers these wicked words: "Faith is for others. Fear is for you."

A few years ago, I was on my way from West Palm Beach, Florida, to Cleveland, Ohio. I had to go through Atlanta, where it was raining cats and dogs. Lightning caused blackouts as storms rolled through the heart of Dixie. Then, no huge surprise, my flight from Atlanta to Cleveland was canceled. I called Delta Airlines, thinking they would rebook me on another flight. Delta, I assumed, would be my calm in the storm. I heard a kind voice pick up my call. "Hello, thank you for calling Delta Airlines." *Fantastic,* I said to myself, *customer service to the rescue!* But then I heard the dreaded, "This call may be monitored for quality assurance."

I was stuck in the Bermuda Triangle of computerized telephone services. "Press one for domestic flights. Press two for international flights. Press three if you know your flight number and the name of your congressman. Press four if you're a frequent flier from the Eastern Time zone and have four children. Press five if the nine digits of your Social Security number totals more than fifty . . . " For the foreseeable future I would be placed in a dark cave, listening to Barry Manilow songs.

But we know a cave that's far worse. The problem for us, though, is that at first it didn't look like a cave. It looked like the promised land! And it even was the promised land—at least for a while. That moral indiscretion? "No big deal!" That financial dishonesty? "No big deal!" That small, little lie? "No big deal!"

Sooner or later, though, "no big deal" becomes a really big deal! What we thought was life becomes death—the death of a job, the death of a marriage, the death of our hope. Satan slams the door shut and says, "You'll never leave!" The result? Fear!

That's what happened to Israelite slaves in Egypt. Fear overwhelmed them. Let's review.

Stage One: State Slavery. Exodus 1:11 says, "Therefore they set taskmasters over them to afflict them with heavy burdens. They built for Pharaoh store cities, Pithom and Raamses" (ESV). Try this. Get water from a canal. Pour the water into a mud pit. Step up and down in the mud pit. Add some straw. Let it dry in the sun and voilà, you've got a brick! Now do this all day, every day—with no time off, ever.

Stage Two: Private Infanticide. Exodus 1:15–16 describes it this way: "The king of Egypt said to the Hebrew midwives, one of whom was named Shiphrah and the other Puah, 'When you serve as midwife to the Hebrew women and see them on the birthstool, if it is a son, you shall kill him, but if it is a daughter, she shall live'" (ESV). God sees two women—Shiphrah and Puah—who obey Him and ignore the pharaoh's command. God puts their names in the Bible. But Pharaoh, the most powerful man on the earth, his name isn't in the Bible. What's going on? God does big things with small stuff.

The Hebrew midwives practice civil disobedience—that is, they follow God when told by the government to reject God's will. When faced with a similar situation, Peter and the apostles say, "We must obey God rather than men" (Acts 5:29 ESV).

Stage Three: Open Genocide. Exodus 1:22 describes the pharaoh's decree: "Every son that is born to the Hebrews you shall cast into the Nile, but you shall let every daughter live" (ESV). It's against the backdrop of this dark cave that Moses is born.

MEET MOSES

"Now a man from the house of Levi [Amram] went and took as his wife a Levite woman [Jochebed]. The woman conceived and bore a son" (Exodus 2:1–2 ESV). The son is Moses, Amram and Jochebed's third child. They already have a daughter, whose name is Miriam, and a son, whose name is Aaron.

Moses' mother, Jochebed, hides her baby boy in the reeds. Moses' rescue from the reeds prefigures Israel's deliverance from the "Sea of Reeds"—a more accurate translation of the Hebrew words. We know this body of water by the title "Red Sea." I prefer *reed*—for obvious reasons! We'll stay with *red*, though. This is how English Bibles translate the phrase. Back to our story!

"When she [Jochebed] saw that he [Moses] was a fine child, she hid him for three months. When she could hide him no longer, she took for him a basket made of bulrushes and daubed it with bitumen and pitch" (Exodus 2:2–3 ESV). The word translated "basket," is the same word translated "ark"—as in Noah's ark—in Genesis, Exodus' backstory. Moses' ark, just like Noah's, is coated with tar and pitch. Noah's ark inaugurated a new beginning for humanity. So does Moses' ark. God is on the move!

But you say, "Noah's ark was so much bigger!" What's God doing? In the Book of Exodus, God does big things with small stuff.

Jochebed places Moses—ark and all—into the Nile River. Miriam runs along the river's edge. Big sister to the rescue! She watches as Pharaoh's daughter bathes with her servants. Then this: "When she [Pharaoh's daughter's servant] opened it, she saw the child, and behold, the baby was *crying*. She took pity on him" (Exodus 2:6 ESV, emphasis added). When God wants to do something really big, He often begins with something really small—like a baby. Recall Isaac, Samuel, John the Baptist, and especially Jesus. Moses' infant tears were God's first strike against the might of Egypt. Tears? God does big things with small stuff.

"When the child grew older, she [Jochebed] brought him to Pharaoh's daughter, and he became her son. She named him Moses, 'Because,' she said, 'I drew him out of the water'" (Exodus 2:10 ESV). The pharaoh's plans are foiled again. Do you think this is becoming a recurring motif? God uses people who have no power to subvert those who do. First it was Shiphrah and Puah, then Miriam and Jochebed. We can add Moses to the list.

The first fifteen chapters of Exodus are about Israel's deliverance from Egypt and, of course, there's no deliverance without a deliverer. His name is Moses. Of the 716 references to Moses in the Old Testament, roughly a third of them appear in Exodus. Moses looms large in the book. He functions as a savior, singer, judge, prophet, intercessor, architect, and builder.

Moses is from the tribe of Levi on both sides of his family (Exodus 2:1; 6:20). This alerts us to one of his main functions in the book. Moses is a priest who has a closeness to Yahweh described as "face to face" (Exodus 33:11 ESV). Through Moses, God not only gives Israel His Word but also a sacrificial system centered in the tabernacle. God goes so far as to say of Moses, "With him I speak mouth to mouth, clearly, and not in riddles, and he beholds the form of Yahweh" (Numbers 12:8, author's translation).

Moses means "draw out of water." Here's another important name in the book whose Hebrew name is "And These Are the Names." Moses' name foreshadows his destiny. Through water, Moses will bring Israel out of Pharaoh's fearful cave. And he will do it with a wooden staff. A wooden staff? God does big things with small stuff.

But why Moses? After all, he's a three-time loser. First, at age 40, Moses murders an Egyptian. Second, he tries to cover it up by hiding the dead man in the sand. Third, fleeing Egypt, Moses ends up in the Midian desert working for his father-in-law for forty years.

When he grows up, Moses doesn't become a hero. He becomes more like a big, fat zero. Rather than dining with heads of state, he will count the heads of sheep—his father-in-law's sheep. Why does God pick Moses to lead Israel out of Egypt? By now you know the answer. God does big things with small stuff!

OUR CAVE

God sees us curled up in our cave, our self-made prison of fear. God also sees us don our Superman or Superwoman cape, thinking we're superheroes who can save ourselves.

I've got bad news. You're not a superhero. Neither am I. We can't fight our way out of fear. We can't think our way out, buy our way out, educate our way out, program our way out, vacation our way out, or blast our way out.

I've got some really good news for you! Jesus frees us from the prison of fear. *And Jesus does it all with small stuff.*

The tokens of Christ's Passion include a chalice, a plate, some unleavened bread, wine, tears, a torch, a lantern, a sword, a whip, thirty pieces of silver, dice, a spear, and a pitcher of gall mixed with vinegar. Jesus doesn't recoil, run, or retreat when He peers into our ugly cave. He comes to us right where we are. To do what? Really big things (set us free), with what looks like really small stuff (His Word and Sacraments).

Sometimes life gets really dark. It feels as though we're on a permanent diet of jungle rats, snails, and frogs. But there's a glimmer of light dawning. Can you see it? It's Easter light. It's Easter deliverance! And it's here, for us, right now. After all, Israel's salvation story is our story as well—free for the taking.

MIGHTY MOSES

Let's get some perspective. According to Stephen's speech in Acts 7:23, Moses was forty years old when we come to Exodus 2:11–25. And, according to Hebrews 11:24–25, Moses was aware of his Hebrew background. Looking ahead, Moses was eighty when he stood before Pharaoh Thutmose III (Exodus 7:7) and age 120 when he died (Deuteronomy 34:7). We might call that a full life—and then some!

The second half of Exodus 2 records Moses' interactions with Egyptians, Israelites, and Midianites. His response to injustice is the thread that weaves these episodes together. Regardless of who's being victimized (a Hebrew slave, a Hebrew neighbor, some Midianite women), Moses steps up to the plate. His sense of fairness transcends gender, creed, and nationality. Moses has a heart for weak and vulnerable people. He also isn't afraid to take decisive action to save them. Beat 'em. Bust 'em. That's his custom!

In the first of these three vignettes, Moses sees an Egyptian striking an Israelite. What does Moses do? He kills the Egyptian, thus foreshadowing Exodus 14 when—thanks to Moses—a whole bunch of Egyptians die in the Red Sea. The next day, Moses sees the same Israelite and thinks he will exclaim, "Thank you, Moses! You saved my life!" But he doesn't. Instead, the Israelite is angry. He asks Moses, "Will you kill me too?" The word is out! The pharaoh finds out! Moses is going to be taken out! Therefore, Moses barrels out of Egypt and ends up working for his father-in-law, Jethro, for forty years.

The Israelite's question in Exodus 2:14 is another sneak preview of coming attractions. "Who made you a prince and a judge over us?" (ESV). As the epic unfolds, the Israelites repeatedly doubt Moses' leadership over them (Exodus 4:1; 5:21; 6:9–11; 14:11–12; 32:1). And, just like the Israelite in chapter 2, others will join this chorus line—accusing Moses of trying to kill them (Exodus 16:2–3; 17:3–4). Exodus 2:11–14, then, summarizes much of the book. *Moses is at odds with the Egyptians and the Israelites are at odds with Moses.*

Moses' mad dash to Midian provides another literary link—this time back to the book of Genesis. After Sarah died, Abraham married Keturah, who had a son they named "Midian" (Genesis 25:1–6). Two generations later, Joseph's brothers sell him to Ishmaelites—nomadic merchants who take Joseph down to Egypt (Genesis 37:25–36). When Moses meets a priest of Midian and his seven daughters (Exodus 2:16), he's connecting with long-lost relatives. The meeting also foreshadows the events of Israel's encampment at Sinai, which is in the land of Midian (Exodus 19–40).

What's up with the multiple names of Moses' father-in-law? You probably know him as "Jethro"—likely his priestly title. However, in Exodus 2:18 and Numbers 10:29, he's called "Reuel." In Judges 4:11, he goes by yet another name, "Hobab." The man gets three of his names in the Bible. That's quite an accomplishment!

Moses' encounter with his soon-to-be-wedded wife, Zipporah, once more takes us back to Genesis. Both Isaac (Genesis 24) and Jacob (Genesis 29) meet their wives at watering wells. Because Moses stands in this patriarchal tradition, the Israelites are expected to receive him as God's gift. They will, at first. But as Exodus unfolds, the relationship becomes strained until it almost ends.

At the watering well, we see Moses—for the third time in the chapter—championing the rights of oppressed people. Earlier it was a Hebrew slave being beaten by an Egyptian. Then it was a Hebrew beating a Hebrew. Now it's a group of women being harassed by evil shepherds. Moses has a big heart for small people.

Surprisingly, while the Israelites reject Moses (Exodus 2:14), the Midianites receive him—and with great acclaim (Exodus 2:19). Consequently, in the span of a few verses, we learn that Moses protects (Exodus 2:11, 17) and shepherds (Exodus 2:17–19). He's also outcast (Exodus 2:15, 22) and rejected (Exodus 2:14). More than that, Moses' actions anticipate what God will do to rescue Israel. The list is impressive. Both Moses and God

- "see" Israel's oppression and subsequently act (Moses, Exodus 2:11; God, Exodus 2:25; 3:7, 9; 4:31);

- "strike" the enemy (Moses, Exodus 2:12; God, e.g., Exodus 12:12, 13, 29); and

- "save" and "deliver" those in need (Moses, Exodus 2:17, 19; God saves, e.g., Exodus 14:13, 30; 15:2; God delivers, Exodus 3:8; 6:6; 12:27).

Yahweh and Moses are on the same page.

This united team of two foreshadows the work of God the Father and God the Son. They are one (John 10:30). In fact, to see the Son is to see the Father (John 14:9). Their plan? Bring salvation. According to this divine strategy, salvation had a place—Golgotha. Salvation had a day—Friday. Salvation had a time—9:00 in the morning until 3:00 in the afternoon. And salvation had a cost—the blood of God's only Son. Thank God, salvation also has a destination—your life and mine.

Stephen connects the dots between Moses and Jesus (Acts 7:39, 51–53). And, like Moses, Jesus is also a shepherd—born not only to tend to sheep (Micah 5:2–4; Matthew 2:6) but, all the more, lay His life down for His sheep. John the Baptists heralds, "Behold, the Lamb of God, who takes away the sin of the world" (John 1:29 ESV).

ISRAEL'S CRY

Do you cry to God when you're in deep pain? Sometimes I do. Sometimes I don't. There are times, unfortunately, when my cry morphs into a complaint. Then I'm tempted to join hands with other complainers—they're easy to find because there're so many of them. Still, on other occasions, when I feel despondent, I cry to people. I end up asking them to be my savior. When that doesn't work, I try crying to myself. After a few more days, I conclude that no one cares.

Then I come to my senses and earnestly cry out to *God*. He listens. He cares. He employs all His power in heaven and earth to meet my needs. This is the message of Exodus 2:23–25. The chapter's last three verses leave Moses and take us back to Egypt. The following expressions describe Hebrew slaves in the land of the Nile: "the people of Israel *groaned*," "*cried* out for help," "their *cry* for rescue," and "God heard their *groaning*" (Exodus 2:23–25 ESV, emphasis added). This repetition of *groan* and *cry* is a lot like Exodus 1:13–14, where Moses uses the same rhetorical strategy to drive home his point—albeit with the word *serve.*

God's absence in Exodus 1–2 (He's only mentioned in Exodus 1:17, 20, 21) creates shockwaves in Exodus 2:23–25, where "God" comes five times. Israel's groans "came up to God," "God heard," "God remembered, "God saw," and "God knew" (ESV). The long night is over. A new day is dawning. Yahweh's kingdom of life will soon defeat Egypt's culture of death. God will come down into the fray through the burning bush.

Let's consider the expression "God remembered" (Exodus 2:24 ESV). You probably recall from my discussion on Exodus 1:8 that the Hebrew idea of remembering implies much more than intellectual activity or recalling information stored away in our brain. *It implies action.* With the pharaoh's death (Exodus 2:23), God is ready to act. The fullness of time has arrived.

GOD KNOWS OUR PAIN

God knows the pain of His people. That's the comforting truth stemming from these last three verses in Exodus 2. Isaiah 63:9 builds upon the idea—stating that God shares His people's sadness. Yahweh isn't detached, aloof, or indifferent. When Israel suffers, Yahweh suffers. Israel's enemies are Yahweh's enemies. Whoever strikes Israel strikes the apple of Yahweh's eye (Zechariah 2:8).

This same line of thinking continues into the New Testament, where, for example, Jesus tells His disciples, "The one who rejects you rejects *Me*" (Luke 10:16 ESV, emphasis added). Christ announces to Paul—who was ravaging the church—"Saul, Saul, why are you persecuting *Me*?" (Acts 9:4; 22:7; 26:14 ESV, emphasis added). God isn't an unmoved mover. When He sees us agonizing over life's harsh realities, His heart is moved with love and mercy. God hears us. Loves us. Forgives us. Empowers us. God comes to us in the most unlikely places—a hill called Calvary and an empty garden tomb.

THE PAIN OF REJECTION

Stephen tells us, "Moses was instructed in all the wisdom of the Egyptians, and he was mighty in his words and deeds" (Acts 7:22 ESV). At age 40, with this pedigree in hand, Moses attempts to rescue a fellow Hebrew from an Egyptian who's beating him ruthlessly. Recall the Hebrew's response, "Who made you a prince and a judge over us?" (Exodus 2:14 ESV). How do you spell that? *Rejection.*

What does society say when we've been rejected? "Get a bigger house!" "Get a brighter blouse!" "Get a brand-new spouse!" "And quit being such a great, big, lazy louse!" Moses offers something much better. Moses tells us that God accepts the rejected.

It takes one to know one. Moses certainly knew the pain of rejection. Try working for your father-in-law for forty years! When his first son is born, Exodus 2:22 reflects Moses' angst: "[Moses] called his name Gershom, for he said, 'I have been a sojourner in a foreign land'" (ESV). Exodus 4:20 indicates that Moses has another child when he and Zipporah leave Midian en route to Egypt. This child—not mentioned by name until Exodus 18:4—is called Eliezer. His name means "my God is a helper." And help is on the way!

God will call and empower Moses. But if God enlists a reject named Moses, why not recruit the forty-year-old version instead of the eighty-year-old version? Moses at forty? Okay! Moses at eighty? No way! But benched at forty, at age 80 Moses is Yahweh's first-round draft pick. His assignment? Get Israel out of Egypt.

There will be a voice and a burning bush and holy ground. It will shock the sandals right off Moses' feet—literally!

CHAPTER 3

The Burning Bush, God's Name, and Moses' Godly Change: Exodus 3–4

Moses and Aaron were among His priests. (Psalm 99:6 ESV)

Let's see where the next few chapters in Exodus will take us. Exodus 3:1–4:17 describes God's call to Moses, while Exodus 6:2–7:7 states the contours of God's plan to rescue Israel. A description of Moses' return to Egypt separates these two sections (Exodus 4:18–31) as does his first confrontation with the new pharaoh (Exodus 5:1–6:1). Through it all, Moses undergoes a dramatic change—something very commendable for an eighty-year-old man!

What about you? What do you want to change about your life? Is it a bad habit? A bad relationship? A bad attitude? A bad situation? What is it that you look at and say, "This just isn't right. It's got to change"?

We live in a society that offers instant transformation. We watch television and change the channel with *click, click, click*. We look at our iPhone and change the screen with *tap, tap, tap*. We put food in our microwave and it's ready to eat with *zap, zap, zap*. Because we change channels, screens, and food so fast, we think we should be able to change our lives with just a click, a tap, or a zap.

Think again.

God changes us using the same process He used with Moses. Note the word *process*. Change—godly change—is a process. Godly change takes time. We can forget the clicks, taps, and zaps.

MOSES' NEED TO CHANGE

"Moses was keeping the flock of his father-in-law, Jethro" (Exodus 3:1 ESV). For forty years, all Moses saw were sheep. For forty years, all Moses heard were sheep. For *forty years*, all Moses thought about were sheep. Talk about getting stuck in a rut. Sheep! Sheep! And more sheep! Moses had to be thinking, "This just isn't right. It's got to change!"

It happens to us, too, doesn't it? We get stuck in ruts. What is it for you? Are you overly critical of other people? Is your spending out of control? Have you lost your ambition to study the Bible, live a life of integrity, follow hard after Jesus? Just like Moses, we look at specific areas in our life and say, "This just isn't right. It's got to change!" But how?

The process (remember it's a process!) of change begins with God's presence. "The Messenger of Yahweh appeared to him [Moses] in flames of fire from within a bush" (Exodus 3:2). This is no ordinary bush. And this is no ordinary Messenger.

YAHWEH'S MESSENGER

God's presence in the burning bush (Exodus 3:2–6) discloses that Yahweh's Messenger and Yahweh/God share the same attributes. Note that the Messenger speaks (Exodus 3:4), Yahweh speaks (Exodus 3:4, 7), then God speaks (Exodus 3:6, 12, 14, 15). Moreover, later in Exodus, this same Messenger goes ahead of Israel to defeat the nation's enemies (Exodus 23:20; 32:34).

What can we say about these connections? *Yahweh and the Messenger are one.* We can also say this: the Old Testament Messenger is a preincarnate form of the Second Person of the Holy Trinity, who became flesh in Jesus.

I know. That's a mouthful—and a mindful! Let me put it this way: Jesus appears throughout the Old Testament. He's predicted in places like Genesis 3:15, where Moses records He will crush the serpent's head. Christ is previewed in people like David, for Jesus is Israel's King and the King of the world. And Jesus is present as the Messenger/Angel of the Lord. The Savior puts it this way: "These are My words that I spoke to you while I was still with you, that everything written about Me in the Law of Moses and the Prophets and the Psalms must be fulfilled" (Luke 24:44 ESV). The Old Testament shows us Jesus through predictions, previews, and His presence.

FIRE ON MOUNT HOREB

If this is no ordinary Messenger talking to Moses from the bush, then this is no ordinary fire within the bush. It's the fire of God. The fire of God appears when God speaks to Gideon (Judges 6:21) and to Amos (Amos 7:4). The fire of God appears when God calls the disciples on the Day of Pentecost (Acts 2:3). John the Baptist even says that we're baptized with the fire of God (Luke 3:16). Why is God present in fire? Wherever there is fire, you can bet something happens every single time. And what is that? Change!

The Messenger in fire appears to Moses on Mount Horeb. In Hebrew, *Horeb* means "desolate wasteland." Mount Horeb is synonymous with Mount Sinai, first mentioned in Exodus 16:1. Today, Sinai goes by the name *Jebel Musa*—a mountain some 7,500 feet above sea level that's 5,000 feet higher than its surrounding valleys.

Warning. Here comes more Hebrew! The Hebrew word for "bush" employed in Exodus 3:2–4 is *seneh*. The term only appears one more time—Moses calls God, "One Who Dwells in *Seneh*" (Deuteronomy 33:16). Moses deliberately chooses the rare term *seneh* for "bush" to stress the importance of Mount *Sinai*. As you can see, the words go together.

God will again descend on Mount Sinai "in fire" (Exodus 19:18 ESV). Exodus 24:17 is even more explicit, "Now the appearance of the glory of the LORD was like a devouring fire on the top of the mountain in the sight of the people of Israel" (ESV). Moses' experience in Exodus 3 portends Israel's experience with God in Exodus 19–24. It will all take place on God's holy mountain, *Sinai.*

Question: Why does the *seneh*/bush remain unconsumed? Answer: In like manner, the Israelites will not be consumed by their horrific suffering in Egypt. Why? God is with them. He isn't above their suffering or beside their suffering. God is *in* their suffering. He is *in* the burning bush!

The burning bush not only demonstrates God's presence and protection with the Israelites during their Egyptian slavery. It also—like several other events in Exodus 3—foreshadows what will happen through the ten plagues and Yahweh's rescue at the Red Sea. Just as bushes normally don't last long when engulfed in fire, rivers normally don't turn to blood, gnats normally don't come from dust, and water normally doesn't turn into walls. The point is clear. When it comes to change, expect the unexpected!

HERE I AM!

God's first words in the book appear in Exodus 3:4, "Moses, Moses!" (ESV). It's fitting for a book titled "And These Are the Names" for God's first utterance to be the liberator's name. What does Moses say to God? "Here I am!" (Exodus 3:4 ESV). The expression means, "God, I'm at Your service." "Take my life and let it be Consecrated, Lord, to Thee" (*LSB* 783). "Lord, I'm ready to change!"

Houston, we have a problem! God is separate, distinct, and different from everything and everyone else. The biblical word for that is *holy.* Will a holy God really take up residence in Israel's unholy life? Indeed! He does so "in, with, and under" a burning bush. Hence, God calls the place holy ground (Exodus 3:5). At God's command, Moses removes his sandals and then gets a crash course on changing from a secluded shepherd into a savvy savior of people.

What follows in Exodus 3:7–10 is a pivotal speech. Yahweh employs six first-person singular pronouns in these verses—accenting that the power of redemption rests in Him, not in Moses, and certainly not in Israel. "*I* have surely seen the affliction of My people who are in Egypt . . . *I* know their sufferings" (Exodus 3:7 ESV, emphasis added here and following). "*I* have come down to deliver them . . . [*I*] will bring them up out of that land" (Exodus 3:8). "*I* have also seen the oppression with which the Egyptians oppress them" (Exodus 3:9). "*I* will send you to Pharaoh" (Exodus 3:10).

In this part of Exodus, Yahweh describes Himself as "the God of your father, the God of Abraham, the God of Isaac, and the God of Jacob" (Exodus 3:6, 15, 16; 4:5 ESV). Yahweh comes down to fulfill His promises to the patriarchs—this includes giving them the land of Canaan (Exodus 3:8, 17). God will come down again repeatedly on Mount Sinai in Exodus 19:11, 18, 20; 34:5. He never becomes weary of coming to the aid of His people!

Chapter 2 ends with this incomplete idea, "And God knew" (Exodus 2:25 ESV). God knew what? God knew the pain of his people (Exodus 3:7). Yahweh doesn't stay safe and secure in the heavenly realm. He doesn't bark out orders, "My people will talk with your people." Instead, Yahweh becomes acquainted with Israel's grief (cf. Isaiah 53:3). After all, He's in the burning bush!

Although Yahweh is the Holy One of Israel and therefore transcendent, He's not so high and mighty that He remains unmoved by human suffering. God chooses to become engaged in the mess of this world. So much so that—even if He must suffer for it—He will not pull back. No wonder biblical writers employ images like husbands and wives, as well as parents and children, to describe God's pain, loss, and grief. Divine suffering, however, doesn't render Yahweh powerless. Far from it! It prompts Him into action.

Israel is one instance of God's concern for marginalized people (Exodus 3:9). Yahweh saves *all* who cry to Him. "You shall not wrong a sojourner or oppress him, for you were sojourners in the land of Egypt. You shall not mistreat any widow or fatherless child. If you do mistreat them, and they cry out to Me, I will surely hear their cry" (Exodus 22:21–23 ESV).

THE PROMISED LAND

In Exodus 3, for the first time in the Bible, God refers to the Promised Land as "a land flowing with milk and honey" (v. 8 ESV). The expression implies abundance, beauty, and plenty. Moses describes the land this way in Deuteronomy 8:7–9: "A land of brooks of water, of fountains and springs, flowing out in the valleys and hills, a land of wheat and barley, of vines and fig trees and pomegranates, a land of olive trees and honey, a land in which you will eat bread without scarcity, in which you will lack nothing, a land whose stones are iron, and out of whose hills you can dig copper" (ESV). To be in the Promised Land, then, is to be where God pours out His gracious gifts.

Do you see the connection? God's plan to change Moses is part of His greater plan to change Israel—to take His people from bondage to bounty, from a prison of hell to a land of abounding hope.

Spoiler alert! Multiple times, when push comes to shove, Israel loses sight of the Promised Land. With Pharaoh and his hordes breathing down their necks, God's people lament to Moses, "Is not this what we said to you in Egypt: 'Leave us alone that we may serve the Egyptians'?" (Exodus 14:12 ESV). The Israelites reject the land flowing with milk and honey not only at the Red Sea but again when they begin traveling in the wilderness. "Would that we had died by the hand of the LORD in the land of Egypt, when we sat by the meat pots and ate bread to the full" (Exodus 16:3 ESV).

Like Israel, when we don't robustly embrace *our* promised land— the new heaven and new earth—we try to turn our world into a promised land. Does this work? You tell me. When we demand that earth must be heaven, we torch relationships, make foolish decisions, and jeopardize our faith. Taking a page from Sisyphus in Greek mythology, we roll a rock up a hill—only to watch it roll down every time it gets close to the top. That's what living with unrealistic expectations looks like. Sheer madness.

Let's face it. This world is a house that's falling apart. The roof leaks, most of the electrical outlets don't work, the front door doesn't close all the way, and the lawn is full of dandelions and weeds. One day, the whole mess is going to collapse. Why, then, do we insist (sometimes vehemently) that things should be so much better in this world?

Work will never turn into a promised land, and neither will friendships, children, or marriage. Dead dreams, wilted flowers, heartbreaking moments, harsh winters, and haunting loneliness remind us this isn't heaven—not even close. True, the New Testament says that in Christ we have the firstfruits of the Spirit (Romans 8:23), a guarantee of our inheritance (Ephesians 1:14); that in Holy Communion we taste the powers of the coming age (Hebrews 6:5). But there's more to come—so much more! For now? Let's lay demanding aside and instead live with buoyant faith in the resurrection of the dead and the life of the world to come.

Our story, then, is Israel's story. God invites us to focus on what we can't see instead of what we can see, to place our hope in the new Jerusalem, where we will be with the triune God in all His glory, fall at His feet, and worship Him forevermore.

Our best days aren't behind us. Our sweetest moments didn't happen decades ago. Our peak performance wasn't in college. Our future is so much brighter than our past. Our future? There will be no more crying or weeping or sighing or sickness because the old order of things will pass away (Revelation 21:4). This promise cheers us in sorrow, strengthens us in trial, revives us in despair, gladdens us in darkness, and kindles in us a passionate devotion to our Savior's shed blood, His empty tomb, and His free gift of eternal life. Jesus will make all things—even you—completely new.

And so, like Moses, we cling to the future, even while pressing on faithfully today. We pray with all our might, "God, here I am. Change me!"

And yet.

WHO IS MOSES?

Like Moses, we have times of hesitation. "Who am I that I should go to Pharaoh and bring the children of Israel out of Egypt?" (Exodus 3:11 ESV). How does God respond? Do you think He said something like this? "Moses, where's your confidence, man? Where's your get-up-and-go? Don't you know you can do anything if you set your mind to it? Come on, Moses, the time is now!"

Of course God doesn't say that—not even close. Why? Because Moses' question "Who am I?" is always the wrong question. When we want to change, "Who am I?" is dead wrong—every single time! What's the right question? "God, who are You?"

Who is our God? He is the God who changes through a process, asking us to live by faith alone. God promises Moses, "And this shall be the sign to *you* [singular], that it is I who have sent *you* [singular]: when *you* [singular] have brought the people out of Egypt, *you* [plural] shall serve God on this mountain" (Exodus 3:12 ESV, emphasis added). The first three uses of *you* in this verse are singular. They refer to Moses. The last *you* is plural. It refers to the Israelites. What's true of Moses will soon be true for Israel. The entire nation will worship God on Mount Sinai.

This is shocking! Moses isn't looking for a *future* sign that will convince him of God's plan. Moses wants a sign right now. So do I! But change is a process. One step, one moment, one day at a time.

God says to us, "You'll see My plan unfold when you keep saying, 'Here I am!'" God wants us to keep taking steps toward getting our finances straightened out, repairing that relationship, getting serious about the words we use. *We'll get to the mountain.*

Have you ever picked up a piece of plywood from your backyard in July? You lift it up and bugs go running. You see all kinds of strange life-forms. Spiders and snakes! What happens next? You throw the plywood and run!

Change often looks like that. It's ugly and scary, with all kinds of strange life-forms. Spiders and snakes, bugs and lizards! We don't want to deal with it, so we run away and settle for a life of plain-Jane vanilla. I wouldn't blame Moses if he had told God, in the words of Samuel Hoffenstein's poem, "Come weal, come woe, my status is quo!"

GOD'S NAME

God gives Moses multiple reasons to trust Him. For instance, in Genesis 15:13–16, Yahweh pledges to rescue His people from oppression, make them rich in the process, and give them the Promised Land. That's quite a package deal!

This is Moses' opportunity of a lifetime—to serve as the General's top lieutenant in a project that can't fail. What's more, Moses now can stick it to Egypt—a regime that wanted him dead not once but twice. Guaranteed victory, acclaim, wealth, and vindication. What does Moses do? His gung-ho "Here I am" (Exodus 3:4 ESV) pivots to "Who am I?" (Exodus 3:11 ESV). How does God respond? From Exodus 3:4 through 4:17, He speaks to Moses thirteen different times. What's behind this back-and-forth? The two need to get on the same page because—as strange as it sounds—God has decided to change an eighty-year-old outcast shepherd into one of the most significant people who ever lived.

What's Moses' first excuse? He doesn't know God's name. With a book whose Hebrew title—translated into English—is "And These Are the Names," we arrive at its most significant name. In Exodus 3:14, Yahweh elusively says, "I AM WHO I AM" (ESV). The other two times in Exodus when God says "I am," He also assures Moses that divine presence will accompany him—come what may (Exodus 4:12, 15).

Yahweh, however, has a much greater goal than simply to rescue Moses. Five times within Exodus 7–14 He announces to Egypt, "I am

Yahweh" (Exodus 7:5, 17; 8:22; 14:4, 18). And five times He repeats this phrase to Moses or Israel (Exodus 6:2, 6, 7, 8, 29). It's not coincidental that there are ten plagues and Yahweh's name appears ten times in the song (*our song!*) in Exodus 15:1–18. And, of course, we all know there are Ten Commandments. Yahweh likes tens!

In the Book of Exodus, the definition of Yahweh's name doesn't unfold all at once. Instead, He defines it incrementally. In an ordered, progressive, and cumulative sequence, Exodus 3:14, 6:2–8, and 34:6–7 teach us about God's name—Yahweh. All three passages employ repetition:

- "I AM WHO I AM" (Exodus 3:14).
- "I am Yahweh. . . . I am Yahweh" (Exodus 6:2, 8).
- "And He proclaimed, 'Yahweh, Yahweh'" (Exodus 34:6).

While we might think that God's statement in Exodus 3:14 is a cryptic nonanswer, it's better to understand it along these lines: "I am what you will discover Me to be." The meaning of God's name will unfold chapter by chapter, plague by plague, miracle by miracle. New aspects of God's name play out in the book. It's a *process.* There's that word again!

"I AM" IN JOHN'S GOSPEL

Jesus gives us the fullest understanding of God's name. Toward the end of His ministry, Christ prays to the Father, "I have manifested Your name to the people whom You gave Me" (John 17:6 ESV). Leading up to this prayer, Jesus defines the "I AM" of Exodus 3:14. He is the "bread of life" (John 6:48 ESV) and the "light of the world" (John 8:12 ESV). Jesus is the "door" who leads to abundant life (John 10:9–10 ESV) as well as the "good shepherd" who lays down His life for the sheep (John 10:11–15 ESV). Jesus is the "resurrection and the life" (John 11:25 ESV), the "way, and the truth, and the life" (John 14:6 ESV), and the "vine" to whom branches are connected so they live and bear fruit (John 15:1–6 ESV).

Exodus 3:21–22 previews this new and abundant life that comes freely in Christ. In these verses, Moses quotes God as saying,

> I will give this people favor in the sight of the Egyptians; and when you go, you shall not go empty, but each woman shall ask of her neighbor, and any woman who lives in her house, for silver and gold jewelry, and for clothing. You shall put them on your sons and on your daughters. So you shall plunder the Egyptians. (ESV)

What went wrong in slavery will be made right when Israel leaves Egypt. Israelite cups will overflow. So says Yahweh!

MORE EXCUSES

Moses, however, has a hard time believing it. In chapter 4, he offers more excuses. Moses is the wrong man at the wrong time with the wrong skill set and wrong background. He doesn't believe dropping the name "I AM" to Israel's elders will get him very far. Recalling Exodus 2:14—when a fellow Israelite questions Moses' leadership—the concern is well-founded. The gist of Exodus 4:1–9 is that Israel's leaders also won't go along with the plan.

God therefore gives Moses two miracles: a rod that turns into a snake and a leprous hand that heals. God even throws in a third miracle, just in case the first two don't convince people: "Take some water from the Nile and pour it on the dry ground, and the water that you shall take from the Nile will become blood on the dry ground" (Exodus 4:9 ESV). Talk about fireworks filling the night sky!

Yet Moses isn't ready to sign on the dotted line. He laments to God, "I am slow of speech and of tongue" (Exodus 4:10 ESV). Yahweh responds by pledging to teach Moses what to say and how to say it. That's it? That's God's response? Why doesn't He correct Moses' speech impediment with a wave of His hand? That's what I'd do. If staffs can turn to snakes and hands can instantly become leprous, surely Moses' words can be made clear. It's time to end this endless back-and-forth conversation!

Do you want to know why God keeps it going? I suggest you sit down. Take a deep breath. Brace yourself. Here it comes. God doesn't correct every flaw before He uses people. God employs Moses—and us—warts and all.

Moses still doesn't believe it. Not for a New York minute.

We finally get to the bottom of things. It doesn't matter how many promises and how much power God gives him. The eighty-year-old exiled shepherd has had his mind made up all along. "My Lord, please send someone else" (Exodus 4:13 ESV). What? Moses' earlier objections were a smoke screen. He was never interested in the job. For the first time in this dialogue, God gets upset. Plan B goes into effect. God offers Aaron's help. Oh no. Not Aaron. Please, not Aaron! This will not turn out well. Remember the golden calf? That will be Aaron's doing and Israel's undoing (cf. Exodus 32).

Aaron's service to Moses is only temporary. As events move along in Exodus, we will see that Aaron decreases while Moses' role increases. Aaron is nowhere to be seen by the time of the Red Sea rescue in chapter 14. For now, though, Moses and Aaron—Levitical brothers by birth—are partners against the land of Egypt. They're not, however, equal partners. Regarding Aaron, God tells Moses, "He shall be your mouth, and you shall be as God to him" (Exodus 4:16 ESV).

OUR EXCUSES

Moses had a list of excuses. What are yours? "I'm too old." "I'm too young." "I'm too messed up." "My ship sailed." "My train left the station." Let me remind you about the voice from the bush. It's the Lord's Messenger. It's Jesus. Jesus says, "I love you. I shed My blood for you. I'm not finished with you. *There's important work to do.*"

In the early nineteenth century, Napoleon Bonaparte was in the middle of a fierce battle. His officers said, "If we don't retreat now, we'll be annihilated."

Napoleon called his bugler and ordered him, "Sound the retreat." The fourteen-year-old began to cry. Napoleon commanded him again, "Sound the retreat!"

The bugler replied, "I was never taught how to sound a retreat. I was only taught how to sound an advance."

"In that case," Napoleon commanded, "sound an advance!" The bugler sounded an advance and Napoleon won the battle.

You may want God to sound a retreat, but God only knows how to sound an advance. It's called the fire of God—first revealed to Moses in the bush, now given to us in Holy Baptism. God is determined to change us. What shall we say? How about this? "Here I am. Send me!" That's what the Bible calls "faith."

MOSES AND FAITH

Moses (finally!) goes along with God's plan to change him—albeit still with some hesitation. He tells Jethro, his father-in-law, "Please let me go back to my brothers in Egypt to see whether they are still alive" (Exodus 4:18 ESV). Really? No mention of the burning bush? His conversations with God? The staff, snake, hand, and blood? "To see whether they are still alive," isn't the job description God gave Moses, but at least he's moving in the right direction—toward Egypt. How? By faith.

If you had to summarize your life in six words, what words would you use? Several years ago, an online magazine asked that question. It was flooded with responses. Here are a few of them: "One tooth. One cavity. Life's cruel." "Savior complex makes for many disappointments." "Thought I would have more impact."[1]

Using just six words, how would you summarize some of the people in the Bible? How about this for Noah: "Loathed the rain. Loved the rainbow." How about these words for Shadrach, Meshach, and Abednego: "King was hot. Furnace was not." What do you think about these

---

1 Adam Phillips, "What Is the Story of Your Life? Please Summarize in Six Words," *Voice of America: Learning English*, March 12, 2008, https://learningenglish.voanews.com/a/a-23-2008-03-12 -voa2-83136407/117417.html.

six words for the prodigal son: "Bad. Sad. Dad glad. Brother mad." Here are words for the Good Samaritan: "I came. I saw. I stopped."

The following six words summarize what Hebrews 11 says about Moses: "Walked by faith, not by sight." "By faith" appears eighteen times in Hebrews 11. The chapter begins with these words: "Faith is the assurance of things hoped for, the conviction of things *not seen*" (Hebrews 11:1 ESV, emphasis added). Walk by faith, not by sight. That's Hebrews 11. That's Moses. And that can be us—more and more. How?

See God's promise ahead of us: "[Moses] considered the reproach of Christ greater wealth than the treasures of Egypt, for he was looking to the reward" (Hebrews 11:26 ESV).

I fly enough to know that most airlines have something along the lines of Executive club members, Gold Star club members, and Silver Star club members. The airline club you belong to determines your seat size, discounts, and flight entry order. Airlines presume we want to be the first to board, sit in first-class luxury, and get a lot of free stuff in the mail.

In Moses' day, Egyptians were in the Executive club flying first class. And the Israelites? They were stuck in coach, at the back of the plane— some of them were even hanging on to the fuselage. But Moses would still rather hitchhike than fly first class with the regime's VIPs (Very Important Pharaohs). He would rather be in the Mud Club with state slaves making bricks and building pyramids. Why? Moses was looking ahead to his reward. His glorious future. The Promised Land.

If we don't look ahead, then we look behind. And if we look behind, the temptation is to get stuck in regret.

Maybe we're not looking ahead or looking behind. Maybe we're looking around. Then the enticement is to allow envy and greed to fill our hearts. "Look at that new truck he just bought!" "Did you hear where they went on vacation over Christmas?" "Take a look at her new home! It must be at least ten thousand square feet!"

Faith doesn't look back. Faith doesn't look around. Faith looks ahead. And what's ahead? The promised land—our heavenly promised land. Given by the Father, sealed in the Savior's blood, and guaranteed by the Holy Spirit. In our promised land, there will be no disease, no divorce, no darkness, and death will be defeated and dead. It's God's gift to you! Claim it and begin living by faith instead of sight.

I must advise you, though. Doing so won't be easy. Moses chose "to be mistreated with the people of God rather than to enjoy the fleeting *pleasures of sin*" (Hebrews 11:25 ESV, emphasis added). Think of the "pleasures of sin" as ugly black cockroaches that scream at us, saying, "You'll never amount to anything unless you crush it in the marketplace and take home a lot of dough!" "If you don't compromise your sexual standards, you'll lose the one person who cares for you the most!" "Only a fool would go on turning the other cheek! Get revenge! Stick it to them!" These are lies. Don't embrace them. Instead, open the window of God's promise ahead of you. Let it shine on all those ugly, black cockroaches. Then watch them head for the hills!

Faith also sees God's presence beside us. "By faith [Moses] left Egypt, not being afraid of the anger of the king, for he endured as seeing *Him who is invisible*" (Hebrews 11:27 ESV, emphasis added). It's tough to persevere. The average human attention span has fallen from twelve seconds in the year 2000 to eight seconds today. (This is not good news for pastors!) Goldfish, meanwhile, have an attention span of nine seconds. Goldfish are more focused than people. How did Moses stay focused and persevere? He saw "Him who is invisible."

Have you ever tried to complete a puzzle with hidden objects? The picture may contain mice, flowers, ants, and sand. Amid it all, we're supposed to find a mushroom, a teepee, an angel, and a penguin. Seeing the invisible isn't something we're very good at. But it can be done. Moses did it. Moses saw God in the burning bush. Moses saw God in the ten plagues. Moses saw God in the tabernacle—filling it with divine glory.

Where do we see God? We study the Bible to see God's presence beside us. Holy Baptism and the Holy Supper of Christ's true body and blood are also where God guarantees He is present to forgive, renew, and strengthen faith.

Moses will soon learn that God's presence comes through a pillar of cloud by day and a pillar of fire by night (Exodus 13:21)—another Exodus story whose backstory is in Genesis. God gave Abram a preview of this miraculous guiding pillar. Once, while the patriarch was asleep, God passed through slain animals to make a covenant, doing so through "a smoking fire pot and a flaming torch" (Genesis 15:17 ESV). This fire and a cloud portend God's leading Moses and Israel in the Book of Exodus.

Faith sees God's promise ahead of us and His presence beside us. Faith also sees God's provision for us. "By faith [Moses] kept the Passover and sprinkled the blood, so that the Destroyer of the firstborn might not touch them" (Hebrews 11:28 ESV). You probably know about the Blue Book for cars. Officially, it's called *Kelley Blue Book*. Open it up and you'll see how much your car is worth. In 2020, my 2004 Honda Odyssey Minivan was worth $3,987. That same year, my 2007 Honda CRV was worth $4,089. Anyone interested in some good deals on some really good cars? Facebook me and I'll give you a price you can't refuse!

Passover blood showed Moses and Israel what they were worth. God loved His people so much that He provided blood to save them. Christ is the final Passover Lamb. We're worth the price of Christ's blood. There's a word to describe us—*invaluable*.

Normally, when someone dies, their impact on the world begins to recede. A few years ago, we had Bob Hope, Johnny Cash, and Steve Jobs. These days we have no Jobs, no Cash, and no Hope! In contrast, Christ's impact on the world after His death was greater than during His life. How can we be so sure? Jesus rose from the dead! Now He shouts from the rooftops, "You are infinitely valuable to Me!" Christ's body and blood given in Holy Communion provide atonement, cleansing, healing, and forgiveness. Where God guides, He provides!

Finally, faith sees God's power leading us. "By faith the people crossed the Red Sea as on dry land; but the Egyptians, when they attempted to do the same, were drowned" (Hebrews 11:29 ESV). This is our story too! God's power leads us—out of slavery and bondage and into freedom and fullness.

Walt Disney was one of the most visionary people in American history. He made ground-breaking movies, took cartoon animation to a new level, and founded Disneyland in California and Disney World in Florida. Disney World opened just after Walt Disney died. Lillian Disney, Walt's wife, was asked to speak at the grand opening. The man who introduced her said, "Mrs. Disney, I wish Walt could have seen this."

Lillian Disney stood up and said, "He did." That's it! Two words and her speech was over. "He did!" Walt Disney saw it all.

So did Moses. Moses saw it all. God's promise, God's presence, God's provision, and God's power. How about us?

Paint six words on your front door. Have them tattooed on your left thigh. Follow them all the days of your life. What are they? "Walk by faith, not by sight."

TAKE YOUR STAFF

As Moses was packing his bags for Egypt, God said, "Take in your hand this staff" (Exodus 4:17 ESV). Why does God need to remind Moses to take a staff? Through his staff, Moses will call down plagues, part the Red Sea, control the east wind, and bring water out of a rock.

In Egypt, a rod or staff implied royalty, power, and authority. Pharaohs are depicted in Egyptian artwork as wielding their mighty staffs. Moses may be done tending sheep with his staff, but his "staff-against-staff" showdown with Pharaoh is just about to begin.

GOD IS OUR FATHER

With staff in hand, what do you think God wants Moses to tell Pharaoh? "Your time is up." "Get a new job." "God has forecasted hell and high water for you and your people." No. The very first thing God wants Moses to say to Pharaoh is that Israel is Yahweh's firstborn son (Exodus 4:22).

Israel is not an ethnic, social, ideological, political, or national movement. Israel is God's son. Yahweh, Israel's Father, created, made, and established His people (Deuteronomy 32:6). God will carry them like a son through the wilderness (Deuteronomy 1:31) for He is compassionate toward His children (Psalm 103:13).

This all points to Jesus.

Christ demonstrates the perfect Father/Son relationship. Following Herod's death, Matthew announces that Jesus is the Son called out of Egypt. "Out of Egypt I called My son" (Matthew 2:15 ESV, quoting Hosea 11:1). When John baptized Jesus, the Father announced, "You are My beloved Son" (Mark 1:11 ESV). At His transfiguration, these words were repeated (Mark 9:7). In the anguish of Gethsemane, Jesus prayed, "Abba Father, all things are possible for You. Remove this cup from Me. Yet not what I will, but what You will" (Mark 14:36 ESV).

Through Christ, the baptized are also privileged to call God "Father." Our Father in heaven loves, listens, corrects, rebukes, forgives, provides, and sacrifices for us. God has high hopes for His children. He also has the authority to redirect our lives when we don't conform to His will. Nothing happens without our Father knowing about it (Matthew 6:4, 6, 8, 18; Luke 16:15). Paul goes so far as to assert that through the Holy Spirit we join Jesus in calling to God, "Abba! Father!" (Romans 8:15; Galatians 4:6).

God isn't an angry tyrant. God isn't out to get us. God isn't an impersonal force. No. God is a Father. God is *our* Father. When we're baptized, God adopts us. We go from condemned orphans with no hope to adopted children with no fear.

Our heavenly Father will never let us down. He's dependable. He's reliable. He's entirely worthy of our trust. James 1:17 states, "Every good gift and every perfect gift is from above, coming down from the Father of lights, with whom there is no variation or shadow due to change"

(ESV). Our Father is never moody. He never has a bad day. He never wakes up in the morning wondering, "Who am I going to zap today?" Our heavenly Father's love is always the same. It is consistent when we are not.

Our Father in heaven is also close. "Through [Christ] we . . . have access in one Spirit to the Father" (Ephesians 2:18 ESV). Some of us grew up with absentee fathers. Maybe they didn't live in our home. Or if they did, they were often on business trips or out with friends. Or even when they were home, they were busy—working in the garage, mowing the lawn, watching television. God, our heavenly Father, isn't detached or distant. In Christ, He's close. "In Him we live and move and have our being" (Acts 17:28 ESV).

God is also a competent Father. He can handle any problem. Nothing is beyond His ability. That's good news because if God was consistent and if God was close but He didn't have any power to do anything about our suffering, He wouldn't be of much help. Imagine our heavenly Father saying, "I can't do anything about it, but I feel your pain."

When my three children were growing up, I was shocked at what they expected me to do. Some days they wanted me to change the weather. Other days they wanted me to shorten the school year. Still other days they wanted me to bring back a television program they had missed. My son, Jonathan, once asked me to fix G.I. Joe's head when our dog Maverick chewed it off. After years, Joe was still headless. My oldest daughter, Abi, asked me to fix her bookshelf. The shelf is still bookless. And my other daughter asked me to repair her bike. Lori Beth is still bikeless. Growing up, my kids expected me to know all things, fix anything, and afford everything. They thought I was Superman. Fat chance! But there is a Father who isn't limited in resources or wisdom or energy.

Is God everybody's Father? Is everybody a child of God? Everyone was created by God but not everybody is connected as His child. There's a lot more to being a father than just creating a child. It takes more than creating. It takes connecting.

How does God connect with us as our Father? By grace, through faith—apart from anything we think, say, or do. Personal faith in Christ's death and resurrection is the only one way to get connected to the Father. Once connected, this Father knows us intimately. He loves us completely. He accepts us unconditionally.

And He wants us.

We can go to our Father for approval and acceptance and advice. He watched us being formed in our mother's womb. He celebrated when we took our first step. He has seen every tear that's fallen, every success we've had, every joy, every regret, every jealousy, every sin. He knows the good, the bad, and the ugly. God still loves us.

I invite you to pour your heart out to God, who through faith in Christ is your heavenly Father. Give Him your pain, your problems, and all your perplexities. Why should you do that? Because this Father is consistent and close and competent—forever. That's Moses' first message to Pharaoh. That's Christ's final message to you.

Moses, however, is about to learn—through a near-death experience—that it's completely foolish to take this Father for granted.

GOD TRIES TO KILL MOSES

When Moses saw an Egyptian beating a Hebrew, he killed the Egyptian (Exodus 2:11–12). When Pharaoh Ahmose I heard Moses had killed the Egyptian, "he sought to kill Moses" (Exodus 2:15 ESV). These aren't difficult circumstances to understand. Moses killed an Egyptian to save a fellow Hebrew. The pharaoh wanted Moses killed as a matter of justice.

The attempted killing at the end of Exodus 4, however, is a different matter altogether. Yahweh meets Moses on his way from Midian to Egypt—doing exactly what God had asked him to do. Then what? "The LORD met [Moses] and sought to put him to death" (Exodus 4:24 ESV). Are you confused?

Three women (Jochebed, Miriam, and Pharaoh's daughter) rescue Moses in chapter 2. Now another woman rescues him—this time, it's his wife. "Then Zipporah took a flint and cut off her son's foreskin and touched Moses' feet with it" (Exodus 4:25 ESV). Zipporah "touched" Moses' feet with blood and he was saved. Are you confused even more?

We're learning that early events in Exodus often preview later events. In this case, part of the Passover ritual in Exodus 12 includes "touching" doorposts with blood. This saves the Israelites from the tenth plague— the angel of death (Exodus 12:13, 22–23). How is this associated with Moses' near-death encounter? *Moses experienced Passover before Passover.* What's true of one rescue through blood will become true of many rescued through blood.

Events in Exodus 3 and 19 bolster the idea that what happens to Moses also happens to Israel. In chapter 3, Moses meets God on Mount Sinai. In Exodus 19, all of Israel meets God on Mount Sinai.

Strategically, Moses' brush with death happens right before he begins his ministry (Exodus 4:29). Though a great hero of faith, Moses still needs the gift of reconciling blood. "It is the blood that makes atonement" (Leviticus 17:11 ESV).

CHAPTER 4

Boldness in the Face of Bricks:
Exodus 5–6

The LORD made His people very
fruitful and made them stronger than their foes.
(Psalm 105:24 ESV)

Moses has his assignment. Check. Moses has three signs. Check. Moses also teams up with his older brother, Aaron. Check. God gives faith so the Israelite people and elders trust Moses and Aaron. Check. Everything is moving like clockwork. What a winning streak! Moses is on a roll!

Turning to Exodus 5, we expect the Israelites to be out of Egypt in no time. We can picture Moses marching into Pharaoh's court and demanding he let the Hebrew slaves go, and that will be that. Exodus 5:1 records Moses and Aaron saying this to the Egyptian king: "Thus says the LORD, the God of Israel, 'Let My people go, that they may hold a feast to Me in the wilderness'" (ESV). Happy days are here again!

Pharaoh Thutmose III puts his foot on the brake—saying, in effect, "No way, José!" The king defiantly asks, "Who is Yahweh?" (Exodus 5:2). The prior pharaoh didn't know Joseph (Exodus 1:8). Now this pharaoh doesn't know Yahweh. Egyptian pharaohs need a remedial course in Old Testament history!

It's as if Thutmose III says, "Yahweh? Humph! He's not a god worth knowing!" We can imagine the pharaoh's tone of voice as he dismisses two old men. "Get lost, you old geezers! I'm a busy bureaucrat with much more pressing issues!" And, unlike Pharaoh Ahmose I in chapters 1 and 2, Thutmose III isn't threatened by the vast number of Hebrew slaves. Instead of trying to reduce their number through murder, he seeks to exploit their growing population for work. Both pharaohs, however, have this in common: they place themselves at odds with the God who made the heavens and the earth. A dangerous position, you think? By saying he doesn't know Yahweh, Pharaoh lays down the gauntlet. He dares to pick a fight with God. God's response? "Game on!"

Pharaoh's taunt, "Who is Yahweh?" (Exodus 5:2) will come back to haunt him—and Egypt. Like a steady drumbeat, we hear about God's plan not only to make sure Pharaoh knows but also with him all the earth (e.g., Exodus 7:5; 8:10, 22; 9:14, 29; 10:2; 11:7; 14:4, 18). It will take the parting of the Red Sea for Egypt's brightest and best to confess, "Let us flee from Israel, for Yahweh fights for them against the Egyptians" (Exodus 14:25).

Pharaoh is a fool for not recognizing this ultimate catastrophe. What isn't foolish, though, is that he puts a wedge between Moses and the Hebrew foremen who are responsible for meeting the daily quota of bricks. This "divide and conquer" strategy will prove to be powerful.

PHARAOH, A DRAGON, AND A SNAKE

Egyptian kings are more than stubborn leaders who lack insight on some finer nuances of Old Testament theology. And they are more than pyramid-makers and empire-builders. The Bible teaches that pharaohs are Satan's minions aligned with every sort of evil. To import Pauline terms, Egypt's leaders aren't merely flesh and blood, but rather rulers, authorities, and cosmic powers of evil in the heavenly realms (Ephesians 6:12).

This is why the prophet Ezekiel equates Egypt's pharaohs with sea monsters. He quotes Yahweh as saying, "Behold, I am against you, Pharaoh king of Egypt, the great *dragon* that lies in the midst of his streams" (Ezekiel 29:3 ESV, emphasis added). Then this: "You consid-

er yourself a lion of the nations, but you are like a *dragon* in the seas"
(Ezekiel 32:2 ESV, emphasis added).

Recall the discussion in chapter 1 where I pointed out that several
Old Testament verses equate *Egypt* with a dragon. Now it's the pharaohs. Behind both dragons is *the* dragon—the ancient snake who is the
devil and Satan (Revelation 12:9; 20:2).

The contest between Moses and Pharaoh's magic-makers in Exodus
7 includes serpents—not only because of the link to Genesis 3:15 and
Christ crushing the serpent's head but also because ancient Egyptian
kings employed serpents to represent their power. The most famous
pharaonic headdress, that on King Tut's coffin, includes a cobra.

John portrays Christ's final triumph using these same images—a
dragon and a serpent. He writes, "The great *dragon* was thrown down,
that ancient *serpent*, who is called the devil and Satan, the deceiver of
the whole world—he was thrown down to the earth, and his angels were
thrown down with him" (Revelation 12:9 ESV, emphasis added).

This story is our story—it's the exodus story. Christ, the slain Passover Lamb, defeats and finally destroys our enemy, who will drown in a
lake of fire (Revelation 20:10).

MORE BRICKS!

As state slaves in Egypt, the Israelites had no legal status, no worth,
and no value. Their sons were murdered, tools of torture brought may-
hem, and the daily quota of bricks meant a life of endless monotony.

In their first rescue attempt, Moses and Aaron run into a brick wall
(pun intended). Israelite slaves continue making bricks—only now with
this pharaonic ultimatum, "You shall no longer give the people straw to
make bricks, as in the past; let them go and gather straw for themselves.
But the number of bricks that they made in the past you shall impose
on them, you shall by no means reduce it" (Exodus 5:7–8 ESV). The
empire's organizational blueprint functioned like their pyramids—a few
at the top benefited through the toil and sweat of masses at the bottom.

And Pharaoh won't let anyone mess with this well-oiled machine. Thus, he spews forth this short but toxic propaganda about the Hebrew slaves: They "are idle" (Exodus 5:8, 17 ESV). In other words, "The Hebrews are a bunch of whining, crying, lazy bums!" Pharaoh's goal? Blame the oppressed instead of the oppressors. "It's their fault that they're in such a mess. If they would get more motivation, organization, and education—they would have such a better life." Such is the twisted logic of all oppressors.

The king's decree is draconian—production takes priority over people. Brick quotas remain while slaves now supply straw. And straw was more than a binding agent. It enhanced the bricks' strength and flexibility. Apart from chopped straw, bricks lost their shape and became useless.

When Egypt stopped providing straw for making bricks, life became unbearable. "Why have you not done all your task of making bricks today and yesterday, as in the past?" (Exodus 5:14 ESV). If you've ever tried to hang wallpaper with one arm, you're beginning to understand how desperate things are becoming.

Pity Moses and Aaron. Israelite foremen meet them, point their accusing fingers, and say, "The Lord look on you and judge, because you have made us stink in the sight of Pharaoh and his servants, and have put a sword in their hand to kill us" (Exodus 5:21 ESV). These supervisors, who sold out to the system, dared to scold their God-ordained leaders. It wasn't enough to ask for divine judgment upon Moses and Aaron. The foremen add insult to injury by blaming these two old men for Egypt's animosity. Really? Hadn't the Hebrews been mistreated since Exodus 1:11–14? Wasn't Moses himself once a target of Egypt's plan to exterminate every Hebrew baby boy? Is this really fair? One thing is certain. Being called by God and having the assurance of His presence doesn't mean immediate results. Moses is now behind the eight ball—despised by both the Egyptians and Hebrews. Tending sheep was so much easier!

By the end of chapter 5, Pharaoh isn't about to let Israel go, there's mutiny in the ranks, and Moses has returned to his skepticism that appears throughout Exodus 3–4. He needs to remember Joseph's up-and-down journey of leadership—after all, he wrote it.

JOSEPH'S STORY

Joseph had two dreams. In the first one, his sheaf arises and his brothers' sheaves bow down to his. In his second dream, Joseph envisions the sun, moon, and eleven stars worshiping him. The interpretation seems simple, doesn't it? Joseph goes up. Everyone else goes down. However, it wasn't going to be that easy. Just like Moses, there are complications. Things for Joseph get worse before they get better.

You know the story. Joseph is his father's favorite, but his brothers despise him. His dad gives him a coat of many colors, but his brothers rip it off and sell him to some Ishmaelites coming from Gilead on their way to Egypt. Once in the land of the Nile, Joseph goes to work for Potiphar, a high-ranking Egyptian official, and ends up in charge of everything. And Genesis 39:6 says, "Joseph was handsome in form and appearance" (ESV).

One day, Potiphar's wife says, "Lie with me" (Genesis 39:7 ESV). But Joseph says, "How then can I do this great wickedness and sin against God?" (Genesis 39:9 ESV). This spurned woman goes for Joseph's jugular. He said! She said! And since there were no sexual harassment laws in Egypt, Joseph is thrown into the slammer. While in prison, he interprets a dream of Pharaoh's chief cupbearer, who is then released (Genesis 40:21). Then Pharaoh has two dreams of his own that no one can interpret. The cupbearer, having forgotten Joseph for two years, finally mentions that Joseph is a master at interpreting dreams (Genesis 41:9–13). God gave Joseph the interpretation, and Pharaoh was pleased. Through it all, twenty-three years to be exact, Joseph finally becomes Egypt's vice-president.

Another member of Joseph and Moses' family also went through a meat grinder. He, too, was called by God, yet was also rejected. "He came to His own, but His own people did not receive Him" (John 1:11 ESV). Jesus was misunderstood by the scribes, hated by the Pharisees, despised by the Sadducees, and handed over to the Romans. Pontius Pilate had Him scourged—just inches short of death. But the most heinous act of rejection came from the Father, who abandoned His Son. The end? I think not! Jesus is alive—bodily, victoriously, and eternally. For you!

Meaning what? Our hell, heartbreak, and hurt are Father-filtered. He has a purpose for our pain. Listen to Joseph speaking to his brothers: "You meant evil against me, but God meant it for good; to bring it about that many people should be kept alive" (Genesis 50:20 ESV).

Paul famously puts it this way: "We know that for those who love God all things work together for good" (Romans 8:28 ESV). Paul doesn't say, "All things are good." *All things are not good.* They hurt us and confuse us and mess with our minds. Neither does Paul say, "We're pretty sure that" or "Wouldn't it be nice if." No. Paul is convinced. We *know* that the God of Abraham, Isaac, and Jacob—the God of Joseph and Moses, the God and Father of our Lord, Jesus Christ—takes life's bitter experiences, works them together, and re-creates people who are humble, kind, courageous, resilient, and spiritually mature.

Like Joseph, Moses had every right to become bitter, feel betrayed, and throw in the towel. *But he didn't.* There's a plan—a divine plan—a plan where all things are working for our good and the Father's glory.

OUR UNPLANNED STORIES

Get ready. Here comes a massive understatement. We have a lot in common with Joseph and Moses. Our lives haven't gone the way we expected. Neither did last year, last month, or last week. Why does life so often seem unfair? Why, despite our careful planning, does the next chapter turn out to be so topsy-turvy?

Here's the answer: we're not the author of our story. God is. David puts it this way: "In Your book *were written*, every one of them, the days that were formed for me" (Psalm 139:16 ESV, emphasis added). The key expression is "were written." The script is already in place. The book has been published. God has composed our story—and it's an exodus story.

It's time to put down our pen or close our laptop. But it's also a time to rejoice. Every twist in the plot is for our good. Every new character is God's gift. Every new chapter advances the divine plan. *Every ending is a new beginning.*

You protest, "Not so fast!" I know. I'm with you. We both want our pen back—along with an eraser—so we can delete all our despair and add happiness, tender moments, and brilliant sunsets. And while we're at it, we can introduce people who pump up our egos, go along with our agendas, fill our needs, and never question our judgment. The story will go our way, according to our timetable, and sidestep all hardships. Yes!

How do you think that story will end? Check out Genesis 3. Adam and Eve sing with Sinatra, "I did it my way." Everything comes crashing down. "Whoever is wise, let him understand these things; whoever is discerning, let him know them; for the ways of the Lord are right" (Hosea 14:9 ESV). It's time again to turn over our will to God's. That's what Moses is about to learn.

GOD ANSWERS MOSES

Moses thinks he knows the story. Chapter 1: The burning bush. Chapter 2: Pharaoh lets Israel go. Chapter 3: Retire in the land flowing with milk and honey—probably on the Mediterranean coast! Yet, since God writes the story and we don't, Moses is going to encounter a few dozen detours and several dead ends. How so?

Pharaoh blames Moses. Pharaoh blames Israelite foremen. The foremen return the favor and blame Pharaoh. The Hebrew leaders then blame Moses. And if there isn't enough blame to go around, at the end of Exodus 5, Moses blames God. "You have not delivered Your people at all" (Exodus 5:23 ESV). God tells Moses something like this, "One strike doesn't mean you're out. Even two is no reason to fear. I'm weaving together a beautiful story—custom-made just for you. How can I be so sure? *My name is Yahweh.*"

GOD'S NAME: 2.0

We're discovering that the Book of Exodus repeats key themes, motifs, and ideas. Moses makes a point, then later develops and expands upon it—often with increased emphasis and added importance. For instance, in Exodus 2:11–14, a solitary Israelite rejects Moses' leadership. In Exodus 5:21, however, a group of Israelite foremen spurns him. Later, when Pharaoh and his army are hot on their heels, the entire group of slaves rejects Moses: "Is it because there are no graves in Egypt that you have taken us away to die in the wilderness?" (Exodus 14:11 ESV).

The most significant reworked topic in Exodus, though, is God's name—Yahweh. The "I AM" of Exodus 3:14 is expanded in Exodus 6:2–8 with a fuller expression, making these verses a more emphatic definition of *Yahweh*.

God's momentous revelation of His name at the burning bush is followed by several setbacks. Moses and Aaron speak God's Word to Israel's elders and people, whose initial response of faith and worship sounds a hopeful note (Exodus 4:28–31). Yet circumstances quickly deteriorate. Pharaoh mocks Yahweh's plan and challenges His authority: "Who is Yahweh that I should obey His voice by letting Israel go? I do not know Yahweh, and I will not let Israel go!" (Exodus 5:2).

Exodus 6:2–8 comes within this context of Pharaoh's defiance, the people's disillusionment, and Moses' dismay. Within these verses, God tells Moses four times, "I am Yahweh" (Exodus 6:2, 6, 7, 8) while Yahweh says "I will" seven times. Do the math and what do you have? *Yahweh's plans will not be thwarted.*

God declares in Exodus 6:3, "I appeared to Abraham, to Isaac, and to Jacob, as God Almighty, but by My name Yahweh I did not make Myself known to them" (Exodus 6:3). Do you see the dilemma in this verse? It appears that God didn't give His name, Yahweh, to Israel's ancestors. If this is the case, what should we do with verses like this: "To Seth also a son was born, and he called his name Enosh. At that time people began to call upon the name of Yahweh" (Genesis 4:26)? Indeed, the name *Yahweh* appears in multiple verses throughout the Book of Genesis.

Exodus 6:3, however, doesn't contradict Genesis. Instead, it announces God's plan to bring greater clarity to His name. The verse has nothing to do with *when* the name *Yahweh* is revealed. It has everything to do with *what* the name *Yahweh* reveals. A more comprehensive definition of God's name becomes clear through His deliverance of Israel from Egypt, as well as His ensuing dealings with His people at Sinai.

The second time Yahweh defines His name in Exodus, He twice promises to bring Israel out of Egypt (Exodus 6:6, 7). These verses challenge Pharaoh's double-reference to burdens in the preceding chapter: "Moses and Aaron, why do you take the people away from their work? Get back to your *burdens*. . . . You make them rest from their *burdens*" (Exodus 5:4–5 ESV, emphasis added).

In Exodus 6:6, the Hebrew verb *redeem* appears for only the second time in the Old Testament (Genesis 48:16). A redeemer acts because a family member is in desperate straits. Yahweh's decision to redeem the Israelites, therefore, is based upon the fact that they're His family members—indeed, the nation is His firstborn son (Exodus 4:22).

Yahweh redeems "with an outstretched arm" (Exodus 6:6 ESV). Several temples that Hebrew slaves built had larger-than-life images of a pharaoh's arm. For instance, the temple at Karnak depicts Thutmose III with a huge, outstretched arm. No wonder the image of God's mighty arm—stronger than any pharaoh—makes a permanent impression on biblical authors (e.g., Deuteronomy 4:34; 5:15; 7:19; 2 Chronicles 6:32; Psalm 136:12; Jeremiah 21:5; 32:17; Ezekiel 20:33). Even Mary, in her marvelous Magnificat, sings of divine power with these words, "He has shown strength with His arm" (Luke 1:51 ESV).

Following the promise to employ His "outstretched arm," for the first time in the book, Yahweh invokes an oath (Exodus 6:8) that includes both the gift of Promised Land (Exodus 6:4, 8) as well as a personal bond: "I will take you to be My people, and I will be Your God" (Exodus 6:7 ESV). Yahweh is deeply committed to Israel. *These are His people!*

The exodus from Egypt, however, didn't establish Israel as God's people. The patriarchal covenant did that (e.g., Genesis 17:7). Hence, before their departure from Egypt, God frequently calls the Israelites "My people" (e.g., Exodus 3:7, 10; 5:1; 7:4, 16; 8:1; 9:1, 13; 10:3).

If this is true, though, what do the future-focused verbs mean in this statement? "I *will* take you to be My people, and I *will* be your God" (Exodus 6:7 ESV, emphasis added). Deuteronomy 4:20 sheds light on this dilemma. "The LORD has taken you and brought you out of the iron furnace, out of Egypt, to be a people of His own inheritance, as you are this day" (ESV). Consequently, the phrase in Exodus 6:7 refers to the exodus event and not Israel's status as God's people—thus emphasizing the fact that the Israelites belong to Yahweh, not to Pharaoh.

Pharaoh's statement that he doesn't know Yahweh (Exodus 5:2) and God's assertion that He didn't make Himself known by the name *Yahweh* to the patriarchs (Exodus 6:3) prompts God's response, "You shall know that I am Yahweh your God" (Exodus 6:7). The plagues and Red Sea victory will accomplish God's intention—Pharaoh, Egypt, and Israel will all come to know Yahweh's incomparable ways (Exodus 7:5, 17; 8:10, 22; 9:29; 10:2; 11:7; 14:4, 18). This God commands the galaxies, moves the stars, rescues His people, and leads them to a land flowing with milk and honey.

To summarize, Exodus 6:2–8—bracketed by the expression "I am Yahweh"—furthers our understanding of God's name by announcing His threefold purpose. First, Yahweh will rescue Israel from Egypt with an outstretched arm and great acts of judgment. Second, He will remove Israel from Pharaoh's authority and place them under His own. And third, God will bring His people into the Promised Land.

Gospel. More Gospel. Additional Gospel. *This is Yahweh!*

LIGHT SHINES IN THE DARKNESS

Sometimes everything goes dark. As Exodus 6 begins, that's Moses' world. And, as Psalm 88 ends, that's Heman's world. Heman has only one recorded psalm, and it's the Psalter's darkest prayer. How dark? The last line includes these words: "My companions have become darkness" (Psalm 88:18 ESV). All is not lost! David counters Heman's anguish with this prayer, "The darkness is not dark to You; the night is bright as the day, for darkness is as light with You" (Psalm 139:12 ESV). Yahweh doesn't leave Moses in the dark. And David won't let Heman stay there either. My aunt and uncle also had a thing or two to say about life's darkness.

A clock for Christmas isn't exactly the kind of gift that thrills a ten-year-old boy. I said thank you to my Aunt Corinne and Uncle Larry, took the clock upstairs to my bedroom, put it on a nightstand, and plugged it in. In those days, snooze buttons hadn't been invented. To silence the alarm, I sometimes envisioned throwing it across the room. That, or borrowing my father's sledgehammer!

Over time, however, I became attached to my alarm clock. Don't tell anyone, but I even took it to college! That's because my alarm clock had one redeeming feature: the clockface glowed at night. When your room is dark, your best friend is a bright light.

Do you know about dark rooms? Loneliness. Depression. Shame. Guilt. Emptiness. Rage. Cancer. Death. They crawl under the door, sneak into the room, and hide under the bed. Everything becomes dark, very dark. Then, just when we least expect him, the prince of darkness shows up, pointing his accusing finger and running down his list of our failures, foibles, and faithlessness.

God shows up in Exodus 6 when Moses is sitting in the shadows. God also shows up when we're groping in the dark. That's what John 1:5 promises, "The light *shines* in the darkness, and the darkness has not overcome it" (ESV, emphasis added). Note the verb *shines*. It's a present-tense verb. John doesn't write, "The light shone." Nor does he write, "The light will shine." John writes, "The light *shines* in the darkness." In your darkness.

In your deep darkness, in the darkest hours of your life, this light shines. "And the darkness has not overcome it" (John 1:5 ESV).

With those last words, John prepares us for Good Friday. Talk about a dark day! Nails. Blood. Sweat. Tears. Darkness. Oh my, the darkness! Three hours of darkness! And then, death. Three days later, though, the light shines (present tense, *shines*!). The darkness will never overcome Jesus. The darkness will never overcome you!

And the darkness didn't overcome Moses. Moses had God's name. "The name of Yahweh is a strong tower; the righteous run to it and are saved" (Proverbs 18:10). In the name of Jesus, we have a strong tower. In the name of Jesus, we are priceless.

ABSOLUTELY PRICELESS

On November 22, 1963, John Fitzgerald Kennedy arrived at Love Field in Dallas, Texas. Later that day, as he was traveling in a motorcade through Dealey Plaza, America's thirty-fifth president was assassinated by Lee Harvey Oswald. Something else in American history also happened on that day.

Looking to buy some land, a man got into a small plane and began flying over central Florida. By noon, he had found a choice spot, where Interstate 4 was going to cross the Florida turnpike. The cross-point of two major thoroughfares, along with a nearby airport, was an ideal location for his new business venture.

However, there was one gigantic problem. The land he wanted to buy was filled with swamps. Throwing caution to the wind, the businessman began buying up land anyway. When word got out, people thought he was crazy. No one buys swampland. That's insane! The locals began warning him, "Listen to us! Cut your losses. Get out while you can! Why, you could lose your shirt!"

The man? Walt Disney. The land? South of Orlando, Florida. The business venture? Disney World. And my point? What some deem worthless others call priceless.

What did Yahweh see? Why would He go to the trouble of calling Moses, wrangling with Pharaoh, and orchestrating ten jaw-dropping plagues? What the Egyptians deemed worthless—Hebrew slaves—Yahweh called absolutely priceless.

CHAPTER 5

Powerful Plagues: Exodus 7–11

> He sent Moses, His servant, and Aaron, whom He had chosen. They performed His signs among them and miracles in the land of Ham. (Psalm 105:26–27 ESV)

Ten plagues appear in Exodus 7:14–12:36. Moses' prelude to these plagues appears in Exodus 7:8–13—a skirmish between Aaron's staff and those of Pharaoh's magicians. The encounter foreshadows the two main features of the plagues. First, through Moses and Aaron, God demonstrates power over Pharaoh. Second, Pharaoh disputes the indisputable—that he's no match for Yahweh. At the end of the plagues, Pharaoh finally concedes. By then it's too late.

The ten plagues are God's punishment against Egypt for the regime's violent mistreatment of Israel. They are Yahweh's "visitation" because of "what has been done to [Israel] in Egypt" (Exodus 3:16 ESV). At the beginning and end of the plague section, they're called God's acts of judgment (Exodus 6:6; 7:4; 12:12). Here's the lineup:

- Water into blood (Exodus 7:14–24)
- Frogs (Exodus 7:25–8:15)
- Gnats (Exodus 8:16–19)
- Flies (Exodus 8:20–32)
- Diseased livestock (Exodus 9:1–7)
- Boils (Exodus 9:8–12)
- Thunderstorm of hail and fire (Exodus 9:13–35)

- Locusts (Exodus 10:1–20)
- Darkness for three days (Exodus 10:21–29)
- Death of the firstborn (Exodus 11:1–12:36)

The plagues come in cycles of three while their movement goes from disease and damage to darkness and death. The first plagues in each cycle are similar; that is, plagues one, four, and seven begin with Moses and Aaron visiting Pharaoh in the morning (Exodus 7:15; 8:20; 9:13). The tenth plague is climactic and lies outside the pattern— announcing God's final and definitive judgment. See Psalms 78:42–51 and 105:28–36 for similar plague lists.

It's tempting to understand the events in Exodus 7–12 as natural— though extraordinary in magnitude. This interpretation is incorrect for several reasons. First, it's hardly natural for Moses to strike his staff on the ground and turn what's in his hand into a serpent. Second, when the Nile turned to blood—note that it didn't merely look like blood—so did the water in vessels throughout Egypt (Exodus 7:19–21). Finally, the plagues were predicted (e.g., Exodus 9:5), discriminated (e.g., Exodus 9:26), and moved from the least to the most intense. The plagues exceed what is normal at various levels, including time, scope, and intensity.

Therefore, God's judgments against the land of the Nile are best deemed "hypernatural." Everything goes way beyond what we would expect. To interpret the plagues as reasonable occurrences, then, is an idea far removed from the Book of Exodus.

What was it like to see every speck of dust turn into a gnat (Exodus 8:16–17)? Or to witness hail so big that it shattered every tree (Exodus 9:25)? And what about the locusts? They were so ravenous that nothing green remained (Exodus 10:15). The words *every, all,* and *whole* are pervasive in the plague accounts—employed over fifty times. Note, for instance, the terms "every tree," "all the fruit," "the whole land." It's not startling, then, that Moses repeatedly writes something to the effect of "This has never happened before and it will never happen again" (Exodus 9:18, 24; 10:6, 14; 11:6).

These divine judgments against Egypt reverse God's plans for creation. They return life to the precreational chaos of Genesis 1:2. For instance, at creation, God's "Spirit/wind" blows over the waters; soon, God begins to form and vegetate the earth. In the plagues, God's "Spirit/wind" blows locusts into Egypt, which devour all vegetation (Exodus 10:13–15). Further, the plague of darkness (Exodus 10:21–29) signals a return to the darkness before God called forth light in Genesis 1:3.

The plagues, however, are primarily judgment upon Egypt's gods (e.g., Exodus 12:12; 15:11). A word of explanation is in order. The Bible mentions pagan deities using two perspectives. From an earthly perspective, the gods of the nations are acknowledged to be real for those who worship them. From a heavenly perspective, they only exist in people's minds. That is, God says pagan pantheons are fake. They're impostors and wannabes. Paul's analysis couples both the human and divine perspectives. "For although there may be so-called gods in heaven or on earth—as indeed there are many 'gods' and many 'lords'—yet for us there is one God, the Father, from whom are all things and for whom we exist, and one Lord, Jesus Christ, through whom are all things and through whom we exist" (1 Corinthians 8:5–6 ESV). Consequently, when Yahweh defeats Egyptian deities through plagues, He does so to witness to people—to show them that their trust is misplaced.

First in line was Khnum—Egypt's creator of water and life. Yahweh delivered a knockout punch when the water in Egypt became blood. At the same time, this was a crushing blow against Hapi, the god of the Nile. The plague of the frogs was Yahweh's frontal attack against Heqet, the goddess of childbirth, portrayed as a frog in Egyptian artwork. Hathor, the mother goddess of the sky, was depicted as a cow. Yahweh took aim at her through pestilence against livestock. He then directed darkness against Egyptian deities connected with the sun—Amon-Re, Aten, Atum, and Horus. Jethro, Moses' father-in-law, arrives at the correct conclusion: "Now I know that Yahweh is greater than all gods" (Exodus 18:11).

If the plagues are attacks against the enemy—the Egyptian pan-theon—then why doesn't Moses clarify things by stating these deities' names? Moses withholds names not to deny Yahweh's victory but to humiliate the gods by ignoring them. Grounds for these omissions are stated in Exodus 23:13: "Pay attention to all that I have said to you, and make no mention of the names of other gods, nor let it be heard on your lips" (ESV). Yahweh's jealousy for Israel's allegiance prohibits the utterance of other gods' names.

During most of the plagues, Yahweh distinguishes between Israel and Egypt, lest the innocent be swept away with the guilty. And, begin-ning with the fourth plague, then climaxing in the death of the firstborn on the night of the Passover, Yahweh sets apart and spares the Israelite region of Goshen—its people, livestock, and houses (Exodus 8:22–23; 9:4, 6–7; 11:4–7; 12:13, 23).

To describe the plagues, Moses writes the terms for "signs" (Exodus 4:17; 7:3; 10:1–2), "miracles" (Exodus 4:21; 7:9), and "wonders" (7:3; 11:9–10)—thus implying that God does more than run roughshod over Egypt. He wants people to believe in His power over all things through ten awesome signs and wonders.

The First Plague: Water Turned to Blood

Without water, Egypt would cease to exist. This becomes obvious when flying over the country. I remember looking down while on a flight from London to Nairobi and seeing a desert wasteland. For hun-dreds of miles, it's not suitable for civilization, except for one ribbon of life—the Nile River. For millennia, people have depended on the regu-lar, annual inundation and flooding of the Nile. Egypt can be summed up in one word—*water*.

When describing the first plague in Exodus 7:17, then, Moses employs five different terms for Egypt's waters, while in Exodus 8:5–7, he uses four words for water. What's going on? Egypt is a land of impris-oning water. That's why Moses structures his book to show that Israel is hemmed in by these waters (ch. 1–2; 14–15). It stands to reason, therefore, that God first strikes Egypt's water supply. In doing so, He foreshadows Israel's salvation from the land's watery abode—made evident through the Red Sea miracle in Exodus 14.

This first plague, water turned to blood, also stands as an indictment against Egypt's drowning of Hebrew sons in the Nile. While an earlier pharaoh used the Nile to kill Hebrew baby boys (Exodus 1:22), now the tables are turned. Egypt's waters become a place of death. And more death through water is on the way. "The waters returned and covered the chariots and the horsemen; of all the host of Pharaoh that had followed them into the sea, not one of them remained" (Exodus 14:28 ESV).

The Second Plague: Frogs

While the first and ninth plagues involve water and the sun, plagues two, three, four, and eight strike people using living things. Exodus 8:1–15, therefore, is the first plague that involves living creatures. When God created the heavens and earth, He declared "swarms" of life good (Genesis 1:20–21). Now, the "swarm" of frogs (Exodus 8:3 ESV) is very bad. Frogs here. Frogs there. Frogs are everywhere—even in ovens and bowls. Ugh!

Egyptians worshiped frogs to secure fruitfulness, blessings, and abundant annual harvests. The god's name was Heqet, depicted with a frog's head. It's as though God says to Egypt, "I hear you like frogs. Here are a whole bunch of them!" If that's not bad enough, all the frogs die. "They gathered them together in heaps, and the land stank" (Exodus 8:14 ESV). Double ugh!

Imagine frogs in your bed, frogs with your cousin Ed, and you can't get images of frogs out of your head! After they're dead, you go out for a walk one evening and all you hear is the constant crunching of dead frogs under your feet. Then, suddenly, you slip on a slimy corpse and fall into a pile of decaying frogs. The entire experience makes you want to croak!

Some dim-witted Egyptian magicians make matters worse. In their quest to show Aaron that they can duplicate his power, they double the number of frogs! Now Pharaoh has twice the number of frogs to deal with. Oops! All the trouble is now doubled.

Had I been employed as one of Pharaoh's magicians, I would have purged the land of its jumping green mini-monsters—lickety-split! But not Egypt's "top drawer" leaders. Their bad decision deserves another. When given the opportunity to rid the land of frogs, what does Pharaoh say in Exodus 8:10? "Tomorrow" (ESV)! *Tomorrow?* Procrastination is my name, and it only causes sorrow. I know I need to change my name. In fact, I will, tomorrow.

Most of the time, it's foolish to begin sentences with the words, "One of these days." "One of these days, I'm going to make amends with my brother." "One of these days, I'm going to finish college." "One of these days, I'm going to read through the entire Bible." Be honest, now. "One of these days" often turns out to be "none of these days."

It's better to begin more sentences with "Today." "Today, I'm empowered to make godly choices." "Today, I will give thanks for God's gifts." "Today, I'll be kind and courteous because Jesus lives in my heart." Why do this? Because *today*, Jesus is the doorway to deliverance, the pathway to peace, and the gateway to glory. *Today*, His mercy is matchless. His goodness is limitless. His love never changes. His grace is sufficient. And His Word is enough.

"Today" is so much better than Pharaoh's feeble "tomorrow." Why fritter your life away surrounded by foul-smelling frogs?

The Third Plague: Gnats

Imagine your water supply has turned into blood. Add innumerable dead frogs throughout the land. On top of that, now there are millions of gnats making everyday life impossible. Had enough? Raise the white flag? Not if you're Pharaoh!

People who directed the 1939 film *The Wizard of Oz* created several illusions that looked real. For instance, the tornado was a big sock while the farmhouse in the tornado was three feet high. The threatening army of monkeys? They were six inches tall and hung by piano wire. And underneath the monkey costumes were small, battery-driven electric windshield-wiper motors making their wings go up and down.

It's hard to distinguish illusions from the real thing—that is, unless you're Moses and Aaron. By the time we come to the third plague, Pharaoh's magicians are seen for what they really are—delusional, thinking they can keep up with Yahweh. Because Egypt was familiar with magic and the secret arts (Exodus 7:11, 22; 8:7, 18), it was natural to label Moses as just another rank-and-file magician. That is, until the gnats stormed the gates.

Egyptian diviners had turned their rods into serpents (Exodus 7:12). They had also duplicated the first two plagues, turning water into blood (Exodus 7:22) and being fruitful with frogs (Exodus 8:7). Now, however, the magicians admit they're weaker than Yahweh—saying of the gnats, "This is the finger of God" (Exodus 8:19 ESV).

The gnats come with no warning, suggesting that they're God's judgment against Pharaoh for not living up to his word in Exodus 8:8—that he would let Israel go and sacrifice to Yahweh. "All the dust of the earth became gnats in all the land of Egypt" (Exodus 8:17 ESV). "Dust," in this case, denotes loose topsoil, meaning scores and scads of gnats!

Recollect that the plagues appear in three groups of three—with the tenth plague coming as the climax. The first series includes blood, frogs, and gnats; the second, flies, livestock, and boils; while the third series is hail, locusts, and darkness. The last plague in each cycle (gnats, boils, and darkness) appear with no warning. Take cover!

The connection between the gnats and dust is important, for dust is sometimes associated with death. Note Genesis 3:19, where Moses writes, "For you are dust, and to dust you shall return" (ESV). The term *dust* also comes alongside death in Job 17:16, Psalm 22:29, and Isaiah 26:19. The God-ordained gnats, therefore, are more than an inconvenience. They point to something much more ominous—

impending death when the tenth plague strikes. Small wonder, then, that the empire's magicians realized they were up a creek without a paddle. Like the sixth plague of the boils, there's no indication that the gnats left Egypt.

The Fourth Plague: Flies

With gnats still buzzing, a new disaster strikes—swarms of flies. And, to state the obvious, this happened long before screened-in porches, insect repellents, and bug zappers! However, God explicitly protects the Hebrew land of Goshen. To see flies stop before entering Goshen— as though they ran into a plexiglass wall—must have been quite a sight to see. God tells Pharaoh the reason for this distinction, "That you may know that I am the LORD in the midst of the earth" (Exodus 8:22 ESV). Even after God removed all the flies that were whizzing around the king's head, he wouldn't budge. "Pharaoh hardened his heart this time also, and did not let the people go" (Exodus 8:32 ESV).

There are several notable features that appear with this plague. First, the flies begin the second cycle of three that includes livestock and boils. Second, for the first time, a plague is introduced without either Moses' or Aaron's staff. In fact, staffs are missing in the entire second sequence. Third, this is the first plague that distinguishes between the Egyptians and the Israelites. Except for the locusts (the eighth plague), this separation continues through and includes the climactic last plague—the death of every firstborn in Egypt where God saves Israel through blood.

The Greek translation of the Old Testament—called the Septuagint—was completed by Jewish scholars living in Egypt. Seen in this light, their Greek rendering of the Hebrew word for "flies" is translated in English to mean "barn fly" or "dog fly." This blood-sucking insect would have brought unspeakable pain to people. Ouch!

The Fifth Plague: Diseased Livestock

God strikes Egypt's livestock with death. Now, for the first time, Yahweh brings destructive power to Pharaoh's front door. His livestock are killed and, as we would expect, Israel's animals are as healthy as a horse (pun intended).

This is the first time Yahweh's "hand" (Exodus 9:3 ESV) appears in the description of the plagues. When paired with God, *hand* in the Old Testament almost always refers to divine power. In the case of the fifth plague, it's the power to unleash death on livestock.

As this is the first plague to directly bring about death, it's both a frightening preview of the tenth plague as well as of the demise of Egypt's army at the Red Sea. When Yahweh takes aim, He shoots straight, and He kills. "He [Yahweh] let loose on them [the Egyptians] His burning anger, wrath, indignation, and distress, a company of destroying angels" (Psalm 78:49 ESV).

The Sixth Plague: Boils

Next, Yahweh unleashes boils upon the Egyptians and their remaining living animals. He commands His two spokesmen—Aaron and Moses—to throw handfuls of ashes from a kiln into the air. This is poetic justice. The kiln is where Hebrew slaves baked bricks. God now turns the tables. Egypt's source of financial gain becomes the origin of their deep pain. This is the last plague that Aaron is directly involved in. Going forward it will be one-on-one—Moses versus Pharaoh.

The Seventh Plague: Hail

Moses uses more words to describe the hailstorm than in any other plague. For what reason? One god in Egypt's pantheon—Baal Hadad—was believed to be the lord of the storm. Wrong. In the Old Testament, lightning and thunder frequently announce Yahweh's presence (e.g., Exodus 19:16–19; Psalm 18:13–14; Habakkuk 3:4, 11). Additionally, within this plague, the fourth "knowing" statement appears. Here's the sequence:

- "Thus says the LORD, 'By this *you shall know* that I am the LORD: behold, with the staff that is in My hand I will strike the water that is in the Nile, and it shall turn into blood'" (Exodus 7:17 ESV, emphasis added).

- "But on that day I will set apart the land of Goshen, where My people dwell, so that no swarms of flies shall be there, that *you may know* that I am the LORD in the midst of the earth" (Exodus 8:22 ESV, emphasis added).

- "For this time I will send all My plagues on you yourself, and on your servants and your people, so that *you may know* that there is none like Me in all the earth" (Exodus 9:14 ESV, emphasis added).

- "Moses said to him, 'As soon as I have gone out of the city, I will stretch out my hands to the LORD. The thunder will cease, and there will be no more hail, so that *you may know* that the earth is the LORD's'" (Exodus 9:29 ESV, emphasis added).

Pharaoh thinks he's holding his own. Nothing could be further from the truth. God boasts, "For by now I could have put out My hand and struck you and your people with pestilence, and you would have been cut off from the earth" (Exodus 9:15 ESV). In effect, Yahweh says, "Pharaoh, I could have wiped you out a long time ago—but I didn't. Why? Because through the plagues, all the world will hear of My great power and might."

Beginning with the plague of hail, Moses also starts to compare God's judgments on Egypt with the past and the future (Exodus 9:18, 24; 10:6, 14; 11:6). The scope and intensity of these latter plagues set them apart from earlier disasters, leading Pharaoh to lament, "This time I have sinned; the LORD is in the right, and I and my people are in the wrong" (Exodus 9:27 ESV). And, for the third time, the king pledges to let Israel go—only to change his mind again. Pharaoh talks the talk but won't walk the walk. As soon as the hail ends, the king goes back to his dirty bag of tricks. "But when Pharaoh saw that the rain and the hail and the thunder had ceased, he sinned yet again and hardened his heart, he and his servants" (Exodus 9:34 ESV).

Before the plague of hail, God uses the Nile, creatures, and sicknesses to curse Egypt. Now, He employs the heavens to send huge hailstones. The storm is an in-your-face taunt against Baal Hadad—a false god the Egyptians believed controlled thunder and lightning. Yahweh's jab against Baal Hadad in Exodus 9 will become a knockout punch in Exodus 14. Stay tuned.

The Eighth Plague: Locusts

Not only does Pharaoh's heart become hard but now his servants join him (Exodus 9:34; 10:1). Egypt will soon add its army to the list of hard-hearted Hebrew haters (Exodus 14:17). While the locusts don't end up with hard hearts, they certainly end up with full stomachs! The sevenfold use of the term *all* in Exodus 10:12–15 underscores the complete destruction caused by these pesky critters.

I know, just the mention of locusts suggests Mr. Locust himself—John the Baptist. Can you imagine eating locusts? Talk about heartburn! Pass the Rolaids! A few years ago, a man in Bloomington, Minnesota, made national news by eating thirty locusts. He ended up in the ER with a rash all over his body. Pastors call that "the theology of the cross." Lay people call that "just plain dumb!" Did you know that there are ten words for locusts in Hebrew? For the next eight pages of this book, I'm going to explore all of them with you—in great detail. Just kidding!

I'm not kidding, though, when I tell you that locusts flap their wings—nonstop—at the speed of twelve miles an hour for seventeen straight hours. Moreover, the locust swarm density is calculated to be 130 million insects per square mile. And boy howdy, do locusts love to eat. Why, locusts can eat their own body weight each day. Just imagine eating your own body weight each day. On second thought, don't imagine eating your own body weight each day!

Like the earlier plague of hail, the locusts are devastating—so much so that Yahweh directs future generations to learn about this unheard-of event (Exodus 10:2). The idea of telling future generations of Hebrews of Yahweh's great acts of salvation picks up steam and appears within the Passover liturgy (Exodus 12:1–30) as well as in the liturgy for the Feast of Unleavened Bread (Exodus 13:3–16).

If you're an Egyptian living through these unprecedented times, the locusts are a preview of coming disasters. In what way? First, God brings both locusts upon Egypt and parts the Red Sea by means of an east wind (Exodus 10:13; 14:21). Second, just as locusts end up dead in the Red Sea, so will Pharaoh's army (Exodus 10:19; 14:29). Hence, whether it's locusts or Egyptians, when God sets out to rid the land of enemies, He will finish what He started.

I pointed out earlier that after the plague of gnats, Pharaoh's magicians jump ship, confessing, "This is the finger of God" (Exodus 8:19 ESV). Now the entire court has had enough. "How long shall this man be a snare to us? Let the men go, that they may serve the LORD their God. Do you not yet understand that Egypt is ruined?" (Exodus 10:7 ESV).

For the second time, Pharaoh confesses his sin. For the fourth time, he asks Moses to remove God's agents of judgment. Moses and God again respond with kindness. But Pharaoh? His heart remains hard as a rock (Exodus 10:20).

The Ninth Plague: Darkness

"Then the LORD said to Moses, 'Stretch out your hand toward heaven, that there may be darkness over the land of Egypt'" (Exodus 10:21 ESV). This plague strikes at the heart of Egyptians who worshiped their sun god, Amon Re—one of the nation's top deities—along with his wife Mut and their son, Khons.

Many of us know what a blizzard is sometimes called—a whiteout. Well, this was just the opposite. It was a blackout. Human movement came to a standstill. All movement was reduced to desperate groping. Pharaoh finally had had enough of Moses. "Get away from me; take care never to see my face again, for on the day you see my face you shall die" (Exodus 10:28 ESV).

Negotiations are called off. Things are at an impasse. Everything has come to a standstill. But not for long.

The Tenth Plague: Death of the Firstborn

The clock finally strikes midnight. God's judgments against Egypt have included blood, boils, locusts, and lightning. Now Yahweh sends death—the death of Egypt's firstborn. The Bible calls death "the king of terrors" (Job 18:14 ESV) as well as "the last enemy" (1 Corinthians 15:26 ESV). It knocks on Egypt's door and enters as an unwanted guest.

The first and last plagues—the Nile turning to blood and the death of the firstborn—are linked to Pharaoh Ahmose I's murder of Hebrew baby boys. Yahweh now exacts an "eye for eye" (Exodus 21:24 ESV)—in this case, a son for a son.

Egypt's loud wailing signals to the Hebrews that they'd better start packing—leaving room for gobs of Egyptian goods. Earlier, God had told Moses that the Israelites will leave Egypt with great wealth (Exodus 3:21–22). And, because God does what He says, the Israelites go from rags to riches (Exodus 11:2–3; cf. Exodus 12:35–36). True, God hardened Pharaoh's heart, but He also softened the hearts of rank-and-file Egyptians. *Yahweh is the Lord of the heart.*

Pharaoh's Hard Heart

Moses employs three verbs to describe God's dealings with Pharaoh Thutmose III and his heart: "harden," "make unresponsive," and "make stubborn." All three indicate varying degrees of obstinacy, single-mindedness, a seared conscience, and a numb soul. Over the course of the ten plagues, Pharaoh became callous and maliciously minded. We might think it's only the oppressed who suffer when they're harshly treated. Not so. Oppression damages the oppressors. They're also dehumanized.

Ten times, Yahweh is the subject of the three hardening verbs. Ten times, Pharaoh (or Pharaoh's heart) is the subject. Yahweh hardens Pharaoh's heart (Exodus 9:12; 10:1, 20, 27; 11:10), but only *after* the king hardens his own heart (Exodus 7:22; 8:15, 19, 32). Yahweh's hardening, therefore, confirms Pharaoh's. How so? God only becomes the subject of hardening in the sixth plague (Exodus 9:12), though His hardening is anticipated as a future action in Exodus 4:21 and 7:3. It's as though

Yahweh tells Thutmose III, "If that's how you want it, I'll help you along the way." Moses describes the Pharaoh's hardening in such a way that both human guilt and divine sovereignty are held in balance. It's not either/or but both/and.

Pharaoh isn't the only person in Exodus with a hard heart. The Hebrew words translated as "harden" in the previous verses are also used to describe Israel (Exodus 32:9; 33:3, 5; 34:9). Tragically, what God did to Pharaoh, He does to His own people. "But My people did not listen to My voice; Israel would not submit to Me. So I gave them over to their stubborn hearts, to follow their own counsels" (Psalm 81:11–12 ESV). In like manner, Paul teaches that God's judgment includes handing people over to their perverse hearts (Romans 1:24, 26, 28). This world's pharaohs live in an ominous place—as do we when a hard heart gets the best of us. But there is hope!

The Heart of the Problem

The heart of every problem is always a problem of the heart. That's true with Pharaoh's problems as well as our problems. Our biggest danger isn't the problem lurking *out* there. Our biggest danger is the problem lurking *in* here. It's the problem of our heart.

I sometimes think my most substantial challenges in life are outside of me—society, government, the big bad evil world. My biggest problem, however, is inside of me. I can finagle out of all kinds of difficult situations, but I can't finagle out of a hard heart. That's what Ezekiel says. I have a "heart of stone" (Ezekiel 36:26 ESV). Sin makes my heart hard as a rock.

Slow down and think about that for a minute. If you had a rock in your hand right now and gripped it with every fiber in your body, what do think would happen? I know. Some of you have bulging biceps and you'd crush it, but the rest of us could squeeze that rock for the rest of our lives and nothing would happen. Rocks resist change. Every sin in your life and mine—whether of commission or omission (what we do or fail to do)—is directly related to our hard hearts. *Pharaoh lives on.*

Our heart condition can't be cured. We can't make our cold, stony, lifeless hearts beat with love any more than we can take a rock and make it live. No matter how good we manage to be, no matter how much we pray, we can't cure our fundamental problem—our rock-solid heart.

And we can forget about heart bypass surgery, a stent, a pacemaker, or a valve. If the doctor does that, the old parts are still there. Our hearts can't be trained, tamed, or taught. They must be totally removed. *We need heart transplant surgery!*

Dr. Evan O'Neill Kane lived from 1861 to 1932. He put his surgical skills to the ultimate test by operating on himself—not once, but three times! In 1921, Kane removed his own appendix. By using mirrors, Kane wielded the scalpel and did the operation all by himself. He then went home and recovered in several days.

Some may self-operate. No one, however, can perform their own heart transplant surgery. It's not something that can be done *by* us. Spiritual heart transplant surgery is something that can only be done *to* us—by a Doctor with special skills and training and equipment. Yahweh is that Doctor. "I will remove the heart of stone from your flesh and give you a heart of flesh" (Ezekiel 36:26 ESV). A heart of flesh implies a heart that's alive, supple, sensitive, and responsive. A heart of flesh means a tender heart toward Jesus and toward people. *A heart of flesh is God's gift to you.*

CHAPTER 6

A Ticket to Ride: Exodus 12–13

He established a testimony in Jacob and appointed a law
in Israel, which He commanded our fathers to teach to
their children, that the next generation might know them,
the children yet unborn, and arise and tell them to their
children. (Psalm 78:5–6 ESV)

Have you ever been booked on a commercial plane and ended
up on the standby list? Every two or three minutes, you look up at a
monitor to see if you have a ticket. And any announcement from the
ticket agent at the gate that doesn't mention your name only increases
your stress level. Ticketed passengers, by contrast, read magazines and
thumb through their iPhones. Oh, to be numbered with the confirmed,
to have our very own seat number and departure time, to be guaranteed
that we're on the next flight!

There are times when I feel stuck on the standby list of life. Others
have a ticket to make the big purchase, but not me. Others have a ticket
to all the fun, but not me. Others have a ticket for perfect families, perfect jobs, perfect bodies, but not me.

We have several options. One is to throw a pity party and whine,
"Why me?" Another is to become jaded and cynical. Still another
choice is to become small, jealous, vindictive, and petty. In every case,
we're still stuck. Trapped. With no way out.

I have good news for you! You have a seat on the final flight home.
Reservations have been made. The fare has been paid for in full. Or, to

paraphrase the old Beatles' song, you've got a ticket to ride! That's what Moses says. That's what Jesus delivers. And that's what Exodus 12–13 teaches us.

THE PASSOVER

The Passover—connected to the last plague—is one of the most important features in the Book of Exodus. Moses indicates this in several ways. The Passover plague is different than the first nine, as it alone is linked to a detailed ritual (Exodus 12). To further imply the Passover's significance, God changes Israel's calendar, making the month of Abib the first month of the year (Exodus 12:2), which, in later Old Testament books, is called Nisan (e.g., Nehemiah 2:1; Esther 3:7). Abib/Nisan falls in springtime, late March to early April. The Passover marks a new beginning. Not only for Israel but also for us. Adios to bricks and bondage!

The Israelites, however, don't leave through the back door, carrying only the clothes on their backs. They march out in full view of their captors, with Egyptian wealth bulging from their bags. The last become first and the first become last. *Israel has a ticket to ride.*

The Context of Passover

The word *every* appears in Exodus 1 and 12—thus linking the Passover to Egypt's earlier crimes against Israel. "Pharaoh commanded all his people, saying, '*Every* son that is born to the Hebrews you shall cast into the Nile'" (Exodus 1:22 ESV, emphasis added). Moses announces in chapter 12 that the Egyptians made their bed and now they must sleep in it. "At midnight Yahweh struck *every* firstborn in the land of Egypt . . . and *every* firstborn of livestock. And Pharaoh arose in the night—he and every one of his servants and everyone in Egypt, and there was a great outcry in Egypt, for there was not a house where there was not someone dead" (Exodus 12:29–30). What do we call that? A boomerang with vengeance. Egypt's punishment fits their crime.

And it isn't as though the Egyptians weren't warned. "Then you shall say to Pharaoh, 'Thus says the LORD, Israel is my firstborn son, and I say to you, "Let my son go that he may serve Me." If you refuse to let him go, behold, I will kill your firstborn son'" (Exodus 4:22–23 ESV). When Yahweh passed through Egypt, striking down the firstborn of both man and beast, in grace He passed over and spared Israelite firstborn sons because of the lambs' blood upon their doorposts (Exodus 12:23–29).

The Liturgy of Passover

The account of Yahweh passing through Egypt and striking down the firstborn appears in just one verse, Exodus 12:29—a verse standing in the middle of the Passover passage in Exodus 11:1–13:16. As a result, most of this section provides instructions that commemorate and retell the Passover through a meal.

And it's so much more than ritualistic mumbo jumbo. The liturgy is God's gift so that future generations (*including us*) may participate in exoduslike salvation. Notice this future-focused viewpoint. The first Passover was conducted "in haste" (Exodus 12:11 ESV), while subsequent celebrations were to last for seven days (Exodus 12:15, 19).

God's rescue transcends time and space to include children and grandchildren—to the end of time. The ancient Jewish Mishnaic writing called Pesachim (Passovers) puts it this way: "In every generation a person must view himself as though he personally left Egypt." Salvation's power from the first exodus is available now from within the context of the Passover liturgy. Its capacity to save doesn't ever run out or hit a dead end.

The Passover liturgy helped Israel recall the exodus as an event that happened. It's also structured so future Israelites may participate in it. Past and present come together. "This day" will function as a "memorial" (Exodus 12:14 ESV) for Israel, a day they are to "remember" by festival and worship rites (Exodus 13:3 ESV).

The Passover Menu

Eating a lamb is the central feature of the Passover meal (Exodus 12:8–11, 43–47). The Israelites are to sacrifice the lamb on the fourteenth day of the first month of spring at twilight—when the day *begins*, by Israelite reckoning (Exodus 12:1, 6; Deuteronomy 16:1). People are to place the lamb's blood on the doorframe of their home. God will pass over that home and not kill any firstborn human or animal (Exodus 12:7, 13). The lamb—representing Israelite firstborn sons—was killed in their place. We call that substitutionary atonement. It's God's gift.

The Israelites are to roast the lamb over fire as opposed to boiling it in water. Why? To boil a lamb implies that—to fit it into a cooking vessel—several of its bones would need to be broken (Exodus 12:46). And broken bones are a curse from God. For instance, when King Hezekiah felt as though the Lord abandoned him, he calls God a "lion" who "breaks all my bones" (Isaiah 38:13 ESV). In a similar way, Jeremiah in Lamentations 3:4 mourns: "He has made my flesh and my skin waste away; He has broken my bones" (ESV). Unbroken bones, conversely, are a sign of God's favor. David, for example, prophesies that God will watch over Christ's bones. "He keeps all His bones; not one of them is broken" (Psalm 34:20 ESV). John completes these Old Testament ideas when he tells us that, because Jesus is the Passover Lamb (John 1:29, 36), our Savior's legs were not broken (John 19:36).

In fact, throughout his Gospel, John teaches about wholeness. For example, the Good Shepherd leads one flock (John 10); Jesus prays for the unity of His disciples (John 17); our Lord's tunic is not torn (John 19:24); and a fishing net is not ripped (John 21:11). These stories, when placed together, announce God's gift of wholeness and peace. The Hebrew word for that is *shalom*.

GOD'S GIFT OF *SHALOM*

Do you hear what people are saying? "Life's too hard!" "This problem is too big!" "I've never been this low in my life." "I'm David against Goliath!" "I don't see God in this at all!"

What does society offer when we're falling apart? "Work more!" "Drink more!" "Party more!" "Eat more!" "Sleep more!" "Spend more!"

But we know, deep down, that this is like trying to nail Jell-O to a wall. It doesn't work! God puts our Humpty-Dumpty lives back together.

Here's His formula for *shalom*: a perfect sacrifice. "Your lamb shall be without blemish" (Exodus 12:5 ESV). The sacrifice must be the very best, the most prized, and the most valuable animal. Forget about getting your lamb at Dollar General, at Walmart, or ordering a used one on eBay. And don't even think about trying to slip in a blind animal or one that's crippled, sick, or on its last leg.

Use blood from the perfect sacrifice. "The congregation of Israel shall kill their lambs at twilight" (Exodus 12:6 ESV). Blood was then applied to doorposts using hyssop (Exodus 12:22)—a plant often employed in the Old Testament when people or objects needed to be purified. The most famous use appears in Psalm 51:7: "Purge me with *hyssop*, and I shall be clean; wash me, and I shall be whiter than snow" (ESV, emphasis added).

Israel's Passover liturgy is a shadow of *shalom*. It's best to have the real deal, wouldn't you agree? Well, here it is. Three times in the Upper Room after Easter—John 20:19, 21, 26—Jesus says, "Peace [*shalom*] be with you!" (ESV).

Can you imagine what Christ's disciples must have thought? "*Shalom*? Really? Here's the perfect sacrifice? Here's the One who takes sin away? His blood was shed for me? What was broken is now made whole? Hallelujah!"

The Italian Baroque artist Caravaggio (he is known by only one name) painted a masterpiece—*The Incredulity of Saint Thomas*—in 1602. In it, Jesus doesn't just tell Thomas to put his hand into His side. Rather, in this painting, Christ guides Thomas' probing finger into the gaping open wound where the spear had been thrust. Caravaggio testifies to Christ's physical, bodily resurrection.

In the seventeenth century, this kind of real-life painting was unheard of. In breaking new ground, Caravaggio depicts this holy moment with all the grime of real life. If you look closely, you can even see dirt in Thomas's fingernails. Brokenness is healed through the love of the unbroken Lamb—Jesus.

God's gift of *shalom*—foreshadowed in Exodus 12 and realized in John 20—is delivered to us in the Holy Supper, where we receive the true body and blood of Jesus Christ. From beginning to end, the liturgy of the Sacrament is designed to deliver peace. Check it out next time you're at church. Even more, claim God's healing promise as you go forward to receive your Savior. "The punishment that brought us *shalom* was upon Him [Jesus]. And by His wounds we are healed" (Isaiah 53:5).

Bitter Herbs and Unleavened Bread

The Passover menu also included bitter herbs (Exodus 12:8)—to remind the Israelites of their harsh bondage in Egypt. Unfortunately, the realities of that bondage were frequently forgotten (e.g., Exodus 16:3; 17:1–3; Numbers 11:1–9; 14:1–5). The Israelites often referred to their slavery in the land of the Nile as the good old days. At one point, they even call Egypt "a land flowing with milk and honey" (Numbers 16:13 ESV). That's what I call being directionally challenged!

Unleavened bread (without yeast) rounded out the Passover menu (Exodus 12:8). This regulation was initially associated with the fact that there was no time to waste—God commanded the Israelites to get out of Egypt ASAP. "In this manner you shall eat it: with your belt fastened, your sandals on your feet, and your staff in your hand. And you shall eat it in haste" (Exodus 12:11 ESV). By the time the New Testament was written, however, leaven implied hypocrisy (Luke 12:1) as well as sinful living (1 Corinthians 5:6–8). Why? Leaven begins the process of fermentation which eventually leads to decomposition. Therefore, it became emblematic of corruption.

The Passover (Exodus 12:1–13), Feast of Unleavened Bread (Exodus 12:14–20; 13:3–10), as well as the Consecration of the Firstborn (Exodus 13:1–2, 11–16) function so people trust and follow Yahweh. All three liturgies

- commemorate the death of Egypt's firstborn (Exodus 12:17, 23; 13:14–15);

- are memorials for coming generations (Exodus 12:25–27; 13:8–10; 13:14–15); and

- enable future generations to participate in the deliverance by reenacting events associated with the exodus.

Agnus Dei

A stunning piece of art lines the halls of the Prado Museum in Madrid, Spain. A seventeenth-century Spanish artist named Francisco de Zurbarán painted it from 1635 to 1640. He called it *Agnus Dei*—that's Latin for "Lamb of God."

The painting is simple. A wooly white merino lamb with curved horns is lying on his side, facing to the left, on a gray slab. All four of his feet are bound together above the fetlock with two strands of a cord. The knot isn't visible.

With his feet tied together, the lamb's back is elevated. Both eyes are looking down, past a pink nose, at the gray slab. There's no blood. The lamb is alive—but not for long.

Still-life paintings from the seventeenth century rarely display emotion. The lamb in this painting, however, shows emotion—the emotion of resignation. He doesn't fight to free himself. He isn't kicking and screaming. The lamb is ready to die.[2]

Light shines down on the lamb from the upper left at a high angle so that only a little shadow is thrown. Beyond the pool of light that bathes the lamb, it's dark—very dark.

Israel's Passover foreshadows this Lamb. Moses writes, "Tell all the congregation of Israel that on the tenth day of this month every man shall take a lamb according to their fathers' houses, a lamb for each household. . . . Your lamb shall be without blemish, a male a year old"

---

2 Francisco de Zurbarán, *Agnus Dei*, 1635–40, oil on canvas, 14.7 by 24.4 inches (37.3 by 62 cm), Museo Nacional del Prado, Madrid, https://www.museodelprado.es/en/the-collection/art-work/agnus-dei/795b841a-ec81-4d10-bd8b-0c7a870e327b.

(Exodus 12:3–5 ESV). The Passover lamb can't be crippled, lame, spotted, or off-color. He must be perfect.

After choosing a lamb, people are to watch him for three days. Then, on the fourteenth day of the month, the entire community of Israel is to gather at twilight. What happens next? They slaughter the lamb. "Then they are to take some of the blood and put it on the two doorposts and the lintel of the houses in which they eat it" (Exodus 12:7 ESV). The blood of the lamb will set people free from Egypt's darkness and death.

The painting's black background serves to highlight the lamb's white wool. The dark background, though, also highlights the reason the lamb was slaughtered. What could that be?

While Augustine first coined the term, Martin Luther made it famous: *incurvatus in se*—another Latin phrase, this one meaning "turned in on self." Determined to live in the dark, we turn in toward our own interests and desires and needs and agendas. Call it individualism. Call it narcissism. Call it selfishness. But whatever you call it, you must also call it what it is in God's eyes—sin.

Have you ever stopped to hear your self-talk? "To turn outward toward God and others is so risky. I'll get hurt and disappointed and frustrated—*again*. It's better, and it's much safer, to turn toward self." We do much of life in a tight, fetal position. This approach seduces us, traps us, then kills us.

People sometimes dream they can enter paintings. You know, take a walk in the *Starry Night* with Vincent van Gogh or listen to the *Mona Lisa* with Leonardo da Vinci. What would you do if you could enter de Zurbarán's masterpiece, *Agnus Dei*? The impulse, of course, would be to untie the lamb. Let him loose. Allow him to go free. He looks so innocent, so kind, so loving. He doesn't deserve to die.

But recall that the knot is out of sight. How come? The lamb *must* be slaughtered, for his blood alone will set people free. "The blood shall be a sign for you, on the houses where you are. And when I see the blood,

I will pass over you, and no plague will befall you to destroy you, when I strike the land of Egypt" (Exodus 12:13 ESV).

The Lamb's blood flowed in Gethsemane when, as Luke tells us, Jesus was in such agony that He did sweat great drops of blood (Luke 22:44). There was more blood when the soldiers blindfolded Jesus and began punching Him in the face. And blood flowed from His scalp as a crown of thorns was mockingly shoved on His head.

But the real bloodbath happened when our Savior was stripped naked and whipped—whipped without mercy. Blood continued to flow from His open wounds as He carried the cross-piece along the *Via Dolorosa*—more Latin, meaning "the Way of Sorrow." Then there were three nails and the final blow—the Roman spear thrust, bringing a sudden flow of blood and water. The result? John tells us in Revelation 1:5. Christ's blood sets us free from *incurvatus in se.*

MARKED!

God gave a mark to liberate His people Israel—blood on their doorposts. He pointed to the stain on the houses and said to the angel of death, "You may go this far, and no further!"

Rob Poulos knows what it feels like to be marked—he's a walking piece of literature. Poulos has a tattoo on his left wrist of the word *back*, followed by a comma and a closing quotation mark. It is part of a bigger story. Several years ago, he joined a worldwide effort to help author Shelley Jackson tell her story on people's bodies. Appropriately titled *Skin*, the "book" has 2,095 words. Each person bears on his or her body just one word. Poulos heard about it in a literature class at the University of Missouri-Kansas City.

God also loves to mark people—and not just in the Book of Exodus with blood. In Genesis 4:15, God marks Cain, while in Genesis 17:10, He gives Abraham and his offspring the covenant mark of circumcision. Deuteronomy 6:8–9 describes the Israelites tying Yahweh's words on their hands and binding them on their foreheads—showing to the world that they're marked as His people. In Ezekiel 9:4, God commands a man with a writing kit to "pass through the city, through Jerusalem, and put a mark on the foreheads of the men who sigh and groan over all the abominations that are committed in it" (ESV).

It all points to the most awesome story ever told on human skin. First the ten disciples, then, climactically, Thomas, saw Jesus alive. Our Savior showed them the scars on His skin (John 20:20, 27). Christ's skin is forever marked with scars, announcing His loyal love for you that knows no limits.

And God has placed His mark on you. When did that happen? Recall the water, remember the Word, and forever cherish this liturgical rite. "Receive the sign of the holy cross, both upon your forehead and upon your heart to mark you as one redeemed by Christ the crucified" (*LSB*, p. 268). Through Holy Baptism, you are marked with one word: *forgiven*.

A FOCUS ON THE FAMILY

The Blackwater River meanders in northern Florida through cypress groves and muddy swamps. Over a period of twenty years, several prized hunting dogs vanished along these waters. Rufus Goodwin solved the case in August of 1995, after his dog Flojo disappeared. Flojo was wearing an electronic dog collar when she dropped out of sight. Goodwin followed the signal all the way to a five-hundred-pound, fifty-year-old alligator and soon figured out how the dogs disappeared. At night, the gator would come out of the river, sit on the trail, and wait for dogs—blinded by the darkness—to run into his gaping jaws.

Children are blindly running into another kind of alligator—secular American culture. And the results are in. Secular American culture is chewing up children's sexuality and attitudes, as well as their hopes and dreams.

Need some convincing?

Judith Rich Harris wrote a book called *The Nurture Assumption*. In it, she argues that parenting doesn't matter. Nothing mothers and fathers do has any long-term impact on their children. Genes and peer-group pressure are the formative factors. The upshot? Parents should relax, take a deep breath, and chill out—after all, they're only bystanders. In the whole debate over nature versus nurture, Harris argues it's nature all the way.

Nature is important. Parental nurture is more important. In the Passover liturgy, Yahweh is not only against Egypt and for Israel but He also addresses Israel's future generations. They're mentioned in explicit terms (e.g., Exodus 12:14, 24–27; 13:8, 14), while the noun translated as "home/household" occurs sixteen times in Exodus 12. Additionally, the final statement in the description of the tenth plague is a father's reply in days to come. Answering his son's question, the father says—not once but twice—"By a strong hand Yahweh brought *us* out of Egypt" (Exodus 13:14, 16). The "us" is enormously significant. A few verses earlier, in Exodus 13:8, God commands the future father to say to his son, "Because of what the LORD did for *me* when *I* came out of Egypt" (ESV, emphasis added). Israel's exodus is historical. Israel's exodus is also personal and therefore transcends history.

These texts are worth looking at—in their entirety.

- "Then the LORD said to Moses, 'Go in to Pharaoh, for I have hardened his heart and the heart of his servants, that I may show these signs of mine among them, and that *you may tell in the hearing of your son and of your grandson* how I have dealt harshly with the Egyptians and what signs I have done among them, that you may know that I am the LORD'" (Exodus 10:1–2 ESV, emphasis added).

- "And when your children say to you, 'What do you mean by this service?' you shall say, 'It is the sacrifice of the LORD's Passover, for He passed over the houses of the people of Israel in Egypt, when He struck the Egyptians but spared *our* houses'" (Exodus 12:26–27 ESV, emphasis added).

What do you tell your children about money? about music? about friends? about movies? about worship? about Jesus? about prayer?

about honesty? about humility? about marriage? about Sunday School? about Bible study?

Am I promoting a new brand of twenty-first-century legalism? Not at all! Jesus preached His harshest sermons against people who said that following God consists of a bunch of dos and don'ts. My fear, though, is that we're sacrificing children on the altar of "Christian freedom" that has become nothing more than conforming to American culture.

Jim Ryffel and his wife, Linda, raised their two sons in Fort Worth, Texas. Jim was the president of Woodcrest Management, a company that owned and managed small shopping centers. Once, a man renting space for his video store vacated in the middle of the night, defaulting on his lease. Jim's company took the man to court. As part of the damage settlement, he received some of the store's inventory—4,000 X-rated, hard-core pornography DVDs. They were worth more than $100,000. What did Jim do?

Better yet, what do we do when faced with a moral choice? Say, a choice between honesty and lying? a choice between generosity and stinginess? a choice between worship and skipping out? a choice between Sunday School and grocery shopping?

Jim Ryffel piled the movies up in a nearby parking lot. Then he took the driver's seat in a thirteen-ton steam roller. His two sons, Travis and Hunter, sat in the cab next to him. Jim opened the throttle, revved the machine forward, and crushed the movies into a black soup of shattered plastic. He later explained to the press, "Pornography devastates marriages and families. Pornography needs to be destroyed." Do you think his sons remember that day? The day their dad steam-rolled 4,000 pornographic DVDs? The day their dad lost $100,000? What acts of moral courage will our children remember us for?

Alexander Pope penned these words in his *Epistles to Several Persons*: "As the twig is bent, so the tree grows." What is bending your children? your grandchildren? What about the children in your church? Is it the story of salvation? One saturated with transforming grace? Does it sound like this? Christ fills us with the Holy Spirit that we don't send. Christ gives us sisters and brothers in the faith that we don't create. Christ gives us the Holy Scriptures that we don't write. Christ gives us the Means of Grace—Baptism and the Lord's Supper—that we don't deserve. Christ changes the way we teach children—who belong to Him.

Warning. Here comes another alligator story!

A twelve-year-old boy named Michael was swimming in a pond near his family's home in Tampa, Florida. Paddling along with a snorkel and mask, Michael didn't realize that a four-hundred-pound alligator was bearing down on him. The gator lunged for his head. When its jaws snapped shut, Michael's mask and snorkel were torn away. Miraculously, Michael's head came free from the gator's mouth. He screamed and his mother raced to the pond. The gator clamped on to Michael's legs. His mother grabbed Michael's arms and pulled. A fierce tug-of-war began between a tenacious mother and ferocious gator. Then, suddenly, miraculously, the alligator let go.

Three months later, Michael showed a friend the scene of the near-fatal attack. He also proudly showed off three huge scars on his right arm. Three marks that weren't left by the gaping gator. Three marks left by his mother's relentless fingernails.

Like Michael, our children are caught in a fierce struggle with all kinds of enemies—spearheaded by Satan himself. What does God call us to do? Keep pulling. Keep on pulling. Never stop pulling children to the one true God. That's what Moses teaches throughout the Passover liturgy, which also previews our Savior's gifts in the Sacrament of Holy Communion.

THE LORD'S SUPPER

A middle-aged and slightly overweight Scottish woman walked out from behind a theater curtain. People in the audience rolled their eyes and several let out sighs of disappointment. That was the way it was on April 11, 2009—the evening Susan Boyle began to sing.

After her song, the very same audience exploded with applause. The video clip of Susan Boyle singing became the most-watched YouTube video at the time. Her first recording broke all sales records. Susan Boyle wasn't what people expected.

Why do I share this story? Because it teaches that what looks ordinary may turn out to be completely extraordinary.

The Lord's Supper is like that. When Christ's words—"Take, eat; this is My body. . . . Drink of it, all of you; this cup is the new testament in My blood" (*LSB*, p. 162)—are spoken over the bread and wine, it's not what we expect. It's so much more.

That's what Paul teaches. "The cup of blessing that we bless, is it not a *participation* in the blood of Christ? The bread that we break, is it not a *participation* in the body of Christ?" (1 Corinthians 10:16 ESV, emphasis added). Paul's Greek in this verse demands an "It is" response to both questions. Through the cup, we participate in Christ's blood. Through the bread, we participate in Christ's body. The bread and wine don't stop being bread and wine, but because of Christ's words, the bread is also His body and the wine is also His blood. When we come to the Communion rail, God gives us both bread and wine as well as the Savior's true body and blood.

Does Paul's word *participation* ring a bell? Like Moses' presentation of Passover, Paul does more than teach correct doctrine or rehearse history. Paul also places us into a story. By partaking of the Sacrament, the Holy Spirit unites us with Christ's story. His death is the death of our old Adam. His resurrection is our rising to new life. His ascension to the Father's right hand is now where we view all of life. And He will "[raise] us up with Him and [seat] us with Him in the heavenly places in Christ Jesus" (Ephesians 2:6 ESV). On the Last Day, Christ's return in glory means we will bask in His glory forevermore.

In the song, "I Love to Tell the Story," the familiar refrain has these words: "I love to tell the story, 'Twill be my theme in glory, To tell the old, old story Of Jesus and His love." His story is our story as well! *We participate in it.*

Paul's chief teaching in 1 Corinthians 10:16, however, is Christ's real presence in the Holy Supper. He begins with the words, "The cup of blessing" (ESV). Most first-century Jewish Passover feasts used four

cups of red wine as reminders of the Passover lambs' blood. The cups stood for the four "I will" statements in Exodus 6:6–7. The cup of sanctification is based on God's promise, "I will bring you out of Egypt." The cup of judgment is based on God's pledge, "I will deliver you from slavery." After the first two cups, participants ate the Passover supper—an unblemished lamb, unleavened bread, and bitter herbs. After the meal, people drank the third cup, the cup of blessing—"I will redeem you." This is where Jesus said, "This cup is the new covenant in My blood, shed for you." We drink from the cup of blessing!

After celebrating the Passover with His disciples, Jesus prays, "Father, if You are willing, remove this cup from Me" (Luke 22:42 ESV). What do we call *this* cup? It's the cup of death. Jesus petitions His Father to take the cup of death from Him. Yet, as the obedient Son of God, Jesus knows the only way to our cup of blessing is through His cup of death. Despite the agony of separation from His Father, Christ was willing to drink it, bear its pain, and suffer its horror. In Christ's blood, we're bought, purchased, and won from all sin and from the power of the devil.

That's not all.

Communion bread participates with Christ's real body. Pause for a moment to reflect on that. The same hands that healed the sick, the same heart that loved the loveless, the same feet that sought out and saved lost people—that same body comes to us to heal, forgive, and save us.

A TABLE FOR TWO

Whenever we go to a restaurant, the hostess wants to know how many are in our party. Can you imagine going to a restaurant and not knowing how many people are with you? Hostess: "How many are in your party?" Me: "I'm not sure." Hostess: "How many will be joining you for dinner?" Me: "I don't know." When it comes to the Lord's Supper, how many are in your party? Do you know? Two. Holy Communion is a table for two!

Jesus reserves a place for you at this table. Jesus gives you His true body and true blood. *What looks ordinary may turn out to be completely extraordinary.* Who wouldn't want to dine at this table?

GOING THROUGH HELL

In 1979, archaeologists were excavating in Jerusalem in a place they thought was ancient *Gehenna*—a word employed in the Greek New Testament that is usually translated "hell." What they found boggles the mind. It was the oldest piece of Scripture in the world—four hundred years older than any Dead Sea Scroll and dating to about 587, BC when the Babylonians ransacked Solomon's temple. It was the Aaronic benediction. The biblical words appear on two silver amulets that you can see in the Israel Museum. Here they are: "The LORD bless you and keep you; the LORD make His face to shine upon you and be gracious to you; the LORD lift up His countenance upon you and give you peace" (Numbers 6:24–26 ESV). Do you see the irony? People found God's blessing in hell!

That's what Moses and Israel experience in Exodus 14. Following the liturgical interlude that runs from Exodus 12:1–13:16, Exodus 13:17–14:31 describes the least likely locale for God's blessings to show up—the Red Sea, a place that looked like hell.

The area around the Red Sea includes rivers, lakes, channels, and even oceanic bodies. Little wonder that scholars have suggested at least nine different sites for God's miraculous sea deliverance of His people Israel!

Earlier, God said that Pharaoh would let Israel go (Exodus 3:20), and that was Moses' first word to the king (Exodus 5:1). Exodus 13:17 now states, "Pharaoh let the people go" (ESV). A ragtag band of slaves pack their bags and leave Egypt—*finally*! How did they leave? With great fanfare! Moses writes in Numbers 33:3, "The people of Israel went out triumphantly in the sight of all the Egyptians" (ESV).

A Hungarian man named András Toma was fighting for the Germans in World War II when the Soviets captured him in 1944. Toma went crazy while in a Russian Gulag. I've read that Russian Gulags can do that to a person. After Toma was transferred to a mental hospital, the Soviets—whose systems were never models of efficiency—eventually forgot who he was.

Everyone else thought he was insane—that is, until 1998. That's when a doctor discovered that Toma was speaking Hungarian. Opening his medical file for the first time in decades, the doctor also found out about Toma's history. He quickly notified authorities in Hungary. The POW returned home in 1999 to a hero's welcome, where he was called the last prisoner of World War II.

Israel certainly felt like that after being in the Egyptian meat grinder. Now they were prisoners set free!

It's easy to chart the route the fleeing Israelites *should* take. Moses calls it "way of the land of the Philistines" (Exodus 13:17 ESV). Isaiah 9:1 calls it "the way of the sea" (ESV). Following this well-worn trail would mean that Moses and company would be in Gaza—about 150 miles away—in ten days. If God unleashes more plagues on the Canaanites, with any luck, the Israelites would be the sole inhabitants of the Promised Land in less than a month. "Thanks be to God!"

God, however, directed the Israelites to leave Egypt through the wilderness (Exodus 13:7). This wasn't a convenient shortcut. It was a long, winding, and dangerous road. For a full itinerary of Israel's trek to Canaan see Numbers 33—it's very sobering! Then look ahead to Joshua

24 and read how Israel finally entered the Promised Land—it's very inspiring!

Why does God lead Israel on a much longer route to the Promised Land? The first reason is that the short way would lead the Israelites into a direct confrontation with Egyptian fortresses. God, therefore, directed Israel to the south and east, "Lest the people change their minds when they see war and return to Egypt" (Exodus 13:17 ESV).

"Hold on!" you exclaim. "Doesn't Exodus 13:18 say the Israelites are 'equipped for battle'?" (ESV). The Hebrew is better rendered "in an orderly fashion." Yahweh's people, therefore, are more like a marching band than they are a combat-ready army poised for victory—making the long way out the best way out.

CHAPTER 7

The Great Escape: Exodus 14

The chariots of God are twice ten thousand, thousands upon thousands; the Lord is among them. (Psalm 68:17 ESV)

Undaunted Courage is a book by Stephan Ambrose about the Lewis and Clark expedition. After facing an onslaught of problems—hunger, fatigue, desertion, illness, and death—on July 25, 1805, the explorers finally reached the headwaters of the Missouri River near Three Forks, Montana.

Advance information led Lewis and Clark to believe that once they reached the Continental Divide—one hundred miles west of Three Forks—they would face a half-day portage, reach the waters of the Columbia River, then float to the Pacific Ocean. The hard part of the journey was behind them. It was time to celebrate! *Or so they thought.*

Meriwether Lewis climbed the bluffs near the Continental Divide, expecting to see the Columbia River. Imagine his feelings when, instead of seeing the Columbia River, he became the first person aside from the American Indians to see the Rocky Mountains. The group couldn't go back. There was no clear way forward. There's a word for that—*trapped*.

Moses and Israel were also on a journey off the beaten track, with no idea where they were going. God directs His people toward the Red Sea where they'll become trapped—hemmed in by the Red Sea on one side and the Egyptian army on the other. Welcome to Exodus 14!

TRAPPED

We all know the feeling of being trapped. Maybe you conquered a bad habit, only to suffer a relapse. Maybe you feel stuck in a dead-end job, a dead-end marriage, a dead-end family, a dead-end life—or all of the above. Like Moses and Israel, you can't go back, and there is no clear way forward. Hedonism says, "Party your way out!" Materialism says, "Spend your way out!" Individualism says, "You are the way out!" Then there's our own voice that says, "There is no way out!"

Do you talk to yourself? Sure, you do. So do I. I talk to myself all the time—I just don't move my lips! No one talks to me more than I do. My conversations with myself cover a broad range of topics—people (alive and dead), biking, Hebrew, baseball, the weather, God, money. The human mind can record, store, and play back over 100 trillion pieces of information. That provides a lot of discussion starters!

As a matter of fact, many of our 100 trillion pieces of information are lies. A good majority of them have been around a long time—since we were children. We've listened to some lies for so long that they feel true, they sound true, they look true—even though they are anything but. These lies, like an invading army, have hijacked our salvation story.

What are some of our sick stories? "If I'm going to be happy, things *always* have to go my way." "If I fail at *anything*, I'm a failure at *everything*." "It's best to avoid problems rather than face them." "My marriage issues are *all* my spouse's fault." "*Nothing* ever goes my way." "The older I get, the worse life gets."

It's high time—in fact, it's past time—to delete these lies.

FLY AGAIN

Hans Babblinger of Ulm, Germany, wanted to fly. Babblinger wanted to soar like a bird. Problem. He lived in the sixteenth century. Flying was impossible. Or was it?

Hans Babblinger didn't think so. He built a pair of wings and tested them in the Bavarian Alps. Good choice. Really good choice. Upward wind currents are common in the Bavarian Alps. On a memorable day, with friends watching, Hans jumped off an embankment and soared down to safety.

A year later, the king came to town. Hans wanted to fly for the king. But this time, Hans chose the bluffs near the Danube River. Bad choice. Really bad choice. There are no upward wind currents near the Danube River. In front of the king, his court, and the local priest, Hans Babblinger jumped. He fell like a rock into the river. Guess what the priest preached about the next Sunday? "Man was not meant to fly." Hans believed him. He put his wings away. Hans Babblinger never tried to fly again.

What lies are telling you "Never fly again"? What voices keep reminding you about the time you fell like a rock into the river? What voices are urging you to put your wings away? You'd be amazed at the number of people who, after failing once, never try again.

"The LORD will fight for you" (Exodus 14:14 ESV). Moses invites us to claim this truth. Not only when we feel trapped by the Red Seas of life, but also when we come to Baal Zephon—a pivotal place in the Book of Exodus.

BAAL-ZEPHON

Exodus 14 commences with God telling Moses where He wants Israel to camp. It's one of the most alarming commands in the Bible. The Israelites have left Egypt, then God tells them to turn back to Egypt? Are you kidding me? Freedom is out of Egypt and God is now telling His people to return?

The Israelites are to camp in front of Pi-hahiroth, between Migdol and the Red Sea, in front of Baal-zephon. This precise description of Israel's campsite is unique within the Book of Exodus. In fact, Exodus 14:2 marks the only time throughout the nation's forty-year travels when God dictates exactly where He wants the Israelites to set up camp.

If that isn't enough to highlight Baal-zephon, in Exodus 14:9, Moses repeats the campsite's location. "The Egyptians pursued them, all

Pharaoh's horses and chariots and his horsemen and his army, and overtook them encamped at the sea, by Pi-hahiroth, in front of Baal-zephon" (ESV). This repetition accents the pivotal role of Baal-zephon—a place that names the only Egyptian deity in the Book of Exodus.

What's Moses up to? He's informing us that Yahweh is about to defeat not only Egypt but also one of Egypt's chief gods—Baal Hadad. You may remember in chapter 5 we learned that many of the plagues display God's victory over Egyptian deities. Now at the Red Sea, Yahweh prepares to undermine the authority of Baal, an ancient storm god who promised megadoses of sex and money.

Please don't misunderstand. Sex and money are God's good gifts. Lest they destroy us, though, God gives boundaries. We are to enjoy sexual pleasure and the blessings of wealth within the moral framework of the Ten Commandments—more on this when we get to Exodus 20. For now, though, it's enough to know that Baal-worship deified sex and money. How so? Through another story, a sinister story, a very seductive story.

Ancient Egyptians and Canaanites saw themselves as participants in a story of gods and goddesses. The myth centered on Baal's supremacy by controlling water. Here's how the story went:

Baal, a son of the supreme god named El whose wife's name was Asherah, was dispatched every spring to bring order to rain, thunder, and lightning. Yamm—the water lord whose name means "sea"—would put up a good fight. Eventually, though, Baal would defeat him.

As spring turned to summer and summer turned to fall, rain became less frequent. Enter another god—Mot, who represented death. In a violent battle, Mot kills Baal and swallows him whole. All seems lost. Yet Anat, a female goddess and Baal's lover, fights and kills Mot. Baal and Anat then have sex. It rains. The crops grow. The harvest abounds. And mucho money overflows. All's well that ends well.

Do you see the story's plot? Baal champions sex and money. They're trumpeted as life's chief goals. The most enticing part of the myth, however, was that ancient people could participate in the story. How? By engaging in illicit sex at a high place—a hill or a mountain—Baal worshipers believed they were coaxing Baal and his consort, Anat, into having sexual relations in heaven. The result of this heavenly encounter? Rain, and with the rain came abundant crops.

This is not our story. This is not our song.

Placing sexual pleasure and financial stockpiling at the center of life has always been a seductive story. Do you see where it all ends?

God did. That's why He locates Israel's deliverance from Egypt within a spiritual battle—the truth of Yahweh versus the lie of Baal Hadad. Who will win?

PHARAOH CHANGES HIS MIND

Pharaoh comes around to letting Israel leave—conceding the battle to Yahweh and letting His people serve Him (Exodus 12:31). However, when the foolhardy king realizes that Israel's "three days' journey" (Exodus 3:18; 8:27 ESV) has turned into a permanent absence, he once again changes his mind. "When the king of Egypt was told that the people had fled, the mind of Pharaoh and his servants was changed toward the people, and they said, 'What is this we have done, that we have let Israel go from serving us?'" (Exodus 14:5 ESV). It dawns upon Pharaoh that if he allows the Israelite slaves to escape, he will destroy Egypt's economy—as if it hadn't already been wiped out by the ten plagues!

Failing to remember he's up against the Creator of the universe, Pharaoh summons his crack troops—thinking that horses and chariots will defeat the God who made heaven and earth. Hadn't Pharaoh Thutmose III learned anything from the frogs, flies, and fleas? Is this guy crazy?

Apparently so. In his frenzied state, Pharaoh again changes his mind. He doesn't want to enslave the Israelites. Now he wants to kill them. As Pharaoh gives chase to Israel, God doesn't remove the Red Sea. Instead, God enables Israel to go through it.

Through. That's a word worth remembering. There are times when God does a miracle and removes a huge problem or deathly sickness. More likely, though, God makes a path through. In most cases, God doesn't take us out of our pain. Neither does He lead us around problems or help us dig a tunnel underneath them. "Even though I walk *through* the valley of the shadow of death" (Psalm 23:4 ESV, emphasis added).

WE CAN STOP FLAPPING OUR ARMS

Picture yourself on a commercial airline flight. When the 747 begins taxiing down the runway, you begin flapping your arms. The flight attendant sees you and concludes you're one wing short of an airplane. She blurts out, "What are you doing?"

You confidently respond, "I'm helping this 747 get off the ground."

"Um, you really don't have to do that."

"Yes I do! I'm committed to making this work!"

"Trust me. You can sit back, relax, and enjoy the flight. This plane will take off without your help."

"No!" you insist. "I've got to help get this plane off the ground!" We often flap our arms when we see horses and chariots in our rearview mirror.

Pharaoh sees Moses and the Israelites pinned in by the wilderness, lost and confused. The king's next step? "[Pharaoh] took six hundred chosen chariots and all the other chariots of Egypt, with officers over all of them" (Exodus 14:7 ESV). Moses mentions the term *chariot* twelve times in Exodus 14–15. Chariots in the ancient Middle East were like today's nuclear bombs.

Horse-drawn battle chariots appeared in Egypt around 1500 BC. They allowed soldiers to shoot arrows or throw a javelin while being shielded by the chariot's frame. In one picture of King Tut riding in his chariot, his bow is stretched back, ready to strike. Bombs away!

Pharaoh Thutmose III has six hundred chariots. How many chariots does Israel have? Zero! Israel's back is against the Red Sea. They face certain destruction. There isn't a thing Moses can do about it. *Flapping his arms won't work.*

You might be elected vice president of Croatia. You might discover a way to email pizza. Cats might fly—or occasionally be nice. A kangaroo might swim. Men might surrender the television remote control. It's not likely, but all of this is possible. What isn't possible, though, is a problem-free life.

Sometimes God is behind the problem. Sometimes God is the One who brings us to the problem, to a dead end. He does this for Israel. *The only way is through.* Why does God do that? "I will get glory over Pharaoh and all his host" (Exodus 14:4 ESV). God knows what He's doing. He's orchestrating events so when Israel is delivered, He will get the glory. They won't.

The Red Sea wasn't the end for Israel. Our Red Sea isn't the end for us!

The Israelites, though, had a difficult time believing this. "Is it because there are no graves in Egypt that you have taken us away to die in the wilderness?" (Exodus 14:11 ESV). Israel stands between the devil and the deep blue sea—literally.

OVERCOMING DESPAIR

This is the first time the Israelites give in to despair. Unfortunately, what begins as a slow trickle will soon become a rushing river. The list is lengthy: Marah (Exodus 15:23–27); the wilderness of Sin (Exodus 16:1–19); Rephidim (Exodus 17:1–7); and climactically at Mount Sinai when they despair over Moses' absence and build a golden calf (Exodus 32:1–35). *Israelites are always going to Israelite.* They will always find something to despair about.

Despair comes from a Latin word meaning "to move down from hope." It's the feeling that things will never get better as we become emotional zombies. Our greatest despair happens when we evaluate

God based on our current circumstances—failing to remember His past mercies and future glories.

Instead of rebuking Israel or chiding them, Moses speaks large amounts of Gospel. He tells the despairing people, "See the salvation of the LORD, which He will work for you today. For the Egyptians whom you see today, you shall never see again. The LORD will fight for you, and you have only to *be silent*" (Exodus 14:13–14 ESV, emphasis added). The expression *be silent* literally means "make yourself limp." Colloquial equivalents include these: "Relax." "Chill out." "Loosen up." "Take it easy." "Be still." "Resign as CEO of the planet." "Take a deep breath." "Don't get your knickers into a knot!"

We can stop flapping our arms now. We can stop trying to help God—or worse, trying to *be* God. Instead, we can buckle our seatbelts, turn off and store all electronic devices, and let God do the heavy lifting. The plane will take off without our help. To believe this, though, takes faith.

FAITH VERSUS FEAR

Experts say that 75 percent of all communication is negative. Who knew? If you don't believe that, then just listen to talk radio! By the time we're four years old, we've heard over 350,000 nos, don'ts, shouldn'ts, wouldn'ts, and who-do-you-think-you-ares. A lot of voices specialize in catastrophizing, awfulizing, and doomsdayizing.

It's much better to listen to God's servant Moses. When the Israelites see the advancing Egyptian army and chariots, Moses says, "Fear not" (Exodus 14:13 ESV). I need this!

We think about work and we're afraid we either won't get the job we want, or we'll lose the job we have. We think about marriage and we're afraid we either won't find the right person or the whole thing will go up in flames. We think about retirement and we're afraid we either won't have enough money or we'll grow feeble, or both will happen at the same time.

Media doesn't help. "Coming up, after this commercial break, the frightening truth about sitting in traffic." "Up next, what you may not know about the water you drink." Television news should begin with these words: "This report is best viewed from the confines of an underground bunker in rural western Nebraska."

There's a big difference between legitimate concerns and fear, between prudence and paranoia. Prudence wears a seat belt. Paranoia won't get into the car. Prudence saves for old age. Paranoia stockpiles and hoards. Prudence calculates the risk and takes the plunge. Paranoia never jumps.

Faith isn't natural. Fear is natural. Doubt is natural. Wanting to manipulate everything to meet our every need is natural. Looking to control situations and people is natural. Giving in to discouragement is natural. Throwing morality out the back door to deal with hurt is natural. Numbing ourselves with food and drinks is natural. Faith, though, is anything but. It takes faith to walk through a newly created water canyon on dry ground. Just ask Israel!

Let me put it this way.

Imagine you're hiking and you come to a narrow, rickety-looking footbridge—one hundred feet above a raging river. The only way to get to the other side is that bridge, but you're not sure it will hold. You slowly begin making your way across, testing each step before moving on. You've got to have faith in the bridge to get to the other side. But it's not your faith in the bridge that keeps you from falling. It's the bridge.

I can have just a little faith in a good bridge and slowly crawl to the other side. Or I can have a lot of faith in a bad bridge, only to have it give way under my feet. Do you see the lesson? Faith is only as good as the object of faith. Moses invites us to make Yahweh—the God of the sea and dry land—the object of our faith.

I know. It's tempting to think that if we could figure it all out, everything would be okay. Yet Yahweh didn't say to Israel, "Believe and you'll understand everything." Yahweh didn't say, "Believe and I'll let you in on every divine mystery and all the secrets in the universe." Yahweh did say, "Fear not!" (e.g., Isaiah 41:10 ESV).

Faith dares to trust these words.

Faith believes Yahweh is never surprised, never walks off the job, and will never worry through a restless night's sleep. Faith doesn't write the story of our life and then ask God to sign His name at the end. No. Biblical faith hands God a blank booklet with our name signed on the last page, then asks Him to write our story as He sees fit.

YAHWEH'S RESCUE

I have an image in my mind. It's the last day of school. My students have felt like prisoners for what seems like eternity. Then what? The last bell rings and they sprint out the door, down the hallway, into the bright spring sunshine. Free at last!

That's Israel. It's the last day of serving as slaves in Egypt.

"In the morning watch the LORD in the pillar of fire and of cloud looked down on the Egyptian forces and threw the Egyptian forces into a panic, clogging their chariot wheels so that they drove heavily" (Exodus 14:24–25 ESV). Have you ever had your car stuck in snow? Did you gun it? Did your wheels end up spinning round and round? Did you go anywhere? If you can relate to any of this, then you have some idea what the Egyptians felt like. All six hundred chariots were stuck in mud. Little did the charioteers know that Yahweh had at His disposal supernatural horses and chariots numbering "twice ten thousand, thousands upon thousands" (Psalm 68:17 ESV). Let's see. Six hundred against at least twenty thousand. I don't like those numbers if I'm an Egyptian!

This is one of the greatest events in the Bible. Moses lifts his staff. The Red Sea parts. The Israelites walk through on dry ground. Pharaoh and his army follow. The Red Sea comes crashing down on them.

When did God accomplish Israel's salvation? "In *the morning* Moses raised his hand over the sea, and the water rushed back into its usual place. The Egyptians tried to escape, but the LORD swept them into the sea" (Exodus 14:27). When does Psalm 46:5 say God delivers? In the morning. When does joy come? In the morning (Psalm 30:5). When did Jesus rise again? In the morning (Matthew 28:1). When does God deliver us from the long nights of life? According to Lamentations 3:23, His mercies are new every morning. What is the last name the Bible gives Jesus? The bright *Morning* Star (Revelation 22:16).

Do you feel stuck? trapped? pinned against the wall? Are you afraid the depression will never lift? the yelling will never stop? the emptiness will never leave? Are you wondering, "Will this gray sky ever brighten? this load ever lighten?"

The God who pinned Israel against the Red Sea is the same God who turned the sea into dry ground. Closed doors turn into open windows. Disasters turn into avenues of hope and healing. Ends turn into new beginnings. Why? Because climactically, the darkness of Good Friday turned into the dawn of an eternal Easter.

God has never lost a battle. Not with Pharaoh. Not with sin. Not with Satan. And not with death. The outcome is inevitable. The victory is assured. The last chapter has been written. The last exodus is on the horizon. Soon we will be free from creation's decay and gut-wrenching brokenness. In that place—the new Jerusalem—we will be eternally enamored with Christ's mercy, glory in His salvation, and dance for joy with endless delight. *This is our story.*

THE NEXT MORNING

As morning breaks, Moses and his motley crew of ex-slaves look back and see the Egyptians caught in a quagmire. Pharaoh's soldiers realize they're in over their heads—literally. How does it all end? Israel moved from fear to faith. "They [the Israelites] believed in the LORD and in His servant Moses" (Exodus 14:31).

On the other hand, Pharaoh and his army move from frenzied chasing to the stillness of death. The humble are exalted and the exalted are humbled. "He brought out Israel with silver and gold, and there was none among His tribes who stumbled" (Psalm 105:37).

REAL VICTORY

The first games in the National Football League are called preseason games. You know, the games in August that don't count in the standings. Coaches use these games to evaluate newly signed players. And the veteran players? They don't play that much.

The first games in Major League Baseball are called spring training games. You know, the games in late February and March down in Florida and Arizona. Ah! Florida and Arizona, where the entire Midwest wants to be in late February and March! These games don't count in the standings either. Coaches use them to evaluate newly signed players. And the veteran players? They don't play that much.

In preseason and spring training games, when you win, you don't really win. When you beat your opponent, you don't really beat your opponent. When you gain the victory, you don't really gain the victory. None of these games really count.

Have you ever felt as though your life is like a preseason football game or spring training baseball game? That what you're doing really doesn't count? That even when you win, it really doesn't matter? That when you work hard, at the end of the day, it all feels pointless?

We know about fake and phony victories, the kinds of victories that don't count for anything. Like when you think you've landed *the* job, but after six months it turns out to be a nightmare. Like when you think you've met Mr. Right, only to find out that he's Mr. Wrong. Like when you work so hard to make the team, only to sit on the bench for the rest of the season. We're all hungry for real victory. For a victory that lasts, that has enduring significance.

There is good news! *Israel's victory at the Red Sea is our victory.* Oh, we fail along the way. We fall victim to the enticements of the world. We make evil decisions, say evil words, and think evil thoughts. After all, we're sinners. But Yahweh has won the great battle. By faith, the victory is ours. This is a settled fact—forever written as our story—never to be altered, tampered with, or changed.

Paul puts it this way: "In all these things we are more than conquerors through Him who loved us" (Romans 8:37). We don't just squeak by. We don't win by one point, in overtime, at the buzzer. We haven't just won the first three games in a best-of-seven series. We're the reigning champions. We're invincible and unconquerable.

In 1798, a British general named Lord Nelson reported to the British king about his victory over the French in the Battle of the Nile. Lord Nelson told the king, "Victory is not a name strong enough for such a scene."

That's true of Israel's exodus. Victory over the enemy isn't a large enough name to describe what took place. And it's all ours!

CONNECTIONS TO GENESIS

I'm sure by now it will not surprise you that God's miracle at the Red Sea employs several motifs from the Book of Genesis. Here are some of them: out of the chaotic waters, God spoke and separated darkness from light (Genesis 1:2–3). Fast-forward to the battle between Egypt and Yahweh where God's Messenger brings darkness over Egypt's forces while shining light on Israel (Exodus 14:19–20). This miracle of separation appears again. How?

Genesis 1:9 records God as saying, "Let the waters under the heavens be gathered together into one place, and let the dry land appear" (ESV). God splits the waters of the Red Sea and, sure enough, dry land appears! Here's another link: the saving wind in Genesis 8:1 comports with the "strong east wind" that made the dry land for Israel to walk upon (Exodus 14:21 ESV). Finally, just as Noah's generation was "covered" in water, so were Egypt's toughest and most determined warriors (Genesis 7:19–21; Exodus 14:28).

What do we learn by comparing these events? Through water and the Spirit, the exodus is God's act of a new creation. If you think this sounds a lot like Baptism, then you're tracking with Paul who writes, "Our fathers were all under the cloud, and all passed through the sea, and all were *baptized* into Moses in the cloud and in the sea" (1 Corinthians

10:1–2 ESV, emphasis added). Through water and the Spirit, first appearing together in Genesis 1:2, God is present when we're baptized in the name of the Father, Son, and Holy Spirit. Through Baptism, God makes us *participants in the exodus story where all things become new.*

Holy Baptism gives us new eyes to see God's beauty, a new mind to understand God's Word, a new voice to sing God's praises, new hands for service to our neighbor, and new feet to run the race of faith. Most importantly, the washing of regeneration and renewal in the Holy Spirit creates in us a new heart, washed in the blood of Jesus. *Born again* is more than a religious cliché. Born again by water and the Spirit means we're part of a salvation story that will never end.

CHAPTER 8

This Is Our Song: Exodus 15

Your way was through the sea, Your path through the great waters; yet Your footprints were unseen. (Psalm 77:19 ESV)

Exodus 7–14 is peppered with statements about God making known His name. Note this impressive list of verses (they're all my translations, emphasis added):

- "The Egyptians shall *know* that I am Yahweh" (Exodus 7:5).
- "By this you shall *know* that I am Yahweh" (Exodus 7:17).
- "That you may *know* that there is no one like Yahweh, our God" (Exodus 8:10).
- "That you may *know* that I am Yahweh in the midst of the land" (Exodus 8:22).
- "That you may *know* that there is none like me in the whole earth" (Exodus 9:14).
- "That you may *know* that the earth belongs to Yahweh" (Exodus 9:29).
- "That you may recount in the hearing of your son and your grandson how I dealt with Egypt and My signs which I worked against them so that you will *know* that I am Yahweh" (Exodus 10:2).
- "That you may *know* that Yahweh makes a distinction between Egypt and Israel" (Exodus 11:7).
- "And the Egyptians will *know* that I am Yahweh, when I have

gained glory for Myself over Pharaoh, his chariots, and his horsemen" (Exodus 14:18).

Through His mighty acts of plagues, Passover, and the Red Sea crossing, Yahweh wants to be known as the incomparable God—incontestably powerful and working wonders as the rightful Creator and Lord of the universe.

The song in Exodus 15:1–18 not only makes God's attributes known but it also serves as a fulcrum in the book—reviewing the first fourteen chapters and giving us an overview of the book's final twenty-four chapters. Moses' so-called "Song of the Sea" became Israel's national anthem. For instance, Exodus 15:2 is repeated—almost word for word—in Isaiah 12:2 and Psalm 118:14.

The Song of the Sea has four parts:

- God's victory celebrated (Exodus 15:1–5)
- God's weapons described (Exodus 15:6–10)
- God's character announced (Exodus 15:11–16)
- God's promises fulfilled (Exodus 15:17–18)

Exodus 14:30–31, by repeating "Yahweh" four times, anticipates the celebration of Yahweh's name in Exodus 15:1–18—a song where Moses responds to two questions posed earlier in the book: "What is His name?" (Exodus 3:13) and "Who is Yahweh?" (Exodus 5:2).

A CLOSER LOOK

The Song of the Sea opens with an array of divine names and titles in Exodus 15:1–2. Then it explicitly introduces the theme of Yahweh's name: "Yahweh is a man of war; Yahweh is His name" (Exodus 15:3). In all, the song mentions "Yahweh" ten times—with ten serving as the number of perfection in the book with ten plagues and ten commandments. Yahweh is the perfect God! He alone moves the immovable, breaks the unbreakable, and accomplishes the impossible. "He saved them for His name's sake, that He might make known His mighty power" (Psalm 106:8 ESV).

Because Yahweh's name is so prominent in the song, Moses' actions—a key element in Exodus 14—disappear. As does *Israel* in the song. Moses simply calls them "people." "The *people* whom You have redeemed" (Exodus 15:13 ESV, emphasis added) and "till Your *people*, O LORD, pass by, till the *people* pass by whom You have purchased" (Exodus 15:16 ESV, emphasis added). What about Pharaoh? He's mentioned only once (Exodus 15:4). And Egypt? The oppressive empire isn't specified at all. The king and his kingdom are referred to as "the enemy" in Exodus 15:6–7, 9 while the term "them" appears in Exodus 15:5, 10, and 12.

What is Moses up to? Why does he, for the most part, delete the specifics of Israel's greatest victory? My! When our team wins the championship or our candidate secures the election, we look for reporters to describe every detail, from every angle. What did he eat for breakfast that day? How many push-ups did he do the day before? Why did she give speeches in Dayton, Denver, and Daytona Beach? Inquiring minds want to know!

But Moses? He gives us bits and pieces, snippets and scraps. Why? If Moses had provided too much detail in his song, it would be difficult for us to make it our own. For example, naming Moses and Egypt would be awkward, as few of us have been led out of Egyptian slavery.

Exodus 15:1–18, therefore, strikes a more universal note because Yahweh wants everyone to see themselves as breaking free from bondage—emotional, relational, financial, but especially spiritual bondage. Do you see? The Song of the Sea is *our* song.

And what a song it is! That a group of slaves revolted and left Egypt would hardly be news of lasting import. However, that these slaves were led by the Creator of heaven and earth and that He places all oppressive systems on notice—now that's something to take note of! It's no surprise, then, that other nations are trembling (Exodus 15:14–16).

Sooner or later, all slave-holding systems will come face-to-face with Lord Yahweh.

The song's lyrics give no hint that Israel did anything. In fact, shortly before their deliverance, the Israelites lamented to Moses that he had taken them out of Egypt (Exodus 14:11–12). Even with that, God's right hand extended over the Red Sea (Exodus 15:12) for He's an awesome Warrior (Exodus 15:3). Everything is under His control.

Most notable is the Song's celebration of Yahweh's mighty power to deliver (Exodus 15:1). The Song of the Sea repeatedly extols Yahweh's greatness, majesty, and strength. His right hand is "glorious in power" and "shatters the enemy" (Exodus 15:6 ESV). He "stretched out [His] right hand" and the earth swallowed the foe (Exodus 15:12 ESV). The nations hear about this and are in terror because of "the greatness of [His] arm" (Exodus 15:16 ESV). Yahweh is a strong and trustworthy refuge for all who are oppressed.

The rhetorical question in Exodus 15:11, which declares Yahweh's incomparability among the gods, is the song's only query. And, standing in the center of the song, Moses intends it to announce a revolutionary idea. The destructive plagues upon Egypt and the victory over Pharaoh at the Red Sea demonstrate that Yahweh is the sole and supreme God— there's no one like Him in all the earth (cf. Exodus 9:14).

The Book of Exodus begins by highlighting the roles of women— Shiphrah, Puah, Jochebed, Miriam, and Pharaoh's daughter. Now, on the banks of the Red Sea, we meet Miriam again along with more women singing the song. "Then Miriam the prophetess, the sister of Aaron, took a tambourine in her hand, and all the women went out after her with tambourines and dancing. And Miriam sang to them: 'Sing to the LORD, for He has triumphed gloriously; the horse and his rider He has thrown into the sea'" (Exodus 15:20–21 ESV).

AWESOME HANDS!

In the Book of Exodus, Moses employs the "hand of God" image twenty-seven times—this includes the words *hand, right hand, arm, finger*, and *palm*. In each case, God shows He alone wields all power in heaven and on earth.

God uses Moses' hand to do miracles in Pharaoh's court (e.g., Exodus 4:2, 4, 20). And, because Israel was stuck in Egypt's clenched hand (Exodus 3:8), the Lord says, "I will lay My *hand* on Egypt and bring My hosts, My people the children of Israel, out of Egypt by mighty acts of judgment" (Exodus 7:4 ESV). Indeed, He brought His people out of slavery with a mighty hand and an outstretched arm.

Christ also demonstrates power and authority through His hands. Note this example: "Jesus stretched out His *hand* and touched him, saying, 'I will; be clean.'" (Matthew 8:3 ESV, emphasis added). On another occasion, the Savior said, "I give them eternal life, and they will never perish, and no one will snatch them out of My *hand*" (John 10:28 ESV, emphasis added). Christ's most deliberate show of hands, however, was on Good Friday when He stretched them out on a Roman cross. His back was covered in spit, sweat, and blood. His head was bruised and swollen. His lungs screamed for air. And then there were His hands— fixed in place, nailed to a cross.

These hands hold us close to the Father's heart, forever.

WHAT ARE THE ODDS?

Let's step back from the details of Exodus 14–15 and ask this question. What are the odds that a group of Hebrew slaves would defeat the most powerful military force on earth—Egypt, led by a mean and mighty pharaoh? What are the odds? A million to one? Ten billion to one?

The longshot story begins in Exodus 1:11–14: "The Egyptians put slave masters over them to oppress them with forced labor who worked them ruthlessly. . . . They made their lives bitter with hard labor in brick and mortar and with all kinds of work in the fields." It gets worse! "No longer supply the people with straw for making bricks, let them go and gather their own straw. But require them to make the same number of bricks as before; don't reduce the quota" (Exodus 5:7–8). Then it gets worse! As the Israelites flee Egypt, they look over their shoulders and see Pharaoh madly chasing after them screaming, "You'll have hell to pay!" But it gets even worse! The Israelites are then surrounded. They said to Moses, "Was it because there were no graves in Egypt that you brought us to the desert to die?" (Exodus 14:11).

Just when the odds were completely against God's people, there is victory—total and complete victory. "Pharaoh's chariots and army He has hurled into the sea. The finest of Pharaoh's officers are drowned in the Red Sea" (Exodus 15:4–5). No wonder the Israelites sing in Exodus 15:2, "The Lord [Ya] is my strength and my song, and He has become my salvation" (ESV).

This is the first use of *Ya* in the Bible. Imagine that! Yahweh's nickname comes in Israel's first song—our song! "Yahweh is a man of war; Yahweh is His name!" (Exodus 15:3). Pharaoh's fiercest and foremost fall like dominos. All of this, though, is a peek, prelude, and preview to the Bible's greatest against-all-odds story.

Opposition began early in Christ's ministry. Just like Exodus 1–2, there was an evil king who, in genocidal fury, gave orders to throw Jesus to the butcher's blade (Matthew 2). Full speed ahead to Holy Week. Pharisees plot with Sadducees. Scribes test him with Torah trivia. The Jewish leaders posture and pose with Pentateuchal pride. It gets worse. *Christ will have hell to pay.*

Once arrested, Jesus is bound, accused, blindfolded, and mocked. But it gets worse. They strip Him naked and beat Him into a bloody pulp. But it gets even worse. Jesus is blood-soaked and spiked to a tree for six hours—to hang like a scarecrow fixed to wood. Jesus is crucified, dead, and buried. Just when everyone thought it was over, the angel announced, "He is not here, for He has risen, as He said" (Matthew 28:6 ESV).

What are the odds that a man, brutally beaten, then crucified by the Roman Empire, would come back to life? It happened! It really happened! Christ is risen indeed! Now the best is yet to come. When Christ returns, we will sing forever at the Lamb's high feast, "The LORD is my strength and my song, and He has become my salvation" (Exodus 15:2 ESV).

Hallelu is a Hebrew word meaning "praise." Add *Ya*—Yahweh's nickname. What do you have? A song that includes an endless and deathless "Hallelujah!"

SINGING THE SONG OF SALVATION

In 1962, a nuclear disaster was as close as the press of a red button—one red button. A Soviet submarine was patrolling along the eastern coast of Florida when the captain began preparing to nuke three American cities. Had it not been for a clear-thinking Russian officer, World War III might have begun in 1962. The officer's name? Vasili Arkhipov.

Back in the day, Soviet subs were designed for cold water—like the North Sea—not the warm water off the Florida coast. Temperatures reached 120 degrees Fahrenheit inside the Russian sub. As it patrolled near the Florida coast, Soviet sailors were exhausted and on edge. The captain finally lost his cool. He issued the order to launch three nuclear missiles—T-minus three minutes and counting!

Vasili Arkhipov asked the captain to reconsider. The captain listened. His anger cooled. The Soviet sub went home. Authorities kept this near brush with World War III secret for decades. It wasn't until 2002 that the public learned of Vasili Arkhipov's heroic stand.

How does this event intersect with our lives? After all, we won't ever spend three weeks in a sweltering Russian submarine—at least I hope we never do! We may, however, spend a semester under a heavy class load. We may fight the headwinds of a financial downturn. We may spend night after night at the bedside of a sick child or a dying parent. We may fight to keep our family together or our business from going under.

In all these scenarios, we'll be tempted to press the red button and launch—not nuclear warheads, but angry outbursts, rash accusations, a hateful retaliation of ugly words. Sometimes we emotionally vomit and deal with the consequences later.

What do you do when the temperature is up, your defenses are down, and you want to go nuclear? How can you keep your finger from pressing the red button? How can you keep your head when everyone else is losing theirs?

Sing.

That's what I said. Sing. Singing is so much better than sobbing, sighing, feeling sorry for ourselves, and then pushing the red button. Asaph knows.

Asaph—a poet who composed twelve psalms—draws from Israel's exodus hymnody. In Psalm 77, he applies Israel's victory to his current crisis. Asaph begins the psalm by questioning Yahweh's Gospel characteristics (Psalm 77:1–9), sounding much like the Israelites groaning and lamenting in Egypt (Exodus 2:23; 14:11). Then he appeals to God's mighty acts of salvation through Moses and Aaron (Psalm 77:10–20), echoing several motifs from the Song of the Sea. Consider, for instance, these links:

- "Steadfast love" (Psalm 77:8 = Exodus 15:13)
- "Right hand" (Psalm 77:10 = Exodus 15:6 [two times]; 15:12)
- "Wonder" (Psalm 77:11, 14 = Exodus 15:11)
- "Holy" (Psalm 77:13 = Exodus 15:11, 13)
- "What god is great like our God?" (Psalm 77:13 = Exodus 15:11)
- "You with Your arm redeemed Your people" (Psalm 77:15 = Exodus 15:16)
- Aquatic imagery (Psalm 77:16–19 = Exodus 15:4–5, 8, 10)

Why does Asaph make water his adversary instead of Egypt? He's using Moses' strategy in Exodus 15:1–18—make the song accessible so it reaches the broadest audience.

Aquatic words are common in the Psalter. Authors employ terms like *water, the depths, waves, the sea,* and the like to refer to chaos and evil. By employing water terminology, Asaph and other poets invite us to think about our enemies that surround us like an overwhelming flood.

When everything looks bleak—like Asaph, dare to sing. Why? Because the end is not the end. I'm going to write those words again. *The end is not the end.* Because Jesus writes our story, the end is never the end. There is death. There's also resurrection. There's Golgotha. There's also Galilee. *Galilee.* That's where Christ promised to show Himself to the faithful.

Now what? That Visa bill is not the end. That diagnosis is not the end. That impossible situation is not the end. That depression stalking and mocking you is not the end. Christ always adds a new chapter to our story—*always.*

As a teenager, one of my jobs was to mow the lawn. Lessing lawnmowers, though, weren't dependable. They were barely a step above garage-sale giveaways. One day, I couldn't start a mower. I kept pulling the chord and sweating, pulling the chord and sweating!

My father walked up to me and said, "Reed, you're not using all your strength."

"What?" I blurted out.

"Reed, you're not using all your strength."

"What do you mean?"

My dad said, "You haven't asked me to help you."

Did I tell you that my father played football at East Denver High School and in college at the University of Denver? Did I tell you that my father, Bullet Bob Lessing, back in the day, had bulging biceps? Did I tell you that my father was as strong as an ox?

Give your problems to your heavenly Father. Ask Him to help. You don't have to pull and sweat. Instead, sing exodus psalms to your God. That's Paul's strategy as well. "Let the Word of Christ dwell in you richly, teaching and admonishing one another in all wisdom, *singing psalms* and hymns and spiritual songs, with thankfulness in your hearts to God" (Colossians 3:16 ESV, emphasis added).

YAHWEH IS KING!

The noun *king* appears fourteen times in Exodus 1–15 (1:8, 15, 17, 18; 2:23; 3:18, 19; 5:4; 6:11, 13, 27, 29; 14:5, 8). These verses refer to the pharaohs' ruthless rule over Israel. In Exodus 15:18, however, Moses announces, "The LORD will reign forever and ever" (ESV). What is the point? In the Book of Exodus, the pharaohs are fakes, frauds, and full-time phonies. Yahweh alone is the King of kings and the Sovereign of all sovereigns. Yahweh is the only true and lasting King. And He proved it by defeating a puny and finally powerless Egyptian king at the Red Sea.

When Israel was poised to enter the Promised Land, another oppressive king tried to exert dominion over God's people. His name was Balak, a Moabite monarch. Balak's lackey, one Balaam, was hired to curse the Israelites. The more Balaam cursed, though, the more God blessed His people. This led Balaam to tell Balak that the shout of a king (Yahweh) is among the people of Israel (Numbers 23:21).

The Old Testament is chock-full of this Gospel—earthly powers and authorities must bow to Yahweh's rule and reign. He has complete command of world history. "Yahweh is the Great King over all the earth" (Psalm 47:2).

Jesus began His ministry by announcing this good news. "The kingdom of God is at hand; repent and believe the gospel" (Mark 1:15 ESV). In Christ, God's kingdom has invaded the world. What a startling claim! Little wonder, then, that the Jews in Thessalonica attacked Paul and Silas, saying, "They are all acting against the decrees of Caesar, saying that there is another king, Jesus" (Acts 17:7).

Over the course of history, countless people have postured themselves as the ultimate authority. On the Last Day, however, every impostor, just like the pharaohs of old, will be exposed. Thank God for His merciful and mighty rule!

PREPARING FOR THE PROMISED LAND

I played football in high school. Check that. I practiced football in high school and walked the sidelines during games—for three sorry seasons. I weighed 140 pounds and wore black, horn-rimmed glasses. No wonder I was never all-state!

The toughest part of my high school football experience was the two-a-day practices in August. I would drag myself out of bed for practice 8:00 a.m.–10:30 a.m., come home and sleep, then show up 2:00 p.m.–5:00 p.m. I got used to sweat. It was in socks, pads, jerseys, helmets—you name it. Everything smelled like sweat. And the lockers? More sweat.

The first week of two-a-days was tough. The second week was tougher. That's when we put on our uniforms and began blocking and tackling—and, if you were me, running from 280-pound defensive ends as fast as you could. I thought to myself more than once, "If I can survive this, I can survive anything." Two-a-days weren't the *destination*. Two-a-days were the *preparation*—in my case, to sit on the bench during every game!

The transition between Exodus 15:21 and 15:22 is abrupt. Singing and dancing are replaced with blowing sand and scorching heat. Overnight, the Israelites find themselves traveling in the desert of Shur. Their victory march slows down to a crawl. What people assumed would be a walk in the park became a marathon in the desert. Think two-a-days. The earlier complaining in Exodus 14:10–12 returns—full throttle.

The desert isn't Israel's destination. The desert is Israel's preparation.

The Israelites didn't believe it. Their journey through the wilderness was so difficult that only two out of the 603,000 who left Egypt made it to the Promised Land—Joshua and Caleb. That's a graduation rate of 0.00000332. Two-a-days almost tanked the entire team! What happened?

EXPECTATIONS MEET REALITY

The sandwich looked good on the menu, but it looked like leftovers when it was served. You thought you had taken a great picture, but can't bear to look at it now. You anticipated that loading the car for summer vacation would be easy, but your children wanted to bring way too much stuff. Expectations meet reality.

That's what happened to Israel after leaving Egypt. Great expectations met bitter realities.

After our baptismal exodus and before we enter our heavenly promised land, we're also surrounded by sand dunes and dust storms. Hope easily evaporates. "It wasn't supposed to be this way!"

I once took two of my children—Abi and Jonathan—to buy a new bike for five-year-old Abi. Abi picked out a shiny purple bike with a banana seat, flared handlebars, and pink training wheels. Jonathan, age 3, also thought he was going to get a new bike. I reminded him, "Jonathan, you're still having problems riding your trike. A new, big-kid's bike would bring you more pain than pleasure. Someday I'll buy you a bike—just not today." Jonathan looked up at me and asked, "Then I don't get a new bike?" "That's right, Son, not today. You don't get a new bike." Then he said at the top of his lungs, "Then I want a new daddy!"

There are times when we want a new Savior. A Savior who instantly takes us out of slavery and into the promised land—who immediately rights our wrongs, heals our hurts, and delivers us from disease, depression, and all sorts of doom and gloom.

Expectations meet reality.

The reality is that you're twenty-seven years old and your 1,100-square-foot starter home is going to be your address for at least the next ten years. The reality is that you just had twins and life won't settle down for decades. The reality is that sometimes prayers go unanswered, hopes are dashed, and deliverance from the blues and blahs doesn't happen fast enough.

It's one thing to sing in church, "Take my life and let it be Consecrated, Lord, to Thee" (*LSB* 783). It's something entirely different to trust God in the hard places in life, in the confusing places, in the places where it doesn't look like God is at work, or where it even looks like God is working against us.

God doesn't take people *out* of the desert. He provides for them *in* the desert. He provides a table of food and water from a rock (Psalm 78:19–20). At the end of it all, Moses says, "These forty years the Lord your God has been with you. You have lacked nothing" (Deuteronomy 2:7 ESV).

God's not working to accommodate our every whim, desire, and want. He isn't orchestrating a group of cheerleaders who will applaud our every success. This doesn't mean God isn't working for our good. It means He's working to make us holy, not happy. That's why God leads us into the wilderness where lessons are learned, character is forged, and wisdom is won. The desert is God's way of making us more like Jesus.

In the desert of Shur, there's so much Israel doesn't have—yet. But there's so much more that they do have—now. Freedom. Direction. Divine presence. A hope and a future. These are also God's gifts to you in Christ Jesus.

CHAPTER 9

Miraculous Manna: Exodus 16

He commanded the skies above and opened the doors of
heaven, and He rained down on them manna to eat and
gave them the grain of heaven. (Psalm 78:23–24 ESV)

I have a theory. It's airtight. No parent, no matter how patient,
can make it past the fourth "Why?" Your child asks, "Why?" And
you explain. Then she asks, "Why?" And you explain. She again asks,
"Why?" And you explain. Then, at the fourth "Why?" what do you say?
"Because I said so!"

It's okay to ask God, "Why?" There comes a time, however, for us
to trust Him. How come? Because God said so. This is where Israel and
God are at in Exodus 16. Elim—where we pick up Israel's journey to
Mount Sinai—was an abundant oasis, "where there were twelve springs
of water and seventy palm trees" (Exodus 15:27 ESV). But the Israelites
couldn't stay there indefinitely. After two weeks, it was time to continue
their march to Sinai, which takes them into the wilderness of Sin. That's
the name of a desert between Elim and Mount Sinai. However, an obvious pun is in order. In Sin, Israel will sin. That's what we'll see in Exodus
16. Even more, though, we'll see Yahweh's incredible patience and fierce
devotion to Israel.

SHAME

Moses begins Exodus 16 by writing that the Israelites are no longer
slaves, but a "congregation" (Exodus 16:1, 2 ESV). This new identity,

however, didn't mean that God's people overcame the power of shame overnight—the shame of being slaves.

Egypt's sick system was geared to demean, belittle, and keep slaves in their place. "You're a slave! You'll always be a slave!" The result was shame—deep and abiding shame. Guilt consumes us when we sin. Shame consumes us when people sin against us.

Our first parents, Adam and Eve, lived before God and each other without shame (Genesis 2:25). They were free to live wholeheartedly before their Creator and one another without posing or pretense. We all know how long that lasted. On the other side of Eden, shame stalks and haunts us. Driven by shame, we cover up, pretend, hide, numb out, blame others, try harder, and, when none of that works, we fall into despair.

When given a choice between freedom and shame, the Israelites choose shame. "Would that we had died by the hand of the LORD in the land of Egypt, when we sat by the meat pots and ate bread to the full" (Exodus 16:3 ESV). Facing shame is very complicated. It's easier to idealize the past rather than come to terms with it. Meat pots and bread to the full? That's utter nonsense!

Breaking free from shame doesn't happen when we perfect ourselves, master ourselves, teach ourselves, or steel ourselves—or, like Israel, lie to ourselves. The way out of shame is to admit our brokenness and fall at the feet of Jesus. We often hear that Jesus stood in the place of offenders, the guilty. Seldom do we hear that Jesus also stood in the place of the injured, the shamed.

Shame is difficult for us. Shame was catastrophic for Jesus. Ancient Roman literature indicates that the heart of crucifixion was its utter and unspeakable shame. What's more, the group of men who were positioned to honor Christ—Pharisees, Sadducees, and scribes—treated Him with malicious contempt. What did this mean for Jesus? Ultimate shame. What does this mean for us? Jesus is present when shame strikes us with all its might. He carried all our shame, in His body, to the cross.

THE AARONIC BENEDICTION

Let me remind you—using the Aaronic Benediction—how God never, ever shames His people. You probably hear these words often in worship. They come from Numbers 6:24–26: "The LORD bless *you* and keep *you* [That line is three words in Hebrew.]; the LORD make His face to shine upon *you* and be gracious to *you* [That line is five words in Hebrew.]; the LORD lift up His face upon *you* and give *you* peace" [That line is seven words in Hebrew.] (ESV, emphasis added).

First, let me explain the italicized word *you*. It's a singular personal pronoun, not plural. It's *you*, not *you all*. Singular *you* denotes a focus that's individual and intimate, particular and personal. God's care is cosmic and universal—to be sure. Yet to emphasize the value God places on you, He employs singular *you* six times in this benediction. It's you, you, you, you, you and you! "I will bless *you*!"

Now, let me clarify the Hebrew word counts. Do you see how the blessing begins small and gets big? The first line has three words. The second line has five. The third line has seven words. God's blessing is a stream that begins small and ends like a rushing river. Isn't that like our God? Do you remember? A small baby in a little ark—that would be Moses—turns the Egyptian empire upside down.

Let's go deeper.

In essence, God says to Aaron, "Tell the Israelites, 'My face doesn't look at you with disgust or dread or disdain. *I will never shame you. I smile at you. My face shines on you always!*'"

God also tells Aaron to say, "And be gracious to *you*" (Numbers 6:25). What had happened a few months before Numbers 6? We will find out shortly—when Aaron builds a golden calf and the Israelites worship it. God could have thrown the book at Aaron, but He didn't. God could have torched Aaron, but He wouldn't. At the end of Numbers 6, God basically says, "Aaron, tell My people that I'm gracious and forgiving. I want it coming from *your* mouth, Aaron, because you're Exhibit A. You're the one who built the golden calf. Tell the people that I'm not harsh, I'm not vindictive, and I don't hold a grudge. I don't rub it in. I rub it out."

The Germans invented the first lead pencil in 1662. When do you think someone came up with the idea to attach a rubber eraser to the top of lead pencils? March 30, 1858. How ironic? For 196 years, people could write but couldn't erase.

That's never been God's problem. Ever since the garden debacle in Genesis 3, He has been forgiving, absolving, taking away—yes, erasing sin. God has wiped our slate clean!

The benediction ends with these words: "The LORD lift up His countenance upon you and give you peace [*shalom*]" (Numbers 6:26). Shalom is the fullness of life: prosperity, happiness, salvation, restoration, repair—the sum total of the Gospel.

Because of Jesus, all these gifts from the Aaronic benediction are yours. Why? On Good Friday, there was no blessing for Jesus—only a curse. On Good Friday, the Father didn't smile upon Jesus—He turned His face away and Christ experienced the full weight of all guilt and all shame, for all people, for all time. On Good Friday, the Father didn't give his Son shalom. Instead, Jesus was pushed into utter darkness. Numbers 6 is an exceedingly precious blessing for us. Numbers 6 is an exceedingly costly blessing for Jesus.

Years ago, my youngest daughter, Lori Beth, would play a game with me. I'd say, "If they lined up all the little six-year-old girls in the world, I mean all of the little six-year-old little girls in the world, and I had first choice, to pick any little six-year-old girl in the world that I wanted, do you know whom I would pick?" Lori would make up names like Amanda, Brittany, Jessica, or Molly. With a big smile I'd say, "No! YOU! I'd pick *you*. Every. Single. Time!"

That's the gist of the Aaronic benediction. God chooses to love you—today, tomorrow, forevermore. Every single time. That's why He gives us this verse. "Behold, I am laying in Zion a stone, a cornerstone chosen and precious, and whoever believes in Him [Jesus] will not be put *to shame*" (1 Peter 2:6 ESV, emphasis added).

COMPLAINING

In the first third of Exodus, the battle between Yahweh and Egypt's pharaohs drives the storyline. The remainder of the book, however, describes the Israelites in the wilderness and at Sinai. Pharaoh is God's chief adversary in the first part of the book. Who is His enemy in the second part of the book? *Israel.* What happened? All they do is complain.

When was the last time you were with someone who whined about everything under the sun? Did you seek them out to have another conversation? Probably not. You likely thought, "I hope I never have to talk to that person again!" We would rather engage people who, when faced with setbacks, center on solutions instead of problems.

Does a positive and upbeat approach to life's obstacles describe you? What do you do when things go south? What do you say when you're hot and bothered? Do you accept it, deal with it, and move on? Or do you run home, lower the curtains, turn on sad songs, and throw a pity party?

There are times when we give in to whimpering and whining. There are even occasions when we find ourselves complaining about the smallest things. "I asked for extra ice in my water!" "My shirts are folded with the crease up!" "How dare you track mud on my clean carpet?!" Job's carping becomes our catchphrase: "I will give free utterance to my complaint; I will speak in the bitterness of my soul" (Job 10:1 ESV).

Though venting can be helpful at times, perpetual protesting damages our spirits and turns others off. If releasing all our raw emotions was cathartic, complaining would free us from the need to complain. Instead, though, it solidifies our stubbornness and hardens our hearts. Complaining is costly, contagious, sometimes catastrophic, and always way too comfortable. Just ask Israel! What did God's people do most of the time in the wilderness? They murmured in their tents (Psalm

106:25). The only thing more shocking is God's response. He doesn't make any threats. Instead, God rains down bread from heaven (Exodus 16:4). This is incredible!

In the wilderness, God carries Israel like a father carries a son (Deuteronomy 1:31). Changing metaphors, in the desert, God courts His people like a bridegroom courts his bride (Hosea 2:14). "Forty years You sustained them in the wilderness, and they lacked nothing. Their clothes did not wear out and their feet did not swell" (Nehemiah 9:21 ESV). Despite these gracious provisions, the nation included at least four kinds of complainers.

First, the martyr. These people interpret every setback as though it's the end of the world. They're frequently known to say, "This is going to kill me!" Just after Israel left Egypt and before crossing the Red Sea, some complained, "It would have been better for us to serve the Egyptians than to die in the wilderness" (Exodus 14:12 ESV). When faced with a challenging situation, martyrs immediately arrive at the worst-case scenario: death.

Second, the whiner. This person's litany is, "It's not fair!" Moses takes the role of "Chief Whiner" when he asks the LORD, "Why have You dealt ill with Your servant? And why have I not found favor in Your sight, that You lay the burden of all this people on me?" (Numbers 11:11 ESV). Even Israel's leader bellyaches that God is unjust. It's not surprising that the Israelites follow suit.

The third kind of complainer is the cynic. The mantra for these folks is "Things will never change!" Some Israelites took up this dirge, "But now we have lost our appetite; we never see anything but this manna!" (Numbers 11:6). God's people became sick and tired of manna waffles, manna hotcakes, manna bagels, and manna soufflé! "Things will never change!"

Fourth, the perfectionist. These folks love to ask, "Is that your best?" They take the role of judge, jury, and prosecuting attorney. Then they condemn us for not measuring up to their expectations. This fits the

Israelites to a T. "But the people thirsted there for water, and the people grumbled against Moses and said, 'Why did you bring us up out of Egypt, to kill us and our children and livestock with thirst?'" (Exodus 17:3 ESV).

This just in—"How to Have a Bad Attitude," inspired by Moses and Israel while in the desert:

- Base your life on current circumstances.
- Adapt "when and then" thinking. "When I get this, buy this, experience this . . . then I'll be happy."
- Wallow in "what if." "What if this happens?" "What if that happens?" Obsess about the worst-case scenario. Get wrapped up in the paralysis of analysis.
- Consistently put your needs before the needs of others. Adopt an "it's all about me" attitude.
- When you don't get your way, throw a fit.

Is there a better way? You bet!

First, stop idealizing the past. "Would that we had died by the hand of the LORD in the land of Egypt, when we sat by the meat pots and ate bread to the full" (Exodus 16:3 ESV). I'm not a psychologist, nor the son of a psychologist, but if you ask me, I'd say the Israelites were suffering from a selective memory. They look back on the past and call it the glory days.

Glorifying the past blinds us to God's current work. "Remember not the former things, nor consider the things of old. Behold, I am doing a new thing" (Isaiah 43:18–19 ESV).

Second, don't stay focused on the current situation. All Israel can focus upon is their arid surroundings, constant sweat, and deadly desert creatures. "You have brought us out into this wilderness" (Exodus 16:3 ESV). If looking back gets us lost in nostalgic angst, then looking around gets us lost in problems. All we see are sand dunes and snakes!

The third way to conquer complaining is to concentrate on where we're going. Early on, in Exodus 3:8, God tells Moses, "I have come down to deliver them out of the hand of the Egyptians and to bring them up out of that land to a good and broad land, a land flowing with milk and honey" (ESV). Yahweh tells His people in every age, "Come and go with Me to that land!" It's a land with no crying, or sickness, or disease, or death. We're traveling to our heavenly land—the new Jerusalem." We won't be a second into our new land when we will turn and ask each other, "Pain, disease, warfare, pandemics, terrorism—what were they?" God says, "Behold, I create new heavens and a new earth, and the former things shall not be remembered or come into mind" (Isaiah 65:17).

GOD TESTS ISRAEL

Moses describes a place called Marah with these words: "There the LORD made for them a statute and a rule, and there He *tested* them" (Exodus 15:25 ESV). God gives Israel another test in the wilderness of Sin: "Behold, I am about to rain bread from heaven for you, and the people shall go out and gather a day's portion every day, that I may *test* them, whether they will walk in My law or not" (Exodus 16:4 ESV, emphasis added).

For the most part, the Israelites fail their tests in chapters 15–17 not only by grumbling and testing the Lord (Exodus 17:2, 7) but also through disobedience to God's specific manna and Sabbath instructions (Exodus 16:20, 27). This gives us a glimpse into the possibility that Israel—like Pharaoh—may exhaust God's patience: "*How long will you refuse to keep My commandments and My laws?*" (Exodus 16:28 ESV, emphasis added). Compare this with what God asks Pharaoh, "*How long will you* refuse to humble yourself before Me?" (Exodus 10:3 ESV, emphasis added). Could it be that the Israelites are becoming like the dreaded Pharaoh Thutmose III? Indeed! The king's heart became hard. So, finally, did Israel's. "Today, if you hear His voice, do not harden your hearts, as at Meribah, as on the day at Massah in the wilderness" (Psalm 95:7–8 ESV).

What about us? How do we respond to God's tests? When we face disappointments and losses, do we conclude that God isn't faithful? When we're in a desert place feeling loveless, do we begin acting like orphans with no Father in heaven? Here's the bottom line—trials and tribulations are foundational to God's plan for our lives.

There. I wrote it. Do you believe it?

Paul and Barnabas put it this way: "Through many tribulations we *must* enter the kingdom of God" (Acts 14:22). The word *must* jumps out. It seizes us by the throat. *Must* means there are no second options, no detours, no other ways around. We must go through hell and high water to enter God's kingdom. Jesus isn't a vacation planner. Jesus is the Sovereign Lord of the Universe whose one, passionate goal is to justify us (declare us not guilty) and to sanctify us (make us like Him).

MIRACULOUS MANNA

While the seventh plague brought divine hail raining down upon the Egyptians and their animals (Exodus 9:13–21), now God rains down bread from heaven for His people Israel (Exodus 16:4). The manna miracle is actually *ten* miracles wrapped up in one:

- Manna fell.
- Manna fell only for Israel.
- Manna followed the Israelites throughout their wilderness journeys.
- Ungathered manna melted but the gathered manna didn't.
- Regardless of how much manna was gathered, everyone had the same amount.
- Fridays were divinely ordained double-manna days.
- Friday's supply of manna was still good on Saturday.
- Uncooked manna tasted like wafers with honey.
- Cooked manna tasted like rich cream.
- Manna stored in a jar, kept for perpetuity, didn't spoil.

Forty years later, reflecting on these multiple miracles, Moses writes, "He humbled you and let you hunger and fed you with manna, which you did not know, nor did your fathers know, that He might make you know that man does not live by bread alone, but man lives by every word that comes from the mouth of the LORD" (Deuteronomy 8:3 ESV).

Did the Israelites appreciate their marvelous manna? "The people of Israel also wept again and said, 'Oh that we had meat to eat! We remember the fish we ate in Egypt that cost nothing, the cucumbers, the melons, the leeks, the onions, and the garlic. But now our strength is dried up, and there is nothing at all but this manna to look at'" (Numbers 11:4–6 ESV).

Oh no! Another company of complainers!

THE MESSIAH'S MANNA

Once, when Jesus was debating with some Jews over God's gift of manna, He boldly asserted, "I am the bread of life" (John 6:35). "Life" is one of John's main thrusts. Life now. Life tomorrow. Life forever. In John's Gospel, the verb *live* or the noun *life* appear fifty-three times. To give you some perspective, *live* and *life* appear thirty-four times in all of Matthew, Mark, and Luke combined. Life is the goal of John's Gospel. "These are written so that you may believe that Jesus is the Christ, the Son of God, and that by believing you may have *life* in His name" (John 20:31 ESV, emphasis added).

Before His bread of life discourse in John 6, Jesus miraculously takes five loaves of bread and two fish and feeds five thousand. The next day, people find Jesus. They think He's the Messiah because Jewish rabbis of the day taught the Messiah would duplicate Moses' manna miracle. A text from this time called the *Midrash Rabbah* states, "What did the first redeemer do? He brought down the manna. The last redeemer will also bring down manna."

That's true! Jesus is the last and the greatest Redeemer and so He gives manna. But Jesus adds something new. "Your fathers ate the manna in the wilderness, and they died. This is the bread that comes down from heaven, so that one may eat of it and not die" (John 6:49–50). Here is that theme again—life.

Unlike Moses' manna, when we eat Christ's bread, we never die. Of course, we physically die. Jesus isn't talking about physical death. Jesus is talking about spiritual death. Spiritual death is life separated from God's love, God's forgiveness, God's mercy. That will never happen— not for the baptized!

Jesus says, "I am the bread of life" (John 6:48). Not "I was." Not "I will be." Not tomorrow, not next week, not next month. Jesus gives Himself to you as living bread. Jesus gives life to the broke, the broken, and the burned-out. Jesus gives life to the overemployed, the underemployed, and the unemployed. Jesus gives life to the emotionally starved and the emotionally dead. *Jesus gives life to you.*

One November, I taught in Russia. Part of the trip included an eight-hour train ride from Moscow to Saint Petersburg. Since I was running low on Russian rubles before the trip, I stocked up on cheese and crackers. They would be my lunch and dinner. I hate to shock you, but Russian cheese and crackers don't taste all that good.

After a few hours, I gathered my remaining rubles and went to a dining car, desperate for a real meal. Imagine my surprise when I discovered that everything in the dining car was included in the cost of the ticket. Everything had been paid for by my Russian church partners!

Everything has also been paid for by Jesus, for you. Jesus gives you the bread of life freely, willingly, completely—at no cost!

DAILY BREAD

Which emoji do you use most often? Can you guess mine? Let me give you some clues. Near equivalents include anxiety, apprehension. The German word *würgen* gets closest to its meaning of "to strangle, choke, and take by the throat." And from *würgen* we get what English word? Worry.

Worry is the emoji that I most frequently use. Worry strangles, chokes, and clutches me by the throat! I'm sure you can relate. That's why Jesus gives us the Fourth Petition of the Lord's Prayer. "Give us this day our daily bread" (Matthew 6:11 ESV). The request has its beginnings in Exodus 16 where God teaches His people about living one day at a time—trusting in His generous provision instead of being strangled by worry.

After all, God is a great Giver.

In the first chapter of the Bible, Genesis 1, God gives us the earth, the sea, and the sky; plants and animals, birds and fish; the moon, the stars, and the sun. Then, in Genesis 1:31, God calls it all "very good" (ESV). The Bible begins with a grand celebration of Yahweh, who gives good and perfect gifts. That's why we confidently pray, "Give us."

In Matthew 7:11, Jesus tells us how much our heavenly Father delights in giving. "If you, then, who are evil, know how to give good gifts to your children, how much more will your Father in heaven give good gifts to those who *ask* Him?" (ESV, emphasis added). *Ask* in Matthew's Greek is a present tense verb. It means to keep on asking. Never stop asking!

We hear a voice, though, that taunts us, haunts us, and messes with our mind. "Why ask? God's stingy. God's a miser. God's a cheapskate. God won't give you a dime." When we believe this voice, worry slips through our back door. It crushes our confidence, sabotages our sanity, strangles our spirits, throttles our thinking, and torpedoes our trust. Worry is worthless! It's better to pray, "Give us." Paul says, "He who did not spare His own Son but gave Him up for us all, how will He not also with Him graciously *give* us all things?" (Romans 8:32 ESV, emphasis added). God graciously gives all things! With confidence we pray, "Give us."

The Fourth Petition continues with these words: "this day" (Matthew 6:11 ESV). After the Israelites left Egypt, for forty years God gave them manna every day—except on the Sabbath Day (Exodus 16:23). For forty years, six days a week, the Israelites would get up in the morning and gather their manna—bread for the day.

But some Israelites didn't want manna for just a day. They wanted manna for a week, manna for a month, manna for many moons. They collected mounds and mountains of manna! "They did not listen to Moses. Some left part of it till the morning, and it bred worms and stank" (Exodus 16:20 ESV). The temptation was to stockpile. It still is today. That's because we think stockpiles bring security. So we hoard. We accumulate. We amass goods and money and stuff—just in case there's a rainy day.

Of course, saving is a good idea. Saving is a grand idea. There's a huge difference, though, between saving and stockpiling. If we're not careful, it's easy to believe that stockpiles will carry us through every rainy day. We tell ourselves that if we just have enough things, we won't have to worry about any high water—ever.

Yet completely depending on stuff only causes us more worry. Because, as it turns out, possessions can be destroyed. Economies can collapse. Investments can go belly up. And manna can become maggots. When our survival hinges on a pile of stuff that can vanish in the twinkling of an eye, we spend our entire lives filled with worry. "Why, just think! We could lose it all!"

Instead, pray these words: "Give us this day." Live for today. Place tomorrow in God's hands.

Jesus continues in the Lord's Prayer with the expression "our daily" (Matthew 6:11 ESV). For almost 1,900, years Bible scholars didn't understand the Greek word *epiousious*—often translated as the English word *daily*. In the late 1940s, however, archaeologists unearthed an ancient Greek text that contained the word *epiousious*. They discovered that it was a word for food that would only be good for a day. *Epiousious* means "for the current day." We don't pray, "Lord, give us this day enough for the next fifty days." No. We pray, "Give us this day enough for the current day." *Epiousious!*

Then there's Costco. Costco isn't the size of a grocery store. Costco is the size of Rhode Island! Employees don't push carts. They drive forklifts. You pick up a basket the size of a small Volkswagen—not for individual items. No sirree! You buy stuff in cases and cartons; bundles, bags, bushels, and huge boxes. Then you haul it all home and think, "Where in the world am I going to put all this stuff?" Do we really need to buy toilet paper 148 rolls at a time? No. "Give us this day our *epiousious*"—enough for the current day.

"Bread" (Matthew 6:11 ESV). That's the last word in the Fourth Petition. *Bread* means necessities, not luxuries. *Bread* means needs, not greeds. *Bread* means what's required, not always what's desired. Martin Luther tells us in his Small Catechism: "Daily bread includes everything that has to do with the support and needs of the body, such as food, drink, clothing, shoes, house, home, land, animals, money, goods, a devout husband or wife, devout children, devout workers, devout and faithful rulers, good government, good weather, peace, health, self-control, good reputation, good friends, faithful neighbors, and the like" (Small Catechism, Fourth Petition).

How can we be so sure God gives bread every day? "God so loved the world, that He gave" (John 3:16 ESV). The extravagant God of Genesis 1 gives us His most extravagant gift in Jesus. And He gives all of Jesus. Every single part of Jesus. His compassion. His kindness. His strength. His humility. His body. His blood. His dying love.

Why let worry strangle, choke, and take you by the throat? Worry can't change the past. Worry can't change the future. Worry can only destroy today. What's the antidote to worry—every time? Seven marvelous words prayed to our loving heavenly Father: "Give us this day our daily bread."

CHAPTER 10

Rephidim to Sinai: Exodus 17–19

He split rocks in the wilderness and gave them drink abundantly as from the deep. He made streams come out of the rock and caused waters to flow down like rivers. (Psalm 78:15–16 ESV)

Have you ever noticed what happens when you don't get enough water? You confuse thirst for hunger. Then what happens? You eat when you don't need to eat. What's that mean? Weight gain. When throttled by thirst, we also become tired, dizzy, and anxious—then our joints and muscles start to ache. What's *that* mean? A bad life.

For 430 years the Israelites—living in Egypt near the Nile River—never experienced a water shortage. Even when God's people left Egypt, they had no problems with water. Need it to form into walls? No problem. Need it to come crashing down on Pharaoh's horses and chariots? Easy as pie. All this changes, though, in Exodus 17:1–6. It's appropriate to consider these six verses using six questions: who, what, where, why, how, and when.

WHO?

I like to call Moses "The Wonderful Wizard of Water Works." You probably recall from my discussion on Exodus 2:10 that the name *Moses* means "draw out of water." As a child, his mother places him into water for safety, and Pharaoh's daughter's servant draws him out of water for salvation. Zipporah—who would soon be his wife—describes

Moses in Exodus 2:17 with the words, loosely translated, "When it comes to drawing water from a well, Moses is a lean, mean, green aqua machine!" At the Red Sea, Moses parts the water, while Exodus 15:25 reports that—when confronted with bitter water—Moses throws a piece of wood into the putrid pool and, presto, instant purified water. That's the who—mighty Moses!

WHAT?

"There was no water for the people to drink" (Exodus 17:1 ESV). The Israelites have been in the desert for a month. They've seen nothing but rocks, sand, and dirt. *Rocks, sand, and dirt.* They longed for water. So do children—almost instantly when their heads hit the pillow at night.

I realized this while raising three small children. These kids could, even on a hot summer day, play all morning, play all afternoon, and even play into the evening without ever needing a drink. "Are you thirsty yet?" "No way Dad!" Miles and miles they'd go, when offered water, they'd say, "No!"

That is, until their little angelic heads hit the pillow. Then it all began. I can still hear my firstborn: "Daddy I need a drink." How cute. Little Abi Joy Lessing wants a drink. It was so entertaining—that is, until eight o'clock became nine and nine turned to ten.

One night I blurted out, "Abi! The next time you ask for a drink, I'll spank you!" "There," I thought, "that should bring quiet to the Western Front." A few minutes later, the golden silence was broken. I heard a voice crying in the wilderness, "Daddy, when you come to spank me, please bring me a drink!"

That's a cute story about physical thirst. There are other kinds of thirst and their stories are never cute. "My loneliness hurts so bad, sometimes I feel like I'm eating glass." "God, if You're so good, why do I hurt so bad?" "When it comes to love, I've struck out too many times to count!"

In Exodus 17, when the Israelites become thirsty, they turn into a murderous mob of dehydrated and demanding people. "Moses cried to the LORD, 'What should I do with these people? They are almost ready to stone me'" (Exodus 17:4 ESV). God's people are resorting to rocks.

So do we.

Do you remember the scene in *Forrest Gump* when Jenny begins throwing rocks at her childhood home? When she runs out of rocks and falls on the ground? What does Forrest Gump say? "Sometimes, I guess there just aren't enough rocks."

Forest Gump was wrong. There are always enough rocks. We thirst for love so much that, when we don't get it, we begin throwing rocks. Verbal missiles. Nuclear words. Silent stares. Angry texts.

WHERE?

Where did the event in Exodus 17:1–6 take place? "They camped at Rephidim" (Exodus 17:1 ESV). Where is Rephidim? Scholars don't know. Archaeologists don't know. No one knows where Rephidim is. All the experts can say is that Rephidim is close to Mount Sinai.

But you know the exact location of Rephidim. So do I. Rephidim is that place where we are burned out with fear too deep to manage, pain too heavy to bear, and doubts too many to number. Rephidim is that place where relationships are dehydrated, dry, and almost dead. Rephidim is where wives are ready to throw in the towel because husbands are working seventy-five hours a week. Others have spotted Rephidim on the job—where it's always the same ol', same ol'. *Boring!* And Rephidim is in every church. It's the place where—try as we might—everything stays dry and dead as dust.

We sing this song at Rephidim. "As a deer pants for flowing streams, so pants my soul for You, O God. My soul thirsts for God, for the living God" (Psalm 42:1–2 ESV). At Rephidim, we echo David's anguish, "O God, You are my God; earnestly I seek You; my soul thirsts for You; my flesh faints for You, as in a dry and weary land where there is no water" (Psalm 63:1 ESV).

WHY?

We now turn to *why*? Why do we become so thirsty? The answer comes in four words: "It might have been." That's what the Israelites are saying to Moses in Exodus 17:3. "You brought us up out of Egypt" (ESV). Translation: "It might have been so much better had we stayed in Egypt."

It might have been.

These words were made famous in 1856 when John Greenleaf Whittier wrote a poem titled *Maud Muller*. One day Maud—a young woman—meets a man her age. After a brief encounter, each of them ponders what it would be like to marry the other. The moment passes and both Maud and the man end up in sad marriages. Both anguish for the rest of their lives over what was lost on that day so long ago. Near the end of the poem, Whittier writes, "Of all sad words of tongue or pen, the saddest are these: 'It might have been!'"

Regret. God-awful, soul-destroying regret.

HOW?

How can we get water? I guess we could get a staff, but it can't be any ordinary, run-of-the-mill kind of staff. It must be *the* staff. Moses' staff. The staff that goes back and forth from a stick to a snake. The staff that struck the Nile River and turned its water into blood. The staff that stretched over the Red Sea to divide its waters so Israel could walk through on dry land.

Hold on! Why does Moses still have his staff in Exodus 17? Because the same divine power that saved Israel from Egypt is still with Israel in the desert. Yahweh is Lord of the Nile. Yahweh is Lord of the Sinai wilderness. *Yahweh is Lord of heaven and earth.*

Yahweh commands Moses, "Take in your hand the staff and strike the rock and water will come out of it for the people to drink" (Exodus 17:5–6). Moses did. Water flowed. And the Israelites lived. Asaph even includes the miracle in one of his psalms: "He split rocks in the wilderness and gave them drink abundantly as from the deep. He made streams come out of the rock and caused waters to flow down like rivers" (Psalm 78:15–16 ESV).

This rock will be with Israel for a long time. Forty years later, once again, God will provide water from it (Numbers 20:1–13; see Deuteronomy 8:15). This was no ordinary rock! Paul, for his part, asserts that the rock was Christ (1 Corinthians 10:4).

On Good Friday, another staff appears. "They put a staff in His right hand and knelt in front of Him and mocked Him. 'Hail, King of the Jews!' they said. They spit on Him and took the staff and struck Him on the head again and again" (Matthew 27:29). For Jesus, any ordinary run-of-the-mill staff will do. Any stick that remotely looks like a king's scepter is just fine. Any piece of wood that won't break if it's slapped repeatedly on someone's head is a perfect fit for Jesus.

And make sure that the piece of wood is carved to make a sharp, pointed end. *The* Rock must be split and opened. "One of the soldiers pierced [Jesus'] side with a spear, and at once there came out blood and water" (John 19:34 ESV). *Water!* Water flowing from the One whose lips are cracked and swollen. Water flowing from the One whose body burns under the hot Palestinian sun. Gushing water from the parched mouth of the One who cries out, "I thirst" (John 19:28 ESV).

"Strike the rock, and water will come out of it, and the people will drink" (Exodus 17:6 ESV). And they did. And it flowed. And we live.

Isaiah describes God's soul-quenching mercy with these words: "The burning sand shall become a pool, and the thirsty ground springs of water" (Isaiah 35:7 ESV). Ezekiel sees it as a body of water teeming with life: "Wherever the river flows . . . everything will live" (Ezekiel 47:9 ESV). Joel writes, "A fountain shall come forth from the house of the LORD" (Joel 3:18 ESV).

WHEN?

Let's review. *Who*? Moses. *What*? There's no water. *Where*? Rephidim. *Why*? Deep regret. *How*? Through Christ, the Rock of Ages. What are we missing? *When*. We're missing when. When does this water flow? When does it come to me? When does it quench my longing, aching heart? It's because Jesus loves you so very, very, very much that His life-giving, soul-renewing water flows from the cross for you. When? *Right now.*

And if we don't take a drink? Then we fall under the judgment described in Psalm 95:7–11—the psalmist's reflection on Exodus 17:1–6. "Today, if you hear His voice, do not *harden* your hearts, as at Meribah, as on the day at Massah in the wilderness, when your fathers put Me to the test and put Me to the proof, though they had seen My work. For forty years I loathed that generation and said, 'They are a people who go astray in their heart, and they have not known My ways.' Therefore I swore in My wrath, 'They shall not enter My rest'" (ESV, emphasis added).

Psalm 95:8 employs the term *harden*—the same word Moses uses in Exodus 7:3 and 13:15 to describe Pharaoh's heart. Agonizing thirst can turn anyone into a hard-hearted pharaoh, even a believer. Yikes!

THE AMALEKITES ARE COMING!

Moses moves us abruptly from thirst and hard hearts to an Amalekite attack. Recalling the battle forty years later, Moses writes, "He [the Amalekites] attacked you on the way when you were faint and weary, and cut off your tail, those who were lagging behind you" (Deuteronomy 25:18 ESV). How treacherous! The Amalekites strike Israel's rear where the weakest and most vulnerable were located—Israel's very young and very old.

It probably won't surprise you that Amalekites first appear in *Genesis* 14:7. There's the Exodus backstory book—again! A certain Amalek is one of Esau's grandsons (Genesis 36:12, 16). It's telling that, among Esau's descendants, Amalek is the only one born from a concubine—implying a lowly status. The Amalekites, however, go from the bottom of the barrel to king of the hill. Balaam describes them as "the first among the nations" (Numbers 24:20).

There are times when God is a one-man-wrecking crew, annihilating Israel's enemies in the twinkling of an eye. For example, in the late eighth century BC, God's Messenger single-handedly strikes down 185,000 Assyrians (Isaiah 37:36). In the second half of Exodus 17, however, God employs a combination of forces—Moses' intercession, Aaron and Hur's assistance, and Joshua's skill on the battlefield.

We meet Joshua for the first time in Exodus 17:9. He will be mentioned over two hundred more times in the Bible. Also, for the first time, we hear about Moses' writing: "Then the LORD said to Moses, 'Write this as a memorial in a book'" (Exodus 17:14 ESV). What book? We call this book the Pentateuch—Genesis, Exodus, Leviticus, Numbers, and Deuteronomy.

Israel's battle against Amalek is described as between Yahweh and Amalek (Exodus 17:16)—not Israel and Amalek. Why? "The battle belongs to Yahweh" (1 Samuel 17:47). Moses' hands are how God's power is unleashed. But Moses needs help—help to keep his hands up.

What kind of leader is *this*?

In Egypt, it's mortifying not to know the answer. It's embarrassing not to make the team or get the grade. In a system where it all depends on you, weakness is something to overcome. In Egypt, all you have is you. Therefore, you'd better get moving, get a plan, and get going.

That's Egypt. But we left Egypt. We've been baptized! There's now something to be feared much more than weakness: strength. Our strength. It gets us into trouble every time. Why? Taking the bull by the horns assumes that we don't need divine power, that we don't need an answer to prayer, that we don't need God's Word.

In God's kingdom, weakness is a virtue and strength is a vice. We all need help—God's help. We're unqualified and unprepared for the unplanned and the unexpected!

What's the only sane thing to do? Admit your weakness. Confess your confusion. Come clean and say, "I'm POH—Plain Ol' Human." Listen to Paul. "I will boast all the more gladly of my *weaknesses*, so that the power of Christ may rest upon me" (2 Corinthians 12:9 ESV, emphasis added).

That's what Moses believes. When the Israelites face the Amalekites, Moses prays—confessing Israel's desperate need for God. He prays "until the going down of the sun" (Exodus 17:12 ESV).

"LORD, TEACH US TO PRAY"

In Luke 11:1, the disciples plead with Jesus, "Lord, teach us to pray" (ESV). This is the only time Christ's followers ask Jesus to teach them anything. They could've asked for instructions on how to multiply bread, still a storm, write a sermon, or walk on water. They didn't. All they ever asked was, "Lord, teach us to pray." Prayer is our most difficult task. Prayer is our most important task.

Jesus once promised, "Ask, and it will be given to you" (Luke 11:9 ESV). At another time, the Savior said, "Whatever you ask in prayer, you will receive, if you have faith" (Matthew 21:22 ESV). Jesus never attached this kind of power to other endeavors. "Plan and it will be given to you." "You will get anything you work for." These words aren't in the Bible. These words, however, are in the Bible:

- "Pray without ceasing" (1 Thessalonians 5:17 ESV).

- "Be constant in prayer" (Romans 12:12 ESV).

- "Call upon Me in the day of trouble" (Psalm 50:15 ESV).

Wives, what if your husband calls you and blurts out: "Pick up the kids at school, get the oil changed in the car, and get some money from the ATM—fast!" That's not the best way to nurture a relationship! Yet that's what happens when I pray. Too frequently, I call out to God saying: "I need new tires on the car, some extra energy, wisdom at work, and a lot of money from the ATM—fast!" I pray as though I'm ordering a burger and fries. "I'll have one solved problem and two blessings. Hold the hassles, please."

Sometimes our prayers zig, then zag, then zig again. Distractions swarm like bugs on a summer night in northern Minnesota. When we pray, we think of a thousand things we need to do, even as we forget the one thing we set out to do—*pray.* If you're like me, you have an acute case of PDD—Prayer Deficit Disorder.

What do you need to pray for? To stay sober? Solvent? Sensitive to your spouse? Is the lump cancerous? Is your boss angry? Is your stomach a raging sea of stress and sorrow? Most of us have a painful history with prayer. Why keep emailing our deepest longings into a silent abyss? "God jilted me once. I won't let Him ever do it again!"

Wouldn't you like to pray better? Deeper? Stronger? With more fire, faith, and fervency? Wouldn't you like to pray like Moses and watch the Amalekites head for the hills?

While the Israelite/Amalekite battle rages on, Moses doesn't pray out of obligation or duty. Moses pours out his soul. He's like Jacob wrestling with God. "I'm not going to let go until You bless me" (Genesis 32:26).

What does Moses do after successfully praying for Joshua and his soldiers to defeat the Amalekites? Does he order a monument built of himself or hire a PR team to get the word out? Not quite. "Moses built an altar and called the name of it, The LORD Is My Banner" (Exodus 17:15 ESV). When we pray, God comes through; He gets all the credit.

ENGAGING THE ENEMY

Israel's encounter with the Amalekites is part of a cosmic war. Behind every Amalekite, every Canaanite, every Jebusite, Moabite, and Edomite; behind every plight, blight, and sleepless night stands *the* enemy. We know him. He's the ancient serpent, the devil. Satan.

The Hague Convention of 1907, the Geneva Protocol of 1925, and the Geneva Convention of 1929 all produced agreements so nations would fight wars in a more humane way. Nerve gas, biological germs, and bullets that expand on impact were prohibited because they produce more suffering than the conferees believed necessary.

Our spiritual enemy knows no rules, no regulations, and no restraints. His weapons inflict maximum pain. Nothing is too cunning or too cruel. And the devil has allies—fallen angels called demons. The Bible speaks about them more than one hundred times. It calls them evil and unclean spirits, rulers, authorities, powers, dominions, thrones, and leaders. This may sound like science fiction to you—but it's all very real.

The Greek word for "devil" is *diabolos. Diabolos* comes from the Greek verb *diaballein,* which means "to split." The devil is a splitter, a divider, a wedge driver. The *diabolos* divided Adam from Eve, Jacob from Esau, Absalom from David. And the *diabolos* divided Judas from Jesus. The *diabolos* divides spouses, families, friends, and churches. Unbelievers? The *diabolos* takes to hell. Believers? The *diabolos* makes life hell.

Do these thoughts sound outdated? Do you place books about the devil in a basement closet labeled "superstition" or "antiquated religion"? If so, you're not alone. According to research by The Barna Group, four out of ten Christians (40 percent) don't think Satan is real.[3] That makes it easier to stroll along, hum a happy tune, and think that the Christian life is pretty much what? A Sunday afternoon picnic.

THROW IT BACK!

Years ago, on a humid night in Arlington, Texas, a young baseball fan learned a painful lesson of what happens when you listen to the wrong voice. It was the first inning of a game between the Texas Rangers and the Toronto Blue Jays. The flame-throwing Nolan Ryan was on the mound for the Rangers while another sure bet for the Hall of Fame,

---

3 The Barna Group, *Most American Christians Do Not Believe that Satan or the Holy Spirit Exist*, April 2009, https://www.barna.com/research/most-american-christians-do-not-believe-that-satan-or-the-holy-spirit-exist/.

Dave Winfield, was at bat for the Blue Jays. It was a classic match-up: an overpowering fastball pitcher with more than five thousand career strikeouts opposing one of baseball's premier hitters. Hitting conquered pitching on this occasion. Dave Winfield launched a Nolan Ryan fastball into the left-field bleachers, right into the hands of an eight-year-old boy. Imagine that! Catching a home run ball that involved two future Cooperstown Hall of Famers!

The ball would have been worth thousands of dollars. *Would have*, that is, if the boy had held on to it. The crowd of Ranger fans around the hapless lad began chanting, "Throw it back!" After some hesitation, the confused little guy did the unthinkable. He threw the ball back onto the field!

Our enemy utters the same words. "Throw it back!" What's he referring to? These words of the apostle Paul: "Take . . . the sword of the Spirit, which is the word of God" (Ephesians 6:17 ESV). When we fail to read, mark, learn, and inwardly digest God's Holy Word, Satan attacks us with his accusations, lies, and half-truths. "Throw it back!" That's Satan's supreme strategy.

Historians exploring Civil War battlefields have found musket after musket with barrels full of gunpowder. The soldiers who carried these weapons became so rattled by the battle's roar, smoke, danger, and confusion that they kept reloading their guns but forgot to fire them. What good is it to have a weapon and never use it?

"The LORD will have war with Amalek from generation to generation" (Exodus 17:16 ESV). We'll be engaged in spiritual warfare until we die, or Christ returns. Our weapon? God's Word. Never throw it down, throw it out, or throw it back!

FROM AMALEKITES TO MIDIANITES

As we come to Exodus 18, the chapter seems like a huge disconnect. How does war against the Amalekites connect with instruction from a priest from among the Midianites?

I'm glad you asked! There are several literary links:

- Amalekites came and attacked (Exodus 17:8) while Jethro—the Midianite priest—comes and greets (Exodus 18:5–7).

- Exodus 17:9 and 18:25 describe men who are chosen for a specific task.

- Moses both sits on a stone (Exodus 17:12) and sits to adjudicate legal matters (Exodus 18:13).

- Both events use the phrase "the next day" (Exodus 17:9; 18:13).

- The main activity in each chapter lasts all day (Exodus 17:12; 18:13–14).

- Moses is worn out and given help (Exodus 17:12; 18:18).

- Amalekites and Midianites are related and often associated with one another (cf. Judges 6:3, 33; 7:12).

What are we to make of these correspondences?

Moses wants us to recall a specific backstory in Genesis 12:3 where God promises Abram, "I will bless those who bless you, and him who dishonors you I will curse, and in you all the families of the earth shall be blessed" (ESV). Because Jethro blesses Israel, he's blessed. Because Amalekites dishonor Israel, they're cursed. According to Galatians 3:29, we're Abraham's seed and heirs to God's promise of spiritual protection all our days. The end result? It's better to be a trusting Midianite instead of an attacking Amalekite!

Not only does God watch over His people but also His plan is to bless the world through them. Jethro, a Midianite priest (Exodus 3:1), comes to faith in Yahweh through Moses' testimony (Exodus 18:8–12). What Moses started, Israel will continue. And what Israel continues, the Church will take up—testifying to God's delivering power and mercy for all people.

JETHRO'S CONFESSION

While more than one hundred of the occurrences of *pharaoh* in Exodus are in chapters 1–15 alone, the book's last three references to Egyptian kings comes in the Moses-Jethro discourse of chapter 18

(Exodus 18:4, 8, 10). Notably, Jethro's exclamation, "Now I know that Yahweh is greater than all gods" (Exodus 18:11), balances a pharaoh's previous rebuff, "Who is Yahweh, that I should listen to His voice by letting Israel go? I do not know Yahweh, and I will not let Israel go" (Exodus 5:2). A Midianite priest exemplifies the way non-Israelite people should respond to Yahweh—with faith. Jethro, as the convert par excellence, is mentioned thirteen times in Exodus 18.

A Midianite becomes an Israelite. This is just the beginning. A Canaanite named Rahab and a Moabite named Ruth also become part of the chosen people. Brace yourself. There's more. By God's grace, you and I have also become Israelites. What? Paul maintains that believers are children of Abraham (Romans 4:11, 16) and that the Church is the "Israel of God" (Galatians 6:16 ESV). We're in!

Jethro's confession concludes the battle between the hand of Yahweh and the hand of Pharaoh. At the burning bush, Yahweh announced, "I have come down to deliver them from the *hand* of the Egyptians" (Exodus 3:8 ESV, emphasis added). Eleven times, the plague narratives mention Yahweh's mighty hand (Exodus 3:19; 6:1; 13:3, 9, 14, 16) or that Yahweh stretched out His hand (Exodus 3:20; 7:4, 5; 9:3, 15). At the Red Sea, "the Israelites saw the mighty hand of Yahweh displayed against the Egyptians" (Exodus 14:31 ESV). Moses praises the triumph of Yahweh's right hand (Exodus 15:6, 12) over the pharaoh who boasted, "My hand shall destroy them" (Exodus 15:9 ESV).

In the text following Moses' recording in Exodus 18:9 regarding Jethro's joy that Yahweh "had delivered them from the *hand* of Egypt," Jethro declares, "Blessed be Yahweh who has delivered you from the *hand* of the Egyptians and from the *hand* of Pharaoh" (Exodus 18:10). Jethro's threefold repetition of "hand" summarizes and concludes this important theme in Exodus 1–18.

AT LAST, MOUNT SINAI

My home state of Colorado has some awesome mountains. The Maroon Bells. Pikes Peak. Longs Peak. The Collegiate Peaks—including

Mount Harvard, Mount Yale, and Mount Princeton. And my favorite—
the Mount of the Holy Cross.

There are also magnificent mountains in the Bible. Take, for instance,
Mount Ararat, where Noah's ark landed. Then there are descriptions of
Christ's Sermon on the Mount, His Mount of Transfiguration, as well as
the Mount of Olives where Jesus ascended into heaven. Certainly, one
of the Bible's most famous mountains—hands down—is Mount Sinai.

Israel's stage-by-stage journey to Sinai begins in Exodus 12:37 and
continues with Moses naming locations in Exodus 13:20; 14:15; 15:22;
16:1; and 17:1. He describes the trek's climactic statement in Exodus
19:1–2, reporting that three months after the exodus, the Israelites
arrived at their destination. After Exodus 19:2, no reference to traveling
appears until the book's closing scene (Exodus 40:36, 38).

Some locate Mount Sinai in northwest Arabia—partly on the
grounds that they believe a volcano is required to explain the events in
Exodus 19:16–25. But the smoke, fire, and clouds are better understood
as components connected to God's miraculous presence. Adherents to
northwest Arabia also point out that, by marriage, Moses was related to
the Midianites (Exodus 3:1; 18:1) whose homeland was in the region
of Arabia. However, more specifically, Moses was related to Kenites, a
nomadic Midianite clan whose presence in the Sinai region is well doc-
umented (cf. Judges 1:16; 4:11).

The truth that Mount Sinai is not in northwest Arabia but in the Sinai Peninsula is substantiated by the additional fact that the locale was
an eleven-day journey from Kadesh-barnea (Deuteronomy 1:2). This
is an exact fit with Jebel Musa (Arabic for "Mountain of Moses"), or
Mount Horeb in the southern Sinai Peninsula—the Christian tradition-
al place for Sinai, dating to the fourth century AD.

The rest of the Book of Exodus describes events at Mount Sinai—as
does the Book of Leviticus. Numbers 1:1–10:11 also takes place on this
sacred mountain. All told, the Israelites camp out at the base of Sinai for
ten days short of an entire year—that's fifty-nine chapters in the Penta-

teuch. It's time to park the car, get out, stretch our legs, and sit a spell at Sinai.

GOD'S TWOFOLD PLAN

Through Moses, Yahweh repeatedly demands that Pharaoh Thutmose III do two things. First, let Israel go. Second, allow them to worship Yahweh (Exodus 4:23; 7:16; 8:1, 20; 9:1, 13; 10:3). When the Israelites arrive at Sinai, Yahweh declares that both demands have been met. "You yourselves have seen what I did to the Egyptians, and how I . . . brought you to Myself" (Exodus 19:4). What Yahweh did to Egypt through the plagues freed Israel—that's the first part of the book. Yahweh now brings the Israelites to Himself at Sinai so they may worship Him. That's the second section of Exodus. As we will see in chapters 19–40, the enemies impeding God's plan will no longer be the Egyptians and the Amalekites, but the Israelites and their leaders—especially Aaron.

THE COVENANT AT SINAI

Here's an important point. The covenant God establishes with Israel on Mount Sinai isn't completely new. It continues God's promises to Abraham while also focusing on one specific feature—*mission*. God adds to an earlier revelation. We've seen this before. For instance, Exodus 6:3 doesn't introduce the name *Yahweh* for the first time in the Bible. Instead, the verse indicates God is about to add a new dimension to His name.

So what's being expanded upon at Sinai? *God's saved people are also His missionary people.* The covenant referred to in Exodus 19:5 isn't a matter of status. It's a matter of vocation. The flow of thought in Exodus 19:5–6 runs something like this: God says, "Listen to My voice and do what I command. In doing so, you will show yourselves to be My people. As for My part, I will be Your God and perform My oath sworn to Abraham, Isaac, and Jacob. The nations will see this relationship and, by faith, some will become part of My chosen people."

The Hebrew verb behind the English expression "you shall be" in Exodus 19:5 (ESV) frequently appears in the context of entering into marriage (e.g., Deuteronomy 24:2, 4; Judges 14:20; Ruth 1:13; Hosea 3:3). The exclusive nature of a marriage between a man and a woman indicates that Yahweh expects absolute devotion from His people. This relationship is rooted in divine love—a love likened to that between Husband Yahweh and His wife, Israel, that will attract unbelieving nations (Deuteronomy 4:6–8).

At Sinai, therefore, Israel's status as God's people and their vocation as His missionaries aren't established for the first time. Instead, God repeats and renews His intention to save the world—a plan initially rolled out in Genesis 12:1–3.

Accordingly, Israel doesn't become the people of God at Sinai. Leading up to their encounter with Yahweh at the sacred mountain, God repeatedly calls them "My people" (Exodus 3:7, 10; 5:1; 7:4, 16; 8:1, 20–22; 9:1, 13, 17; 10:3–4 ESV). In the Pentateuch, the expression "My people" reappears once more, in Leviticus 26:12 (ESV). What does this teach us? God reiterates His unconditional covenant love when Israel needed to hear it most—when they're caught in the clutches of Egyptian slavery. There's a phrase for that—unconditional grace.

ALL THE EARTH

God's redemptive activity is not just on behalf of Israel and the nations. It also stands in service to the entire creation. In fact, Moses builds a robust emphasis on creation into the Book of Exodus. We see this in several parallels between Exodus and Genesis 1–9. Both share these motifs:

- A creational setting (Genesis 1:28; Exodus 1:7)
- Anti-creational activity (Genesis 3–6; Exodus 1–2)
- The word *ark*, which for Noah denotes a boat (e.g., Genesis 6:14), while for Moses means a basket (e.g., Exodus 2:3)
- Noah's flood and the ten plagues are ecological disasters
- Death and deliverance appear in and through water (Genesis 6–9; Exodus 14)

- The covenants with Noah and with Israel are confirmed with creational signs (Genesis 9:12–13; Exodus 24:8)

- The tabernacle's construction mirrors the seven days of creation

Consequently, within Yahweh's missional mandate, He announces, "All the earth is Mine" (Exodus 19:5 ESV). God's actions in the Book of Exodus—indeed, in the rest of the Bible—are to restore all the earth. Paul puts it this way: "Creation itself will be set free from its bondage to corruption" (Romans 8:21 ESV). What's that look like? No more water turned to blood, or oceans turned to oil slicks, or forests burned by fire. The day is coming when Jesus will sit on His throne and say, "Behold, I am making all things new" (Revelation 21:5 ESV).

SEGULAH

God calls Israel His "treasured possession," "a kingdom of priests," and "a holy nation" (Exodus 19:5–6 ESV). Our identity—based upon who God says we are—is a priceless gift.

The painful truth, though, is that all of us, to some degree or another, have a distorted view of who we are. Many of us have negative images of ourselves because people have put us down—some even slamming us to the mat. The person who coined the phrase "sticks and stones may break my bones, but names will never hurt me," didn't have the slightest idea of how life works. Negative names hurt—deeply.

Dr. Charles Cooley, who taught at the University of Michigan, is considered the Dean of American Sociology. Cooley said that self-worth is determined by what the most important person in our life thinks about us. For Israel and for us, that person is Yahweh.

Yahweh values His people, calling them a "treasured possession" (Exodus 19:5 ESV). The Hebrew word is *segulah*. Twice the term refers to a king's treasure (Ecclesiastes 2:8; 1 Chronicles 29:3), while six times in the Old Testament, *segulah* is how God refers to Israel (Exodus 19:5; Deuteronomy 7:6; 14:2; 26:18; Psalm 135:4; Malachi 3:17). *Segulah* denotes a one-of-a-kind treasure—a prized, priceless possession.

Growing up, I had two *segulahs*—my baseball card collection and my stamp collection. I had to hide them from that neat freak on the block, also known as my mother. Some days, without warning, she would invade my room, and like a Marine sergeant—possessed with an illness called "organization"—bark out the orders, "Out with the old, in with the new!" I would guard my prized possessions with my life! That's essentially what Yahweh says to Israel. "I will guard you with My life!"

Egyptians sneeringly said to their Hebrew slaves, "You're nothing in our eyes!" The regime was distant, aloof, cold, and calculating. It saw God's people as cogs in their vast and growing political/military machine. The Israelites were nameless numbers and state-owned statistics.

God's response? "Not so!" He sends frogs, flies, and finally freedom! How could Yahweh abandon His *segulah*?

A *segulah* isn't loved because it's valuable; a *segulah* is valuable because it's loved. That's worth writing again. A *segulah* isn't loved because it's valuable; a *segulah* is valuable because it's loved. Because we're loved by Yahweh, we're absolutely invaluable. Incredible!

Several years ago, on the first day of a college class I was teaching, a student walked to the front of the room and softly said to me, "You weren't my first choice."

"I wasn't?" I asked.

"No, a professor teaching the same class went on sabbatical."

"Oh."

"But thanks for teaching."

"Sure. Anytime."

When you were baptized, God made you His first choice. His selection wasn't obligatory, required, compulsory, forced, or compelled. God chose you because God loves you. God looks at you and with great love says, "You're prized and priceless! You're My *segulah*!"

A KINGDOM OF PRIESTS

You're valuable. You're God's *segulah*. You're also capable. You're God's priest. What does that mean?

As "a kingdom of priests" (Exodus 19:6 ESV), the Israelites were to be intermediaries between God and the nations. This calling is hinted at in Exodus 4:22: "Then you shall say to Pharaoh, 'Thus says the LORD, Israel is My *firstborn* son'" (ESV, emphasis added). Israel's status as God's firstborn son implies more children will be in the family—the nations of the world. Israel wasn't an only child, just the firstborn. The nation was God's instrument to bring more people into His family.

We learn more about Israel's priestly calling from Aaron's garments. Aaron—Israel's first high priest—had clothes sewn from the same fabric that adorned the Most Holy Place (Exodus 25:21–9; 26:34). Implying what? God was present, "in, with, and, under" Aaron's high priestly ministry. Moreover, in the Book of Exodus, the term *glory* is only related to Yahweh (Exodus 16:7, 10; 24:16–17; 28:2, 40; 29:43; 33:18, 22; 40:34–35). However, there's one exception. The high priest's garments were made "for glory and for beauty" (Exodus 28:2, 40 ESV). Aaron—and every high priest after him—radiated God's glory.

Not only did Aaron's clothing show God to Israel. His ephod showed Israel to God. The two stones upon the ephod were engraved with the names of Israel's twelve tribes. It functioned as a remembrance before God (Exodus 28:12). In similar fashion, the high priest's breastplate was adorned with twelve stones—each engraved with the name of an Israelite tribe (Exodus 28:15–30). Further cementing the idea that the high priest represented Israel before God is the fact that he bore Israel's judgment (Exodus 28:30) and sin (Exodus 28:38).

As priests, therefore, the Israelites were empowered to reflect God to the nations and bring the nations before God—specifically through witness and prayer. *Israel is Yahweh's missionary to the world.*

A HOLY NATION

Who does God say we are? We're valuable (His *segulah)* and capable (a kingdom of priests). We're also God's holy nation. Moses' use of *nation* for Israel in Exodus 19:6 takes us back to Genesis 12:2 where Yahweh promises Abram that he will become a great nation. The connection is clear—both are missionary texts. Through Israel, Abram's offspring, Yahweh calls the nations to faith. For this to work, Israel needs to become holy.

The Hebrew term for *holy* appears ninety-three times in the Book of Exodus with seventy-eight of them linked to God's presence in the tabernacle. The Israelites, therefore, will derive their holy status as they embrace their liturgical life centered in God's delivery of Gospel gifts in their place of worship—the holy tabernacle.

BACK TO THE FUTURE

To drive home what God says about us, let's switch gears. Let's pretend we're going back in time. Recall the movie *Back to the Future.* Remember Marty McFly, the DeLorean, Doc Emmett Brown, and the flux capacitor? Once in a time machine, we travel back through U.S. history, back to Jesus and the disciples. then back to Moses and Israel, and then all the way back to Adam and Eve. We even go back further, past Genesis 1:1, to see what God was doing before He created the world. And what would that be? "He [God the Father] chose us in Him [Jesus] before the foundation of the world" (Ephesians 1:4 ESV).

What's our identity? We're God's *segulah*, His priests, and a holy nation. When did God make that decision? Before the creation of the world.

How do you like them apples?

WHAT DOES PETER SAY?

Like Moses, Peter also clarifies our identity. Combined with Isaiah 28:16 and Psalm 118:20, 1 Peter 2:4–5 puts it this way: "As you come to Him [Jesus], a *living stone* rejected by men but in the sight of God chosen and precious, you yourselves like *living stones* are being built up" (ESV, emphasis added).

I've never seen a live stone. Have you? "Living stone" sounds oxymoronic—like "jumbo shrimp," "political ethics," or "government efficiency." "Living stone," though, isn't a contradiction. Christ, our stone, was dead. Now He's alive forevermore!

Here's Peter's point. What's true about Christ's identity is true about ours. He is the living stone and we are living stones. Jesus was rejected, now He's chosen, precious, and vindicated. When we're rejected, that's also not the last word. Like Jesus, we're chosen and precious. *And vindication is coming on the Last Day.*

In fact, 1 Peter 2:5–10 conveys seven images that describe our baptismal identity in Christ. Each of the seven originally applied to Israel in the Old Testament. The titles are as follows:

- A spiritual house (1 Peter 2:5; Exodus 19:3)
- A chosen race (1 Peter 2:9; Exodus 19:4)
- A royal priesthood (1 Peter 2:9; Exodus 19:6)
- A holy nation (1 Peter 2:9; Exodus 19:6)
- God's own people (1 Peter 2:9; Exodus 19:5)
- People of God (1 Peter 2:10; Hosea 2:23)
- Received mercy (1 Peter 2:10; Hosea 2:23)

Dietrich Bonhoeffer embraced his baptismal identity in Christ. Bonhoeffer was a Lutheran pastor who was executed on April 9, 1945, by Heinrich Himmler—the head of the German Nazi SS and Gestapo—by order of Adolf Hitler himself. They stripped Bonhoeffer naked, put wire (not rope) around his neck, and hanged him. Days before his death, Dietrich Bonhoeffer composed a short poem titled *Wer Bin Ich*, or "Who Am I." Toward the end of the reflection, Bonhoeffer writes that whoever he is, he belongs to Jesus. *So do we.*

MISSION

Peter—again like Moses in Exodus 19—affirms our identity within the context of mission. At the end of 1 Peter 2:9, the apostle affirms that God has done everything in Christ for believers so that "you may proclaim the excellencies of Him who called you out of darkness into His marvelous light" (ESV). Peter further instructs Christians to live "as sojourners and exiles" (1 Peter 2:11 ESV) and to conduct themselves honorably among unbelievers—who will, in turn, "see your good deeds and glorify God on the day of visitation" (1 Peter 2:12 ESV). All of which is to say, I think I can reduce the Bible into one sentence. Here it is: God makes Himself known *to* His people with the goal of making Himself known *through* His people. What do you think?

At first glance, it doesn't appear that God's mission is a major theme in Exodus. Yet a closer look uncovers that this is a significant thrust. Exodus 9:14–16 is an important section. Moses relates these words of Yahweh to Pharaoh:

> For this time I will send all my plagues on you yourself, and on your servants and your people, so that you may know that there is none like Me in all the earth. For by now I could have put out My hand and struck you and your people with pestilence, and you would have been cut off from the earth. But for this purpose I have raised you up, to show you My power, so that My name may be proclaimed *in all the earth.* (ESV, emphasis added).

It's not surprising, therefore, that when the Israelites leave Egypt, "a mixed multitude" (i.e., a group of believing Egyptians) leaves with Israel (Exodus 12:38 ESV). It wasn't just ethnic Israelites who left Egypt. There was a whole group of Egyptians that said, "Your God is real who offers the grace deal." They saw the light.

And would you believe it? In a later text, Yahweh dares to say, "Blessed be Egypt My people" (Isaiah 19:25 ESV). There's redemption for all the Egypts of this world who repent and believe the Gospel. Now that's mercy!

ISRAEL SAYS YES

Yahweh laid claim to Israel, calling them His "firstborn son" (Exodus 4:22 ESV). During the plagues, God set Israel apart from Egypt (Exodus 11:7), then He redeemed them from bondage (Exodus 15:13), brought them to Himself (Exodus 19:4), and honored them as His *segulah*, kingdom of priests, and holy nation (Exodus 19:5–6). How did Israel respond to their new identity? They uttered a resounding yes! Moses records their words, "All that the LORD has spoken we will do" (Exodus 19:8 ESV).

Yet, as we have already seen, the Israelites vacillate between faith, worship, and obedience (Exodus 1:17; 4:31; 12:28, 50; 14:31; 16:24) and grumblings, despair, panic, accusations, and disobedience (Exodus 5:21; 6:9; 14:11–12; 16:2–3; 17:2–3, 7; 18:13–16). Israel gives new meaning to the word *fickle*.

A certain amount of suspicion, therefore, hangs over Israel's pledge, "All that the LORD has spoken we will do." They say virtually the same thing in Exodus 24:3 and 7. Sandwiched between the bold assertions of faith in chapters 19 and 24 (that will crumble in Exodus 32) is one of the foremost sections of the Bible—the Ten Commandments.

CHAPTER 11

God's Top Three: Exodus 20:1–11

The earth quaked, the heavens poured down rain, before
God, the One of Sinai, before God, the God of Israel.
(Psalm 68:8 ESV)

Israel has been liberated and set free. Egypt is now in their rear-view mirror. What's ahead? Freedom to write their own rules, follow their own hearts, write their own story? Not quite. A new King has claimed them, freed them, and captured their hearts. Now Israel has the best freedom possible. The nation is free to live the way Yahweh intends—to follow, serve, and submit to His will. Freedom, then, is living a life of service to God whose love is jaw-dropping, earth-rattling, and life-transforming. True freedom is a gift to celebrate, not a license to do whatever feels good.

The Book of Exodus, therefore, has two parts—freedom *from* and freedom *for*. Freedom from Pharaoh and Egypt happens early one morning at the Red Sea. Freedom for living in love, however, is a long, drawn-out process. It begins with the Ten Commandments.

TRUE LOVE

In Matthew 22:37–40, Jesus summarizes the Ten Commandments by breaking them down into two sections—love God and love people. Paul chimes in, teaching in Romans 13:8 that love is the fulfillment of the Law.

I once looked at how the word *love* is used in songs on Billboard's top 100 list. In several songs, *love* is what? Lust. That's all love is for some people—sexual lust. Yet in most songs, love is a feeling. Love comes and love goes. Love runs hot and loves grows cold. "I've lost that lovin' feelin.'" That's why 50 percent of the couples who say, "I do," one day will say, "I don't. The feeling's gone; I just can't get it back."

When Jesus and Paul summarize the Ten Commandments with the word *love* they aren't referring to a feeling. Biblical love is a choice to act. Biblical love is something we do.

A movie called *The Four Feathers* takes place in Africa during the late 1800s. A young British army officer is lost in the Sahara Desert and collapses in the sand. An African tribesman rescues him and becomes a friend for life. At different times in the movie, the British officer asks the tribesman why he keeps helping him. The tribesman tells him God put him in his path.

God doesn't call us to love people because they're lovable. The divine mandate isn't to love people for what they can do for us. We are to love people because God put them in our path.

A teacher in a creative writing class asked her students to write something that said "I love you" without using the word *love*. Here's what her students came up with: "Honey, your hair looks just great dyed purple and bright orange." "These cookies you cooked are hardly burned at all." "Sure, I'll go to the tractor-pulling event with you. Looking forward to it!" "You take the last piece of apple pie with vanilla ice cream and caramel on top." What do all these ways of saying "I love you" have in common? They all involve what? *Sacrifice.*

There once was a woman who was driving her husband's new red sports car and got in an accident. The woman broke into tears. It was all her fault, she admitted. How was she ever going to face her husband? It was his brand-new car.

The man in the other car was sympathetic but insisted that they exchange car insurance information. The teary-eyed woman reached into her glove compartment to retrieve the documents and the first paper to fall out had these words written on it: "Honey, in case of an accident, remember it's you that I love, not the car."

What does God do when we've made a mess of things? When we sideswipe people and dent and ding them? God has written a note—a very long note—called the Bible. "Jesus loves me, this I know, for the Bible tells me so." Try singing these lyrics too. "Jesus loves me, this I *show*, for the Bible tells me *grow*." How do we grow in love? By following the Ten Commandments.

THE TEN COMMANDMENTS IN CONTEXT

One pharaoh calls Israel a "people" (Exodus 1:9 ESV), but Yahweh calls them "My people" (Exodus 3:7 ESV). What does it mean to belong to Yahweh? How is Israel to live after their deliverance at the Red Sea? And what will life look like now that they're no longer under the cruel reign of Egypt but under the loving rule of Yahweh? Whatever this newfound freedom looks like, it's not altogether new.

Before arriving at Mount Sinai, Moses helps the Israelites "know the statutes of God and His laws" (Exodus 18:16 ESV). In fact, after the Red Sea and before Sinai, God gives Israel statutes and ordinances in Exodus 15:26 and 16:5, 23, and 25–30. Even earlier, God says, "Abraham obeyed My voice and kept My charge, My commandments, My statutes, and My laws" (Genesis 26:5).

The Ten Commandments, therefore, weren't completely new. We can trace several of them back to the Book of Genesis—the backstory is still in play! For instance, murder was reprehensible from the start, as indicated by God's response to Cain killing Abel (Genesis 4:10–12). Further, it was wrong for Abraham to lie (Genesis 12:10–20) and for Shechem to rape Dinah (Genesis 34).

Another feature of the Ten Commandments is that God gives them *after* saving His people. I can't emphasize the modifier *after* enough. The Ten Commandments aren't isolated tidbits on how to live a moral life to gain God's favor. *Nothing could be further from the truth.* Nowhere in the Book of Exodus does Moses suggest Israel was saved from Egypt because of the nation's adherence to the Law. *Nowhere.* Had God given Moses the Ten Commandments from the burning bush in Exodus 3, and then told him to give them to the Hebrew slaves as conditions they must obey to be delivered, there wouldn't have been an exodus from Egypt.

God gives His directives to people who are already rescued, already saved, and already delivered. God doesn't give the Law so Israel may become His people. The Israelites are already His people, His chosen nation. God's election of Israel goes back to Abram in Genesis 12, who was saved by grace through faith apart from obedience. Here's the bottom line. The Israelites were to love God (Deuteronomy 6:4–5) because God first loved them (Deuteronomy 7:6–8).

Consequently, divine Law from Sinai comes within a relationship. In the Ten Commandments, the expression "Yahweh your God" appears in Exodus 20:2, 5, 7, 10, and 12. Mandates don't derive from a god, some god, any god, their god, her god, or his god; they come from the heart of "your God." And this relationship—like every relationship—has expectations. God doesn't keep us in the dark, wondering what He wants. Yahweh is no passive-aggressive deity!

THE LAW IS GOOD

How are the Ten Commandments working for people today? Not so well. A 2020 survey of 1,200 people ages 15–35 found that 90 percent of those polled could name no more than two commandments. Then there's the Danish newspaper *Ekstra Bladet.* Some years ago, it reported the results of a telephone survey of one-hundred pastors in the Lutheran State Church of Denmark. A reporter asked pastors whether they could recite the Ten Commandments. Eighty percent couldn't remember all of them. Three pastors even broke the Eighth Commandment ("You shall not bear false witness against your neighbor" [Exodus 20:16 ESV]) by telling their wives to tell the reporters they weren't home!

God gives His Law not to make our lives miserable but to protect us from another kind of bondage—sin and self-destruction. God also wants to keep His people from becoming another Egypt, which would negate His mission to the world. The Law, then, is good. Moses says as much. "The LORD commanded us to do all these statutes, to fear the LORD our God, for our good always, that He might preserve us alive, as we are this day" (Deuteronomy 6:24 ESV). Divine mandates aren't an imposition. Far from it. They preserve life and well-being.

The Ten Commandments are good in another way. They're to keep Israel's communal life from falling apart. For instance, the Law not only expressly forbids murder (Exodus 20:13; cf. 21:12–14), but also accidental death from a dangerous ox (Exodus 21:29). Likewise, the community prospers when weak and vulnerable people are treated with kindness and justice (Exodus 22:21–24; 23:3, 6–9). God's will that people live harmoniously is further expressed in the commands not to charge interest (Exodus 22:25), to return a garment taken in a pledge before the sun goes down (Exodus 22:26), and to be kind to enemies (Exodus 23:5).

Israel's experience in Egypt provides an impetus to abide by divine Law. "You shall not oppress a sojourner. You know the heart of a sojourner, for you were sojourners in the land of Egypt" (Exodus 23:9 ESV). Paul puts it this way: "For the whole law is fulfilled in one word: 'You shall love your neighbor as yourself'" (Galatians 5:14 ESV).

FOLLOW YAHWEH

Most of us realize that when we're listening to a speaker, what they say gives us insight into what kind of person they are. Words indirectly show others something about character. In like manner, the Ten Commandments provide an inside look into God's heart. They show us His moral compass. And they invite us to follow suit. Take the Third Commandment—keep the Sabbath Day holy (Exodus 20:8). Just as Yahweh rested and refreshed Himself on the seventh day (Exodus 31:17), we are to imitate Him by setting aside a day each week for refreshment and recreation.

The idea of imitation extends throughout the Second Table of the Law, Commandments 4–10. Here's one example from the Seventh Commandment: you shall not steal. "If ever you take your neighbor's cloak in pledge, you shall return it to him before the sun goes down, for that is his only covering, and it is his cloak for his body; in what else shall he sleep? And if he cries to Me, I will hear, for I am compassionate" (Exodus 22:26–27 ESV). Compassion flows from Yahweh. Jesus also exhorts us to mimic our Maker: "Be merciful, even as your Father is merciful" (Luke 6:36 ESV).

THE PROLOGUE: EXODUS 20:1–2

Yahweh rescued Israel from Egypt and brought them to Himself on Mount Sinai. Accompanied by clouds, lightning, fire, smoke, and earthquakes, Yahweh speaks like thunder to the shaking Israelites assembled at the foot of the mountain—backing as far off as possible (Exodus 20:18, 21).

The prologue reprises Yahweh's credentials as Israel's deliverer. While the people's Song in Exodus 15 elaborated this theme profusely, the claim here is more succinct and to the point: "I am Yahweh, your God, who brought you out of the land of Egypt, out of a house of slaves" (Exodus 20:2). The Ten Commandments are preceded by affirming God's deliverance of Israel out of Egypt—from bondage and bricks to safety and salvation.

Narratives and laws never appear together like this in ancient literature. They're rarely connected in modern texts. When was the last time you prepared to take a driver's license test by reading a booklet that combined regulations with stories? In the case of divine mandates in Exodus, the God who gives the Law is the same God who rescues and delivers His people. God doesn't say, "Do this because I said so." No. God says, "Do this because I love you." *Yahweh is a Gospel God.*

In fact, Moses weaves instruction and narrative side by side through-out the book. God's instructions don't stand alone as an external code. Instead, they're integrated into Israel's Gospel story. The book takes us on a topsy-turvy journey from story (Exodus 1–19), to instruction (Exodus 20:1–17), to story (Exodus 20:18–21), to instruction (Exodus 20:22–23:22), to story (Exodus 24), to instruction (Exodus 25–31), to story (Exodus 32–34), and finally to instruction (Exodus 35–40).

This movement of the Book of Exodus teaches these truths:

- A life of faith isn't a response to instruction as instruction but a response to the great acts of Yahweh's salvation.

- The Law is for the redeemed; acts of kindness don't achieve salvation.

- Instruction's shape is defined by the shape of the saving action of Yahweh.

- The motivation for following divine mandates comes from Yahweh's salvation of Israel—not from abstract ethical arguments or philosophical imperatives.

I once heard about an aging grandmother who, one Christmas, decided to send checks to her nine grandchildren instead of buying each of them gifts. She signed the checks and wrote in the Christmas cards, "Buy your own gift." Imagine her shock when, on New Year's Day, she found all the checks still under a book on her desk!

When Yahweh sends the Ten Commandments, He includes the check—Gospel power to walk in His ways (Exodus 20:2). Motivation to follow the Ten Commandments derives from Yahweh's mighty hand and outstretched arm when He saved Israel from Egyptian bondage. Moses weaves Law and Gospel together. "When your son asks you in time to come, 'What is the meaning of the testimonies and the statutes and the rules that the LORD our God has commanded you?' then you shall say to your son, 'We were Pharaoh's slaves in Egypt. And the LORD brought us out of Egypt with a mighty hand'" (Deuteronomy 6:20–21 ESV).

THE FIRST COMMANDMENT

Who's on first? That's a question made famous in a skit by Bud Abbott and Lou Costello. Since the first baseman's name is Who, the statement "Who's on first" is ambiguous. It could be a question—"Which person is playing first base?" Conversely, it could be an answer—"The name of the first baseman is Who."

Who's on first? That's easy for Israel. Moses says it's Yahweh.

Exodus 1–15 describes a contest between Yahweh and Egypt's gods—deities that included Horus, the sky god portrayed as a falcon; Aten, portrayed as the sun-disk; Sekhmet, the lioness-headed goddess; Hatmehit, a fish-goddess; and Heqet, portrayed with the head of a frog. Yahweh's defeat of these fake gods—vis-à-vis ten plagues—demonstrates that He alone is the true God. This fact, testified by the plagues (Exodus 8:10; 9:14), is celebrated in the Song of the Sea (Exodus 15:11) and confessed by Jethro (Exodus 18:11). Other verses in Exodus reiterating the First Commandment include the following:

- "Whoever sacrifices to any god, other than the LORD alone, shall be devoted to destruction" (Exodus 22:20 ESV).
- "Pay attention to all that I have said to you, and make no mention of the names of other gods, nor let it be heard on your lips" (Exodus 23:13 ESV).
- "You shall worship no other god, for the LORD, whose name is Jealous, is a jealous God" (Exodus 34:14 ESV).

In the ancient world, the Israelites were unique, as their allegiance was to be singular. They were to worship one God. Every other culture—be it of Egypt, Babylon, Assyria, or Canaan—worshiped many gods. If Israel jettisons the First Commandment, the whole covenant relationship will come to a screeching halt. This is the thrust of Exodus 32 and Aaron's golden calf.

SIGNS AND REALITY

When my three children were little, I planned to take them to Destin, Florida. Destin has a beautiful beach—filled with white sand and emerald water. Unparalleled glory awaited us! My kids had never seen a beach. To say they were excited would be a massive understatement. "Are we there yet?" they asked every hour as we drove down the interstate.

Imagine that when we get to Birmingham, Alabama, I see a sign that says "Destin, 260 miles." I park the car and say, "Kids, we're here!" Many of you already think I'm not playing with a full deck of cards—but now you say this proves it!

Here's the point. The sign to Destin isn't the reality. It directs people to the reality. The sign to Destin can't give white sand and emerald water. Only Destin can do that.

Here's the next point. Creation is a sign. Creation is an amazing sign of God's power, wisdom, and glory. Creation gives us utterly delightful tastes, touches, smells, sounds, and sights. Creation, like a road sign, points us to the reality behind it—the Father, Son, and Holy Spirit.

Here's my question. Will we stop at the sign or continue to where the sign leads? Will we search for ultimate satisfaction horizontally (in creation) or vertically (in the Creator)? Nothing against Birmingham, Alabama, but the Florida coast is much more inviting!

Here's how idolatry works. My longing for a good thing becomes a bad thing when that longing becomes the ruling thing. Take food, for example. What a gift! Can anyone say "pecan pie"? But when love for food becomes everything, we end up overweight and out of shape. Or money. When our love for money becomes everything, we neglect relationships and become workaholics.

We need this truth hammered into our heads: God didn't design creation to fill our deepest longings. Creation's role is to be a huge sign pointing us to the One who alone satisfies. Bottom line? When we love the Giver more than the gifts, our hearts are free. Conversely, when we love the gifts more than the Giver, we'll never reach our God-given destination—life now and life forever with Him.

The acronym *FIRST* helps us stay on the right road. It helps us become more intentional about keeping the First Commandment. Let's see what that looks like.

FIRST

Finances

"Honor the LORD with your wealth, with the firstfruits of all your produce" (Proverbs 3:9 ESV). Money is a huge test of our priorities. Our checkbooks reveal what's most important. And the results are in. We're consumed with consuming.

Let's get some perspective. In 1950, about 10 percent of all income in America was spent on luxuries. By 1980, that figure was 30 percent. In the last forty years, that figure has climbed to 40 percent—that's about $500 billion a year spent on stuff we don't really need. Our new religion is Transcendental Acquisition! We should rewrite the constitution to read, "We believe in life, liberty, and the *purchase* of happiness."

I was once in the middle of a series of sermons on financial management when a woman told me, "You know, Pastor Lessing, I really need this series. In the past few years, I've racked up a lot of credit card debt."

Feeling like a mighty Hebrew prophet of yesteryear, I asked, "Well, what are you going to do about it?"

She replied, "I'm making the minimum monthly payments until I pay it off."

Feeling more and more like famous Amos, I asked, "How much do you owe?"

She responded, "$3,000."

"Well," I said, "that's not catastrophic. The average American owes about $7,000 on their credit cards. Have you figured out how long it's going to take you to pay off your balance if you only make minimum payments?"

She said she hadn't. Getting a tad nervous, she looked at her watch and said, "Oh my, I've got to go!" As I recall, she took off running!

Do you know how long it takes to pay off $3,000 at 18 percent interest making only minimum payments of $50 each month? Twelve years and nine months. At the end of that time, you will have paid a total of $4,733 in interest alone.

Any serious response to the First Commandment begins by aligning my finances with God's Word. My reason for living needs to be more than desire, perspire, acquire, then retire!

Interests

"Whether you eat or drink, or whatever you do, do it all to the glory of God" (1 Corinthians 10:31 ESV). Living for God's glory means we do things with an attitude of gratitude. When we're gardening, water skiing, or watching sports, we say, "Thank You, Lord!"

Living for God's glory also implies that my interests won't compromise biblical truth. I won't get involved in activities where people willfully and repeatedly break God's Word. It's also worth noting that my interests won't intentionally break the Third Commandment: "Remember the Sabbath day, to keep it holy" (Exodus 20:8 ESV).

Relationships

"Do not be deceived: Bad company ruins good morals" (1 Corinthians 15:33 ESV). Have you noticed that we become like the people we spend the most time with? Some people come to church and then spend time with unbelievers, agnostics, and atheists; they hang out with casual Christians, compromising Christians, caustic and complaining Christians. Then what happens? It's called the law of gravity. It's a lot easier to be pulled down than it is to be pulled up. If the God of Abraham, Isaac, and Jacob is first in our life, there are some relationships that are dead wrong. It's time to get out of them quickly, yet gracefully.

Schedule

"Make the best use of the time" (Ephesians 5:16 ESV). Horace Whittle, a dockworker in England, hated his alarm clock. Every workday for forty-three years, its bell jarred him awake. For forty-three years, Whittle longed to ignore it. He finally got revenge. On the day he retired, Horace Whittle flattened the clock under an eighty-ton hydraulic press. "It was a lovely feeling," he said. "Now I can begin to live!"

Those are six of the saddest words in the world. What are you waiting for so you can begin to live? A new job? A new home? A new relationship? Putting God first means I make the most of every opportunity. The average person in America lives about 28,000 days. Begin investing those days in your family, people who are hurting, and your church's ministry. Make this your daily prayer to Jesus: "Teach us to number our days that we may get a heart of wisdom" (Psalm 90:12 ESV).

Troubles

Who or what we turn to when trouble comes knocking also reveals our allegiance to the First Commandment. God says, "Call upon Me in the day of trouble" (Psalm 50:15 ESV). I was once visiting a church member in the hospital when someone in her family told me, "Pastor, all we can do now is pray." Honestly? Prayer is your last resort?

Did you get undercut by a competitor or slammed by your spouse or torched by your teenager? Call upon the Lord. Do you feel depressed and melancholy? Call upon the Lord. Are you overwhelmed with guilt and shame and emptiness? Call upon the Lord.

Jesus summarizes the First Commandment with these words: "Seek *first* the kingdom of God and His righteousness, and all these things will be added to you" (Matthew 6:33 ESV, emphasis added). That's quite a promise!

THE SECOND COMMANDMENT

The Eighth Commandment wants us to protect people's names. Its twin appears in the Second Commandment where God mandates that we protect His name—Yahweh.

God's name is a major motif in Exodus. He wants it to be spread abroad, to the ends of the earth (e.g., Exodus 9:16). The Book of Psalms also makes it clear that a primary use of God's name is connected to His missional plan for the world (e.g., Psalms 18:49; 48:10; 86:9; 96:2–3). David prays, "O LORD, our Lord, how majestic is Your name in all the earth!" (Psalm 8:1, 9).

God's name is taken in vain when we use it to insult people, things, animals, sports teams, and the like. America is the most foul-mouthed country in the world, and it's getting worse. Frequently members of the media invoke God's name mindlessly and callously.

On other occasions, the temptation is to use God's name in vain to excuse ourselves. "The Lord didn't want me to pick up my room." "I didn't feel led to get out of bed." "God doesn't want me to honor that contract." "God told me what you should do. God told me what's wrong with you. God told me that your next car must be Chicago-Cub-blue."

In the world what's this called? Forgery. That's when you use someone else's name to get what you want. There are spiritual forgers who misuse God's name by saying, without any biblical basis, "God told me . . ." Allow me to clarify things. *The will of God is only revealed in the Word of God.*

THE THIRD COMMANDMENT

In 1793, the French replaced the old clock in favor of French Revolutionary Time: a ten-hour day with one hundred minutes per hour, one hundred seconds per minute. The goal of "decimal time" was to increase productivity. Did it work? Not even close. Productivity collapsed. The suicide rate skyrocketed. Why? People need rest. The French officially stopped using decimal time after just seventeen months.

Without rest, we become lethargic, angry, cynical, and sarcastic. Our immune system also begins to falter. But we're Americans, not AmeriCANT'S. That's why we ignore our bodies and press on. Up the hill. For another endless day. We used to call this workaholism. Then it changed to ambition. Now we call it drive. Whatever we call it, it's still lunacy.

The Sabbath is God's way to break our bondage to work, quotas, and busyness. *Sabbath* comes from the Hebrew *shabbat*, which means "cut off." God says, "Don't let your highest values become professional and financial. If they rule your heart, you will end up destroying yourself as well as those you love." God offers a break every week for wonder and celebration to rest from our constant need for production.

God's command to *remember* the Sabbath Day expects more than cognitive recall. The Hebraic idea of "remember" implies action. "God heard their groaning, and God *remembered* His covenant with Abraham, with Isaac, and with Jacob" (Exodus 2:24 ESV, emphasis added). The next thing we know, God is speaking with Moses in a burning bush. *Remembering leads to acting.* Ask any husband about his wedding anniversary and he'll tell you his wife is looking for concrete demonstrations of love. "Thoughts" don't amount to much.

Before arriving at Mount Sinai, the Israelites didn't know anything about taking a Sabbath. They never had a day off. In Egypt, they were numbers, items on a spreadsheet, bought and sold like cattle. They worked until they died. Because God's gift of the Sabbath had no known analogy in the ancient world, this was brand new!

Do you notice that the Third Commandment is longer than the rest of the commandments? A whole lot longer. In fact, if we arranged the Ten Commandments into a pie chart, the third would consist of more than 30 percent of the pie. What are we to make of that? *It's very important.*

Unlike the other six days, when it's easy to define people by means of their productivity, the Sabbath is an equal-opportunity event overriding all distinctions (Exodus 23:12). God even calls Israel to treat their slaves with kindness, remembering that they were once slaves in Egypt (Exodus 23:9). Consequently, the Sabbath reinforces our primary calling—to be neighbors. Sabbath time, Sabbath practice, and Sabbath freedoms are neighborly because they depart from pharaonic brick quotas that produce fear, competition, anxiety, and death.

Remembering the Sabbath is an alternative to Egypt. It protests the regime's unreachable production goals. Resting one day in seven is a countercultural lifestyle in a society that believes in more technological inventions, more economic expansion, and more military armament. "Is not life more than food, and the body more than clothing?" (Matthew 6:25 ESV).

I Was Glad

The Sabbath is also a moment when we cease from our addiction to work and learn about Yahweh's Word. That's what the psalmist celebrates: "I was glad when they said to me, 'Let us go to the house of the LORD!'" (Psalm 122:1 ESV).

When you get up on Sunday morning, just how glad are you? With what eagerness do you awake and say, "Good! Today is church-going day!" How joyful does your heart beat to that first call to worship shouted from the bottom of the stairs, "We leave in ten minutes!"

I suspect many of us go out of duty. "Ya gotta do what ya gotta do." Maybe you stay home and finish a weekend painting job or that garden project. Or you may think, "Well, let's get this over so I can have the rest of the day to myself!" Or maybe it was all the rush and rumble, punctuated with such typical but rather unliturgical prechurch statements such as the dad's, "I'm starting the car in two minutes!" Or the teenage son's, "Aw, what's wrong with these shoes?" Or the daughter's, "I'm having a bad hair day!" Or the mom's, "Who's putting the dog out?" And on it goes, with order restored only as you walk into church, a minute late—with everyone staring at you, of course! Sometimes we're galaxies away from being glad to go to the Lord's house.

And even once you're in church, don't you occasionally think, "With a bit of luck, a short sermon, no Communion, and no Baptism, we could be out of here in less than an hour." Oh, the longing for the fifty-five-minute special!

That quick glance at the watch, that impatient look during the sermon, that wanting to get back to the project in the basement—all these point to the most serious of all sins: a lack of love for Jesus. After all, what would we say of someone who goes to meet the love of his or her life only out of a sense of duty, or occasionally, or just to keep the children in line, or hoping the time spent together will be as short as possible?

Let me come out and say it. Parents, it's a myth that we teach values to our children. We don't teach them; we model them. If you moan and groan and drone and pick a bone as to why you're not going to church, that makes a huge impact on your children. Example isn't the main thing. Example isn't the first thing. Example isn't the best thing. *Example is the only thing.*

Jesus Loves to Go to Church

A Sunday School teacher asked her children to take some time on Sunday afternoon and write a letter to God. They were to bring their letter to class the following Sunday. One little guy wrote, "Dear God. We had a good time at church today. Wish You could've been there!"

We may go to church dragging our feet, but that's not Jesus. Our motives may be questionable, but not His. Our concentration may wander all over the place, but not His. Jesus loves the verse, "I was glad when they said to me, 'Let us go to the house of the LORD!'" (Psalm 122:1 ESV).

Jesus goes to church to forgive our sins. The apostle says, "Let it be known to you therefore, brothers, that through [Jesus] forgiveness of sins is proclaimed to you" (Acts 13:38 ESV). Jesus also attends church to heal hurts. The evangelist writes, "All the crowd sought to touch [Jesus], for power came out from Him and healed them all" (Luke 6:19 ESV). And Christ is present in worship to give rest for our weariness. Mark reminds us, "He said to them, 'Come away by yourselves to a desolate place and rest a while.' For many were coming and going, and they had no leisure even to eat" (Mark 6:31 ESV).

Suppose you were to come upon someone in the forest working feverishly to saw down a tree. "What are you doing?" you ask.

"Can't you see?" comes the reply. "I'm sawing down this tree."

"How long have you been at it?"

"Over five hours. I'm beat."

"Why don't you take a break for a few minutes and sharpen your saw?"

"I don't have time to sharpen the saw. I'm too busy sawing!"

How smart is that? Even God needed to be refreshed.

The only commandment in the Decalogue that Yahweh Himself observes is the Third Commandment—keep the Sabbath day holy. God blesses the Sabbath day and makes it holy, thus implying that Israel was to imitate His rest (Genesis 2:2–3). Exodus 31:17 makes this more apparent: "[The Sabbath] is a sign forever between Me and the people of Israel that in six days the LORD made heaven and earth, and on the seventh day He rested and was *refreshed*" (ESV, emphasis added). Literally, the term *refreshed* means "revived His soul." This is stunning! God needed rest and refreshment after six days. So. Do. We.

CHAPTER 12

More Divine Directives: Exodus 20:12–23:33

Oh how I love Your law! It is my meditation all the day.
(Psalm 119:97 ESV)

The first three commandments lay the foundation for the last seven. Expressed more fully, we love other people (Commandments 4–10) when we love God (Commandments 1–3), who first loved us (Exodus 20:2; cf. 1 John 4:19).

We're all lovers. That's the way God made us. We're custom-made to love. A moment doesn't pass when we're not loving. Here's the rub. God created us to love people and use things. We tend to love things and use people. "Self" ends up ruling the roost.

Most public libraries have subcategories under the word *self*. Here are a few of them: Self-actualization. Self-analysis. Self-assertion. Self-awareness. Self-confidence. Self-control. Self-defense. Self-discovery. Self-enrichment. Self-esteem. Self-expression. Self-fulfillment. Self-help. Self-identity. Self-image. Self-improvement. Self-indulgence. Self-love. Self-realization. Self-reliance. Self-respect.

I think you get the idea! Americans are obsessed with four letters: *S-E-L-F*.

I once saw a guy wearing a T-shirt that said, "I'm in it for me." I once saw another guy wearing a T-shirt that said, "Galileo was wrong. The universe does revolve around me." I know, I look at too many T-shirts! We live in a world that evaluates everything through a singular, all-consuming word: *me*!

Tom Wolfe wrote a best-selling book called *The Bonfire of the Vanities*. In it, Sherman McCoy—a highly successful investment banker—gets up every morning, looks in the mirror, and boasts, "I'm the master of the universe!" There's a part in us that loves to call our own shots, make our own plans, forge our own future—that bows low in front of full-length mirrors.

Moses points us in a different direction—toward people. Galileo was right. The universe doesn't revolve around me. It revolves around God and the people He places into my life.

THE FOURTH COMMANDMENT

The cornerstone of how we love others is how we love our parents—or, in Moses' words, honor them. The verb *honor* denotes giving someone esteem and value. Parents (no matter how imperfect they are) are to be treasured. How?

If you're living at home, practice the attitude of cooperation. Do what your parents say willfully, joyfully, and immediately.

A teenager says to her friend, "I'm really worried. Dad slaves away at his job so I'll never want for anything. He keeps working just so I can go to college. And Mom is always washing and ironing and cooking and cleaning. She even takes care of me when I'm sick."

Her friend says, "What's the big deal? What are you concerned about?"

The worried teen responds, "I'm afraid they might try to escape!"

Most children have no idea how much parents spend on them. Today, it costs about a quarter-million dollars to raise a child. Therefore, the next time parents ask you to take out the trash, pick up your room, haul a load of dirty clothes to the washing machine, mow the yard, be in by 10:30 p.m.—and brace them before you do this so they don't pass out—say, "Sure Mom, I'd be glad to! Dad, I'd love to give you a hand!" You'll be amazed at what a little cooperation does to the atmosphere of your home.

If you're no longer dependent upon your parents, work on an attitude of appreciation. In their original setting in Exodus 20, the Ten Commandments are directed toward adult men—implying that their parents are older people.

As we all know, the older we get, the more chinks we see in our parents' armor. And yet! "If one curses his father or mother, his lamp will be put out in utter darkness" (Proverbs 20:20 ESV). Bitterness toward parents is self-destructive.

For many of us, we're responsible for our parents' gray hair. That's true for me in my mom's life. What's that gray hair? "That's when Reed was three years old and tried to flush the cat down the toilet." What's that gray hair? "That's when Reed was in high school and was arrested by the Denver Police." What's that gray hair? "That's when Reed rode his mountain bike over a cliff in northwest Arkansas." You have your stories. I have mine!

Joseph cared deeply for his aging father, Jacob. After Joseph's season of heartache and deep hurt, he could have said, "Dad? Where were you when my brothers—*your sons*—sold me into slavery? Dad? Why didn't you come looking for me? Dad? What gives?" Instead, Joseph honored his father. After not seeing him for more than twenty years, Genesis 46:29 describes Joseph hugging and weeping over Jacob.

In my extended family, on two different occasions, adult children have cut off all connections with their parents. *Two times.* This is insidious. This isn't Joseph with Jacob.

Finally, if your parents are dependent upon you, show an attitude of consolation. A few years ago, *Newsweek* magazine had an article titled, "And You Must Be Mom?" There was a company in New York called Family Efficiency Headquarters. For $1,200 a year, people rented actors who visited their parents. For a few hours every month, these actors played the part of family members. And the elderly—in these cases— were so fragile they didn't know the difference. *This is insidious as well.* Paul writes, "But if a widow has children or grandchildren, let them first learn to show godliness to their own household and to make some return to their parents, for this is pleasing in the sight of God. . . . If anyone does not provide for his relatives, and especially for members of his household, he has denied the faith and is worse than an unbeliever" (1 Timothy 5:4, 8).

Milk has an expiration date. So do eggs. Almost everything in the refrigerated section in grocery stores has an expiration date. The Fourth Commandment, though, never expires. We're to honor—respect, esteem, show affection, appreciate—our parents when they're young, middle-aged (even!), old, and when they're deceased. The obligation is never removed. "Grandchildren are a crown to the aged, and the glory of children is their fathers" (Proverbs 17:6 ESV).

THE FIFTH COMMANDMENT

A few years ago, in Dadeville, Alabama, two men got into a Bible-quoting contest. It turned into a shouting match between Gabel Taylor and Scott Lee. They were fighting over a Bible verse and Scott Lee, who lost the contest, went to his house, got a gun, shot Gabel Taylor, and killed him. Scott Lee knew a lot about the Bible, but he didn't know about the Fifth Commandment, "You shall not murder" (Exodus 20:13 ESV).

The Hebrew verb employed in the Fifth Commandment isn't precise. In some contexts, the term means "murder" (1 Kings 21:19). It can also denote unintentional killing (Deuteronomy 4:41–42) or executing a convicted murderer (Numbers 35:30). Exodus 21:12 is helpful where Moses writes, "Whoever strikes a man so that he dies shall be put to death" (ESV). Any act of hatred that ends in taking someone else's life— that is, acting in God's stead—breaks the Fifth Commandment. Yahweh alone is the Lord and Giver of all life (Genesis 9:6; Leviticus 17:11).

The Fifth Commandment also applies to suicide. David prays, "My times are in Your hands" (Psalm 31:15 ESV). My times are not in my hands. My days, months, and years are in God's hands. Yet, in 2019, there were 47,511 self-inflicted deaths reported in America, making suicide the tenth leading cause of death in our country. Someone died by suicide every eleven minutes.

The Fifth Commandment likewise applies to abortion. Note how Luke uses the Greek word *brephos*. "When Elizabeth heard Mary's greeting, the baby [*brephos*] leaped in her womb" (Luke 1:41 ESV). *Brephos* describes a baby—in this case, John the Baptist—in his mother's womb. Compare this with these words: "This will be a sign to you: you will find a baby [*brephos*] wrapped in cloths and lying in a manger" (Luke 2:12 ESV). Here, *brephos* describes Jesus after He's born. The lesson? God doesn't differentiate between a child inside the mother's womb and a child outside the mother's womb. Both are of infinite value to God. It follows, then, that God inspires Solomon to record these words, "Open your mouth, judge righteously, defend the rights of the poor and needy" (Proverbs 31:8 ESV).

If you have a loved one who committed suicide or know someone who had an abortion, these are not unpardonable sins. The only unpardonable sin is rejecting the cleansing blood of Jesus and the free grace of God. Listen to their story and, as the Holy Spirit guides the conversation, invite them into another story—God's exodus story of redemption and new life in Christ.

Anger Kills

You might be thinking at this point, "Finally, here's one commandment I've kept. I've never killed a person. Praise God!" Hear the Word of the Lord: "Everyone who hates his brother is a murderer" (1 John 3:15 ESV). Oh no! What does John mean? Anger kills people. Anger kills their countenance. Anger kills their spirits. Anger kills their hope and joy and peace.

Anger experts say that 20 percent of the general population has levels of hostility high enough to be dangerous to health—their health and the health of others! A study from the University of Tennessee found that, on average, women lose their tempers three times a week. The average man loses his temper six times a week. More often, women get angry with people. Men tend to get angry more often with things (flat tires, tools, cars, etc.). And men are more physical in expressing their anger.

Guess where we're most likely to vent our anger? At home. Guess who we most often express our anger toward? Family members. Do you recognize this anonymous saying? "To live above with saints we love; oh that will be glory. But to live below with saints we know; well that's a different story."

When it comes to expressing anger, perhaps you're like a maniac. Maniacs are walking time bombs; they have a hair-trigger temper. These people throw things. They curse and cuss. They yell and they raise hell. Remember Woody Hayes? He was the head football coach for the Ohio State Buckeyes. In the last game he coached, a Clemson player intercepted a pass. Woody ran on the field and slugged the guy! Then there's longtime Indiana University basketball coach Bobby Knight. Enough said.

You've probably heard this myth: "Taking out my anger gets rid of my anger." But a series of studies indicate that expressions of anger create more anger. Anger begets anger.

The mute is the exact opposite of the maniac. Hold it in. Deny. Clam up. Conceal how you feel. The mute is a slow cooker version of anger. Stew and simmer. "I won't say a thing, so you'll need to guess why I'm angry. And if you don't guess it correctly, I'll become angrier."

Perhaps you're not a maniac or a mute. Instead you're a manipulator. Have you ever heard this line: "I don't get mad, I get even"? It's called the law of the jungle, the survival of the fittest. "You hurt me, so I'm going to hurt you twice as much. You won't see it coming until it's too late. Then, *pow!*"

I invite you to follow the ABCs of anger management:

- **Admit my problem.** The Bible says, "Whoever conceals his transgressions will not prosper, but he who confesses and forsakes them will obtain mercy" (Proverbs 28:13 ESV). Denying your anger is like storing dynamite in an attic. Sooner or later, there will be a spark and the house will explode.

- **B**elieve in change. Jesus once called James and John *boanerges* or "Sons of Thunder" (Mark 3:17 ESV). How would you like to attend a church potluck with those guys? Jesus softens their hearts. In time, James and John became loving and compassionate Christians.

- **C**laim forgiveness. Christ forgives you. Cleanses you. He washes away *every* sin.

THE SIXTH COMMANDMENT

When I was in my late teens and early twenties, I would frequently drive from my home in Denver, Colorado, to Winfield, Kansas—the home of St. John's College. I'd begin going east out of Denver. The towns along Interstate 70 became familiar: Limon, Flagler, and Burlington, Colorado; then Hayes, Russell, Goodland, and Salina, Kansas. I apologize to my eastern Colorado and western Kansas friends, but that stretch from Denver to Salina felt like "The Land of No Return." Several times, I ran out of gas. Once I was caught in a blizzard. And on one late August afternoon, it was so hot my car overheated and almost blew up!

There's another fateful place called "The Land of No Return." I'm talking about adultery.

Someone once said, "Marriage is like a three-ring circus. First comes the engagement ring, then the wedding ring, then the suffering." More than half of the spouses in our nation have had an affair and America has the highest divorce rate in the world. More than half of all divorces in the world occur right here, in the U.S. of A. The landscape is littered with the victims of divorce. Ex-wives raising their children alone, former husbands trying to start new lives and still care for children they only see sporadically, and children themselves often torn between warring parents. I once asked my mother, "Mom, did you ever consider divorcing Dad?" She answered, "Divorce? No! Murder? Yes!"

There are powerful forces that encourage adultery. The first is called humanism. Humanism says, "Man is the measure of all things." Here's some good marriage advice: "Bury the I and raise the we." Humanism counters, "Raise the I and bury the we."

Add materialism. Materialism maintains, "Money is the measure of all things." Spouses become financially overcommitted to keep up with the Joneses—then they don't have time for each other. Think about it. Just about the time we catch up with the Joneses, they refinance! J. Paul Getty, who was the wealthiest man of his era, once lamented, "I would give my entire fortune for one happy marriage!" His thirst for money destroyed all five of his marriages.

Hedonism is another powerful force that destroys marriages. It says, "Pleasure is the measure of all things." There's nothing wrong with pleasure. Hedonism, though, is the love of pleasure above everything and everyone else. Hedonism lies at the root of pornography—an annual $12 billion business in America, the pornographic capital of the world. *Pornography destroys marriages.*

We see God's utter seriousness on the Sixth Commandment when He mandates that adulterers must face the death penalty (Deuteronomy 22:22). Even kings aren't exempt (2 Samuel 12:13). God knows the beauty of a one man/one woman marital commitment. God knows the pain when sexual expression occurs outside of the marriage bond.

How shall we respond to a society that says, "Me first, money first, and pleasure first"? We need to monitor our media. Job says, "I have made a covenant with my eyes not to look lustfully at a woman" (Job 31:1). Sex is sold all over: television, radio, movies, social media, and billboards. "But," we protest, "I'm just looking." Who are we kidding? Adultery begins in the head before it ends up in the bed.

To follow God's guidelines for sex, we also must maintain our marriage. Breaking news! I once shot an eighty-five on eighteen holes of golf. There's something I should mention, though. It was a par-three course. Most holes were only 120 yards long. I'm dynamite at 120 yards.

It's those 480-yard par fives that sock it to me. Why? Error increases with distance. What's true in golf is true in marriage. *Error increases with distance.*

Stay close to your spouse. Find things in common. Have a date night once a week and keep it—come what may.

If you've traveled a million miles from God's plan for sexual expression, hear this loud and clear: adultery isn't the unforgivable sin, divorce isn't the unforgivable sin, premarital sex isn't the unforgivable sin.

When a woman was caught in the act of adultery, what did Jesus say? How did He respond? What was God's Word to her? More pressing, what is God's Word to us? "Neither do I condemn you; go, and from now on sin no more" (John 8:11 ESV).

Jesus doesn't leave us in "The Land of No Return." He loves us too much. Jesus claimed us in baptismal waters where He delivered the gifts of salvation won at the cross—forgiveness and mercy and radical, amazing grace. So we can do what? So says Martin Luther in the Small Catechism, "Lead a sexually pure and decent life in what we say and do, and husband and wife love and honor each other" (Small Catechism, Sixth Commandment).

THE SEVENTH COMMANDMENT

I once read about a London man who was the victim of fifteen car thefts in eight years. One car was returned, only to be stolen again. The next year, he was called to a police station to pick up a laptop computer that had been stolen and recovered. While he was in the police station, somebody stole his car, again. He should have had a bumper sticker that said, "This car is protected by a pit bull with COVID-19." Many of us know what it feels like to get ripped off.

Theft in Israel was a tort—that is, the violated party had a right for his or her property to be restored. For instance, "If a man steals an ox or a sheep, and kills it or sells it, he shall repay five oxen for an ox, and four sheep for a sheep" (Exodus 22:1 ESV; see Exodus 22:7, 9). In addition to unlawfully taking animals (Exodus 22:1, 12) and property (Exodus

22:7), stealing also refers to confiscating people, or kidnapping (Exodus 21:16).

Israel's problems pale in comparison to stealing in America. For starters, employees take $50 billion a year from their businesses. And this doesn't include what is called "time theft," which includes faking sick days and making personal phone calls at work. This costs an additional $400 billion each year. There's more. U.S. retailers lose an average of $32 billion per year due to shoplifting. In fact, in the average grocery store in America, one out of every fifty-two customers steals something. It's amazing the number of different ways we steal. I looked up the word *steal* in the dictionary and found 138 synonymous terms. Let's consider two.

First, we steal by deceiving customers. The prophet Amos quotes the businessmen of his day who were saying, "When will the new moon be over, that we may sell grain? And the Sabbath, that we may offer wheat for sale, that we may make the ephah small and the shekel great and deal deceitfully with false balances?" (Amos 8:5 ESV). The prophet indicts people who are religious, but also those who steal with their wheeling and dealing. Israel's businessmen divided their lives into watertight compartments, one marked "religion" and the other labeled "business." Religion, after all, is religion. As for the rest? Business is business!

When a repairman makes unnecessary repairs, when a doctor orders unnecessary tests, when someone sells a house and hides broken screens in the attic, when a salesperson skips over the fine print, and when we sell a car and don't mention all its problems, saying, "Oh it's always been a jewel"—all of this is stealing.

Then there's deceiving the government. This is as all-American as baseball, hot dogs, and apple pie. Paul makes it clear, "Pay to all what is owed to them: taxes to whom taxes are owed" (Romans 13:7 ESV). A man once cheated on his taxes, and then felt guilty about what he had done. He sent the government $500 with this note attached: "Here's $500." He wrote at the bottom. "PS: If I still feel guilty, I'll send the rest." The IRS estimates that 17 percent of taxpayers cheat in significant ways.

Paul provides the solution for stealing. "For you know the grace of our Lord Jesus Christ, that though He was rich, yet for your sakes He became poor, so that you by His poverty might become rich" (2 Corinthians 8:9 ESV). The Gospel is a riches-to-rags story. Because of Christ's poverty—His lowly birth and appalling death—our spiritual bank account is astronomically high. God has "blessed us in Christ with every spiritual blessing in the heavenly places . . . which He *lavished* upon us, in all wisdom and insight" (Ephesians 1:3, 8 ESV).

How often do I say, "poor me"? "Poor me, I don't have the resources to deal with this. Poor me, I don't have the ability to handle this. Poor me, I don't have the wisdom to solve this. Poor me, I don't have the power to conquer this." That's not true. The Greek word in Ephesians 1:8 translated "lavished" means an exceedingly great measure, something way beyond the ordinary. God's spiritual blessings in the Gospel aren't squeezed out from an eyedropper. They aren't carefully rationed like water during a drought. These blessings are a Niagara of super-abundance.

We're blessed!

We have what money can never buy. Yesterday's sin is forgiven. Today's gifts include God's peace, purpose, and plan. Tomorrow's celebration in the new Jerusalem will never end. Content in Christ, I'll respect other people's property. Always.

THE EIGHTH COMMANDMENT

America is a nation of talkers. We have television talk shows, radio talk shows, and cell phones out the wazoo! The average American has thirty conversations a day, and we spend a fifth of our lives talking. In one year, our conversations fill sixty-six books with eight hundred pages in each book. If you're a man, you speak on average twenty thousand words a day. And if you're a woman, on average you speak (wait for it) . . . thirty thousand words a day.

The Eighth Commandment is all about words. "You shall not bear false witness against your neighbor" (Exodus 20:16 ESV). Originally, this commandment's focus was upon lying in a court of law (Exodus 23:2). Early on, though, the mandate was expanded to address every kind of lying. "You shall not go around as a slanderer among your people" (Leviticus 19:16 ESV).

Dr. Leonarde Keeler, the man who invented the Lie Detector Machine, tested over 25,000 people. He concluded that human beings are basically deceptive. No kidding! The Oxford Dictionary's word of the year in 2016 was *post-truth*. What shapes our speech? A quiver in my liver; my ocean of emotion. Not truth.

Some lies are cruel. They intentionally destroy. Proverbs 25:18 states, "A man who bears false witness against his neighbor is like a war club, or a sword, or a sharp arrow" (ESV). "Loose lips sink ships." Loose lips sink relationships too.

First Kings 21 tells us about King Ahab, who yearned for a vineyard owned by a man named Naboth. Naboth wouldn't sell, so King Ahab's queen, Jezebel, hired two wicked men who falsely testified that Naboth had cursed both God and the king—leading henchmen to stone Naboth to death. Ahab got his vineyard based on a cruel lie.

Peter is famous for another type of lie—the cowardly lie. "I don't know the man!" (Matthew 26:72). Rather than confess Christ, Peter caved in. We know about these kinds of lies. "The dog ate my homework." "I really did try to call." "The check is in the mail."

There was a teenage boy who had to be home by midnight. He arrived at 2:00 a.m. Everyone was asleep. While creeping up the stairs, he stepped on a squeaky one.

His dad woke up and asked, "Is that you, Bobby?"

"Uh . . . yes," Bobby blurted.

His dad asked, "What time is it?"

Before Bobby could say a word, the cuckoo clock struck twice. He said it was the most ingenious moment of his life when he stood there and cuckooed ten more times!

Let's not forget the convenient lie. Years ago, my son, Jonathan, was doing a project for school. He asked me, "Dad, how come Saturn has eighty-two moons?"

I was too lazy to look up the answer, so I told Jonathan, "Saturn has eighty-two moons because Jupiter is aligned with Mars and peace will guide the planets."

At other times, we lie out of convenience in social settings. "We've got to go now. Ralph has a business trip in the morning." When, in fact, we're bored stiff and looking for any reason to cut and run!

How, then, should we use our words? Paul to the rescue! "Speaking the truth in love" (Ephesians 4:15 ESV). Don't use truth as a club to beat someone over the head. An old Arab proverb puts it this way: "If you shoot an arrow of truth, first dip the point in honey." Making a point doesn't mean making an enemy.

I think I know what you're thinking: "Where can I find the willpower to tell the truth, the whole truth, and nothing but the truth?

Credit cards have a limit. Some limits are $10,000, some $20,000, and some go as high as $50,000 or $60,000. Does that mean God has a limit? Will there ever be a time when His love comes to an end? Will God ever say, "That's it! You've reached your lifetime limit of grace. You've broken the Eighth Commandment one time too many. There's no more forgiveness for you!" You'll never hear God say this. *Not on your life.*

Hear the truth, the whole truth—and it is nothing but the Gospel truth. There's no end to God's forgiveness. For you. *Ever.* This Gospel provides the "want to" to use words wisely.

THE NINTH AND TENTH COMMANDMENTS

The Ten Commandments begin with our relationship with God, move to God's chief representatives (our parents), continue with how we're to live with social equals, and end by addressing envy and greed—often called coveting. "You shall not covet your neighbor's house; you shall not covet your neighbor's wife, or his male servant, or his female servant, or his ox, or his donkey, or anything that is your neighbor's" (Exodus 20:17 ESV).

What's the most populated prison in the world? Leavenworth? Rikers Island? San Quentin? None of the above. The world's biggest prison is called "I Want." "I want stuff that's bigger, faster, prettier, newer, and nicer. *I want.*"

We don't want much, right? Just one will do. One new house. One new car. One new boat. And when we have one, we're happy. We leave the prison. Then it happens again. The new house gets old. The big boat gets small. The sizzle fizzles, and before we know it, we're back in the prison called "I Want"—consumed with coveting. We would be wise to listen to rapper The Notorious B.I.G., who said, "Mo Money Mo Problems."

The verb *covet* sometimes appears in this sequence: see, covet, take, die. For example, a man named Achan in Joshua 7:21 says: "I *saw* among the spoil a beautiful cloak from Shinar, and 200 shekels of silver, and a bar of gold weighing 50 shekels, then I *coveted* them and *took* them" (ESV, emphasis added). Later in Joshua 7, Achan and his family die. See, covet, take, die. The sequence most famously appears in Genesis 3:6: "When the woman *saw* that the tree was good for food, and that it was a delight to the eyes, she *coveted* it for gaining wisdom, then she *took* and ate it" (ESV, emphasis added). Adam and Eve then spiritually die.

In 2002, Jack Whittaker won a lottery worth $314 million. After paying Uncle Sam, Whittaker took home $83 million. He gave millions away and even bought a house and car for the woman who sold him the winning ticket.

Then his life began falling apart.

Thieves broke into Whittaker's car and stole $500,000 in cash. A young man died in his home from a drug overdose. His granddaughter was reported missing and was later found dead. Whittaker was arrested for DUI and sued by a casino for bouncing $1.5 million in checks. His marriage ended in divorce. Jack Whittaker got remarried and ran two struggling businesses. Each week, he spent $600 on lottery tickets, trying to regain his lost wealth.

If left unchecked, coveting kills.

Mine

Having survived the toddler years—three different times—the following Toddler Property Laws bring back memories. "If I like it, it's mine. If it's in my hand, it's mine. If I can take it from you, it's mine. If I had it a little while ago, it's mine. It must never appear to be yours in any way because it is always and forevermore mine!" A famous proverb put it this way, "The heart wants what it wants." Translated? "I want it all to be mine!"

What's the leading cause of coveting? Here are some hints. It launched in 2004. It's a two-syllable word. Today it has over one billion users. It's called Facebook. Facebook has created a new level of coveting.

We're scrolling through our Facebook newsfeed and see someone from our high school class driving a new BMW. Next, we see someone from our hometown vacationing in Hawaii—for the 117th time. Then, we see that perfect family of five, so happy, so together, so tanned—so *not* my family!

There's nothing wrong with wanting something. Coveting, though, isn't just wanting something; it's a desire strong enough to take another's life, or house, or wife, or anything that belongs to our neighbor. Coveting says, "I'll do anything to get that. I'll break any commandment, any statute, any ordinance, any law—just to get what I want." See. Covet. Take. Die.

When we covet our neighbor's trophy spouse, it brings death to marital joy. When we covet each other's skills, intellect, popularity, family connections—you name it—it brings death to inner peace. When we covet our neighbor's Rolex watch, looks—pick your poison—it brings death to our relationship with Jesus.

Don't tune me out because of what I'm about to write. Coveting is blasphemy. Blasphemy? Yes, blasphemy because coveting accuses God of being unfair. Coveting is blasphemy because it says, "God, You made a mistake by giving that person that gift and withholding it from me. God, You don't know what You're doing. God, if You would just let me run the universe, everything would be so much better!" We can't build a life of faith on a foundation that doubts God's goodness and wisdom.

When coveting, this is what we need to say: "God, in Your perfect wisdom and sovereignty, You gave that person exactly what You want that person to have. God, in Your perfect wisdom and sovereignty, You gave me exactly what You want me to have."

Aren't you tired of envious "when and then" thinking? "When I get a house like his, then I'll be happy." "When I land a job like hers, then I'll be happy." "When we have a bank balance like theirs, then we'll be happy." Happiness isn't getting what we want; happiness is enjoying who we have. Who do we have? Who do we have that conquers coveting every time?

Jesus.

THE IMPLICATIONS OF THE TEN COMMANDMENTS

Following the Ten Commandments, Yahweh's further instructions in Exodus 20:22–23:33 comment on them. This section of Exodus begins and ends with an emphasis on worship. That is, God commands Israel to worship Him with proper altars and to forsake false gods of silver and gold (Exodus 20:22–23). He then orders His people not to become enslaved to the gods of the Canaanites and never make a covenant with them (Exodus 23:24, 32–33). This part of Exodus reiterates an essential truth—the First Commandment is the cornerstone commandment.

Yahweh's goal in Exodus 20:22–23:33 is also to give Israel a vision for living as equals—thus commenting on Commandments 4–10. The high and mighty are no different than the weak and lowly. Of note is that secular and sacred laws regarding new life with Yahweh appear side by side. For instance, Moses addresses the sin of taking bribes (Exodus

23:8) then shifts to Israel's three yearly worship festivals (Exodus 23:14). Following Yahweh consists of one piece—a seamless web encompassing all of life. To compartmentalize invites disaster.

The Gospel is the power for walking in God's ways. Exodus 22:21, 29 and 23:9, 15 announce Israel's divine deliverance from Egypt. God also commands the Israelites to remember their toil and hardship in Egypt—not to gain sympathy from others, but to identify with those in need.

SHOWING MERCY

Another theme within this section that expands upon the Fourth through the Tenth Commandments is God's mandate to show mercy. Here's one example: "You shall not mistreat any widow or fatherless child. If you do mistreat them, and they cry out to Me, I will surely hear their cry, and My wrath will burn, and I will kill you with the sword, and your wives shall become widows and your children fatherless" (Exodus 22:22–24 ESV). Woe!

Israel could become another Egypt! In fact, any nation, any business, any institution, any person, could turn into a demanding, slave-driving pharaoh. Call it Egypt-déjà vu or Egypt 2.2. *Just don't let it happen to you.*

HOLY WAR

Exodus 23 concludes with Yahweh's instructions concerning warfare. He says, "I will set your border from the Red Sea to the Sea of the Philistines, and from the wilderness to the Euphrates, for I will give the inhabitants of the land into your hand, and you shall drive them out before you" (Exodus 23:31 ESV).

Israel fights sixty battles from the exodus (1441 BC) to the Babylonian exile (587 BC). About one-fourth of these campaigns contain clear references to what the Bible calls in Hebrew *herem*. For instance, Moses commands the people, "When the LORD your God has delivered them [Israel's enemies] over to you, and you defeat them, then you must destroy them totally [*herem*]. You shall make no covenant with them and show them no mercy" (Deuteronomy 7:2).

"Show them no mercy"? How does this square with my discussion above about just that—showing mercy? How does "destroy them totally" comport with New Testament admonitions like "love your enemies" (Matthew 5:44 ESV), "turn the other cheek" (Luke 6:29), "walk the extra mile" (Matthew 5:41), and "bless, and do not curse" (Romans 12:14 ESV)? If genocide and ethnic cleansing are morally reprehensible in the twenty-first century AD, wasn't this also wrong in the fifteenth BC? How are the atrocities of our day—sometimes done in the name of religion—different from the killing of Canaanite men, women, and children?

It's tempting to respond, "Don't you get it? That's the Old Testament—all blood and guts! Thank God we're in the New Testament era and can ignore these ancient warfare texts!" Yet, by marginalizing Israel's holy war texts, we can no longer affirm with Paul that all of Israel's Scriptures are "profitable for teaching, for reproof, for correction, and for training in righteousness" (2 Timothy 3:16 ESV). What's more, if we drive a wedge between the Old and New Testaments, we will overlook the fact that "the LORD is a man of war" (Exodus 15:3 ESV), but so is Jesus, who "judges and makes war," is "clothed in a robe dipped in blood," and out of whose mouth "comes a sharp sword with which to strike down the nations" (Revelation 19:11–15 ESV). Further, the Savior calls down curses upon His enemies (e.g., Matthew 11:20–24; 23:13–39; Mark 11:14), as does Paul (Galatians 1:8–9).

But back to the Old Testament. Why the Canaanites? Was it because they were always raising Cain at night? Hardly. God promised Abraham, "I will bless those who bless you, and the one who curses you I will curse" (Genesis 12:3). Canaanites, then, are one example of God protecting His people from their foes. He curses them, and others as well. The list of Israel's adversaries is long—Philistines, Assyrians, and the big, bad Babylonians. Our list includes *the* enemy, Satan, as well as our last enemy, death.

No doubt, there's discontinuity between the *herem* texts in the Old Testament and new life in Christ. We are never called upon to resort to physical violence (Matthew 26:52). *Never.* Love and forgiveness are always our first responses to adversaries. But what's our response to sustained violence and unthinkable acts of hatred against believers? Martin Luther puts it this way: "We should pray that our enemies be converted and become our friends and, if not, that their doing and designing be bound to fail and have no success and that their persons perish rather than the Gospel and the kingdom of Christ."[4]

What's Luther saying? We're in a battle, but not with "flesh and blood" (Ephesians 6:12 ESV). Rather, our fight is "against the rulers, against the authorities, against the cosmic powers over this present darkness" (Ephesians 6:12 ESV). A *spiritual* war is going on. It's a battle of opposing powers with eternal consequences. In this war, the baptized experience terror, traitors, and triumphs.

Behind every Old Testament Canaanite, Moabite, Edomite, and the like, is *the* enemy—Satan himself. While Israel fought evil with spears, clubs, and arrows, "the weapons of our warfare are not of the flesh but have divine power to destroy strongholds" (2 Corinthians 10:4 ESV). The Gospel is how we put the devil to flight, rebuke his accusations, and call people out of darkness and into Christ's marvelous light. Our weapon? "The sword of the Spirit, which is the word of God" (Ephesians 6:17 ESV).

---

4 Ewald M. Plass, comp., *What Luther Says: A Practical In-Home Anthology for the Active Christian* (St. Louis: Concordia Publishing House, 1959), 1100.

CHAPTER 13

Come, Let Us Worship the Lord: Exodus 24–31

Exalt the L ORD our God, and worship at
His holy mountain; for the L ORD our God is holy! (Psalm
99:9 ESV)

In the Book of Exodus, freedom isn't an abstract idea. It's not a positive virtue floating in the air. And freedom doesn't describe autonomous people making independent choices. In the Book of Exodus, freedom means worship—worship Yahweh who abides in His tabernacle.

Moses asks God: "How will I know that You are with me?" God answers: "When you have brought the people out of Egypt, you will *worship* God on this mountain" (Exodus 3:12). A frequent refrain in Exodus is, "Let My people go so that they may *worship* Me" (e.g., Exodus 7:16; 8:1). Exodus 4:23 states it slightly differently: "Let My son go, so he may *worship* Me."

Exodus 24–31 takes up God's goal of worship. His gift is singular—access.

CERTAIN VICTORY

After the laws and regulations in Exodus 20–23, God shows up in Exodus 24—in stunning and spectacular ways. Moses and Aaron, Nadab and Abihu (two of Aaron's sons), and the seventy elders of Israel see Yahweh. "They beheld God, and ate and drank" (Exodus 24:11 ESV).

Let me illustrate the meaning of this vision by going back to the 1980 Winter Olympics.

Hockey fans! Remember the "Miracle on Ice"? When a rag-tag group of amateur U.S. hockey players defeated the "invincible" team of U.S.S.R. pucksters? Watching the game on television, many viewers thought they were seeing the game live. They weren't. It was tape-delayed. Those in the know had heard—probably on the radio—that the U.S. had won the game. These people, confident of the outcome, didn't sweat when the U.S.S.R. scored a goal or when a U.S. skater landed in the penalty box. The victory was a done deal.

That's what's going on with this vision in Exodus 24. *Victory is assured.* As the Israelite leaders eat and drink in God's presence, they get a foretaste of the future heavenly banquet—heaven comes down to earth! On the Last Day, God will triumph over every enemy. Christ gives a similar vision to Peter, James, and John—also on a mountain. It happened when Jesus appeared in divine splendor on the Mount of Transfiguration—along with the glorified Moses and Elijah. The message? "Thanks be to God, who gives us the victory through our Lord Jesus Christ" (1 Corinthians 15:57 ESV).

God sees us, frazzled about the final score, and says something like this: "You can take a deep breath and relax. It may look dire and desperate, but I've defeated death and every enemy. Most assuredly, even *now* you have access to the final victory. Heaven comes down to earth through the Divine Service where Gospel gifts are freely given!"

WORSHIP THE LORD

Israel's elders—the ones beholding the victorious vision in Exodus 24—first appear in Exodus 3:16. This group of seventy is present at other crucial junctures in the book—the Passover (Exodus 12:21), when Moses draws water from a rock (Exodus 17:5–6), when Moses needs help with legal matters (Exodus 18:12), and at Mount Sinai (Exodus 19:7). In every case, the leading men are passive. They follow Moses, who in chapter 24 functions as a priest and worship leader.

Worship also appears at important points in the book (Exodus 4:31; 12:27; 15:1–21; 18:12). Exodus 24 provides additional insights into Israel's life of singing and celebration. Set after detailed laws and regulations in chapters 20–23, it's striking that God wants the Israelites to focus on Him. The laws are important. Yahweh is more important. It's Israel's relationship with God that provides motivation to follow divine teaching.

Exodus 24:1 states, "Then [God] said to Moses, 'Come up to the LORD, you and Aaron, Nadab, and Abihu, and seventy of the elders of Israel, and worship from afar.'" The gist of this verse is "Come near to Me, but don't get too close!" Israel's leaders don't have immediate access to God's presence. There are far too many barriers between Yahweh and them.

Yahweh is the holy, infinite, eternal, all-powerful, all-knowing, and only God. He's in a league all His own. Sure, He has descended upon Mount Sinai in a cloud and in glory, but Israel's leaders must still "worship from afar." Why?

The Bible says people are born dead in transgressions and sins (Ephesians 2:1). The Bible says that by nature we are God's enemies (Romans 5:10). The Bible says we're fading leaves (Psalm 103), empty cisterns (Jeremiah 2:13), and flowers quickly fading (1 Peter 1:24). The Bible shows repeatedly that we're rebels, prodigals, prone to wander, hard-hearted, selfish, and lost sheep.

Moses gets to come near God because he's the mediator, the go-between, between Yahweh and Israel. "Moses alone shall come near to the LORD, but the others shall not come near, and the people shall not come up with him" (Exodus 24:2 ESV). Moses will bridge the gap between Israel's leaders and God. To accent this, Exodus 24 describes his ascent to Sinai by employing the Hebrew verb for "go up" seven times. *Moses had access.*

ACCESS

A few years ago, I called to check on my car insurance. This is what I got: "For a new policy, press one. For an existing policy, press two. For the weather in Anchorage, Alaska, press three. To speak with a claim's adjuster from outer banks of Pago Pago, press four." For a half-hour, I was stuck in the Bermuda Triangle called computerized telephone services. I just wanted access!

As a child, I remember the first time I watched the St. Louis Cardinals play baseball at Busch Stadium. It was 1968, and the Cards fielded the likes of Orlando Cepeda, Julian Javier, Mike Shannon, Tim McCarver, Lou Brock, Curt Flood, and Bob Gibson. I wanted to tell these Cardinals that I had their baseball cards. I wanted to get their autographs. But our seats were three miles west of Kansas City. I just wanted access!

Access to God's presence comes only through blood.

BLOOD

Satan knows about God's gift of access. That's why he whispers, "Access is for others. Guilt is for you." Wrong! Blood breaks down every barrier between God and people. "Moses took the blood and threw it on the people and said, 'Behold the blood of the covenant that the LORD has made with you in accordance with all these words'" (Exodus 24:8 ESV). Blood is how the Israelites get out of Egypt—the Passover lamb's blood. Blood is also how the Israelites gain access to God.

And what amazing access it is! The Israelite leaders see God's feet and the pedestal He's standing on. "There was under His feet *as it were* a pavement of sapphire stone, *like* the very heaven for clearness" (Exodus 24:10 ESV, emphasis added). The expressions "as it were" and "like" are similes. Moses employs them because the vision is too overwhelming to describe literally. Divine pavement is similar to sapphire—a transparent blue gem. The second simile corresponds with this first one. The place of God's abode, heaven, is also blue in color.

Blood, though, is no simile. Literal blood provides access—for Moses and crew, as well as for you. I'm talking now about Christ's blood. Calvary wasn't a sudden tragedy. Christ's execution wasn't God's knee-jerk reaction to a world spinning out of control. No. Revelation 13:8 states, "The Lamb was slain from the creation of the world."

On Good Friday, the Jews wanted Barabbas. Herod wanted a show. Pilate wanted out. Caiaphas wanted death. The soldiers wanted to have some fun. And the executioners? All they wanted was Christ's blood.

Their strategy was singular: beat Jesus within an inch of death and then stop. With His back lacerated by lashes, they shove the crossbeam on His shoulders. When He comes to Calvary, they nail Him to wood. And there He hangs. "Behold, the Lamb of God, who takes away the sin of the world!" (John 1:29 ESV). All is not right with the world because God is in His heaven. All is right with the world because Christ was on His cross.

Hebrews 10:19 is an apt application of Exodus 24:1–11. "Therefore, brothers, we have confidence to enter the Most Holy Place by the blood of Jesus." The word *confidence* appears thirty-one times in the Greek New Testament. From Matthew to Revelation, the message is singular. The blood of Jesus gives us confidence to live, confidence to speak, confidence when we suffer, confidence when we pray, and even confidence when we die. And by the blood of Jesus, we have confident access to the throne of Almighty God.

Unlimited access. This is Yahweh's gift to Moses, Aaron, Nadab, Abihu, and the seventy elders of Israel. They see the God of Israel and they eat and drink—a preview of Christ's real presence in His Holy Supper.

The Last Supper

It took three years to complete. It's one of the most recognizable paintings in the world, with its image found on carpets, carvings, and multiple canvases. With lifelike facial expressions, unable to be captured by anyone else at the time, the 15 × 29-foot painting became an instant masterpiece. I'm describing *The Last Supper*.

When Leonardo da Vinci was forty-three years old, the Duke of Milan asked him to paint the scene. The artist worked three years on the assignment, grouping the disciples into threes with two groups on either side of the central figure, Jesus.

When the masterpiece was finished, da Vinci said to a friend, "Look at it and give me your honest opinion."

"It's wonderful!" exclaimed the friend. "The cup is so real I can't take my eyes off of it!"

Immediately, da Vinci took a brush and painted over the cup. As he did so, he exclaimed, "Nothing shall detract from the figure of Christ!"

Nothing shall detract from Jesus. And why is that? Because Jesus was betrayed. Let that soak in. Jesus was betrayed. "For I received from the Lord what I also delivered to you, that the Lord Jesus on the night when He was *betrayed* took bread" (1 Corinthians 11:23 ESV, emphasis added). The Words of Institution for the Holy Supper begin, "On the night when He was betrayed" (Small Catechism, Sacrament of the Altar). We hear these words so often that we really don't hear them.

Hear them again, as though for the very first time. "On the night when He was *betrayed.*" Betrayed by Judas, one of the Twelve. Betrayed for thirty pieces of silver. Betrayed with a kiss—imagine that! Betrayed in a garden east of Jerusalem called Gethsemane. "Nothing shall detract from Jesus!" Why? Jesus was betrayed for us.

For us. When spoken by God, these are two of the most powerful words on the planet. God isn't against us. God isn't our opponent. God isn't our enemy. God is for us. Not just for her and him, for those and them. God's love is intensely personal. It's for us!

God is for us, in the past. "The Lord brought *us* out of Egypt with a mighty hand and an outstretched arm" (Deuteronomy 26:8 ESV, emphasis added). The Last Supper begins with Jesus reviewing this exodus story. Yahweh used lamb's blood on doorframes to save *us* from the angel of death. God led *us* out of Egypt with a pillar of cloud by day and a pillar of fire by night. God defeated Pharaoh's horses and chariots in the Red Sea while *we* walked through on dry ground.

This is still our story!

Did you know that since its completion in 1498, *The Last Supper* has been falling apart? Leonardo da Vinci—always the inventor—tried employing new materials for the painting. Instead of using the customary wet plaster, he used dry plaster, which worked well artistically but not well for the painting's sustainability. Experts have been trying to restore the original ever since.

How fitting! The Lord's Supper is for people whose lives—like da Vinci's painting—are always falling apart. In this life, we never get it right. But we have the Gospel. God is for us in the past. He performed a Red Sea–like deliverance for all the baptized.

God is for us in the present. Referring to the Lord's Supper, Paul records these words of Jesus: "Do this in *remembrance* of Me" (1 Corinthians 11:24 ESV, emphasis added). Remembrance helps us recall our story—our exodus story. Remembrance also brings Calvary to us—God's current mighty act. What do I mean?

As I've pointed out several times, the Hebrew word rendered "remember" denotes a fresh presentation, a reactualization, God's current action. In the Lord's Supper, God acts. He delivers Christ's true body and blood in the here and now. Holy Communion is the opposite of remembering a dead man. *Holy Communion is a meal with a Man who lives.* Because of His resurrection victory, Jesus is present in, with, and under the bread and wine with His true body and blood.

When the Savior says, "This is My body. . . . this is My blood" (Matthew 26:26–28 ESV)—*is* means "is." *Is* doesn't mean "signifies," "represents," or "symbolizes." The latter view didn't arise until the eleventh century. It was promoted by a man named Berengar of Tours whose Latin watchwords were *confugere ad rationem*—"flee to reason." No. Flee to Scripture! "This is!"

"This is My body . . . for you" (1 Corinthians 11:24 ESV). And how we need it!

In Matthew 5:13, Jesus tells His disciples, "You are the salt of the earth" (ESV). Prompted by this verse, da Vinci painted a spilled salt-shaker next to the elbow of Judas Iscariot. Judas lost his salt because of greed. We lose our salt because of greed. The Lord's Supper is for people who lose their salt!

The artist drives home our need for forgiveness in another way. He chooses herring for the disciples' meal. In his northern Italian dialect, the word for herring was *renga*. *Renga*—in da Vinci's northern Italian dialect—also describes someone who denies religion. Peter denied Jesus in the high priest's courtyard. The disciples denied Jesus in Gethsemane. *Renga!* All of them! *Renga!* All of us! The Lord's Supper is for people who have denied Jesus and need to taste His redeeming love.

Holy Communion announces baptismal redemption in our past, forgiveness for our present guilt, and hope for our future. "For as often as you eat this bread and drink the cup, you proclaim the Lord's death *until He comes*" (1 Corinthians 11:26 ESV). We eat bread, participating in Christ's body. We drink wine, participating in Christ's blood. But only until He comes.

The artist includes a beautiful blue sky in the background of his masterpiece—it points toward heaven. The Lord's Supper is a foretaste of the feast to come. When Jesus returns to restore all things, He will make us perfect. At the heavenly banquet, we will no longer be downcast because we can't share the Lord's Supper with those we love. In heaven, God will gather us together with angels, archangels, and all the company of heaven. We will see Jesus face-to-face, and He will fill us and all believers with unspeakable joy that will never end!

Just like the Israelite leaders in Exodus 24, God invites us to eat and drink in His presence. Both meals preview the Lamb's high feast in the new Jerusalem. And if that doesn't light your fire, you're working with wet wood!

GOD CONSECRATES THE ISRAELITES
TO BE MISSIONARIES

Exodus 24 offers amazing insights into our final victory. Exodus 24 offers amazing insights into our access to God—particularly through Holy Communion. Exodus 24 also offers amazing insights into mission.

"The blood of the covenant" referenced in Exodus 24:8 doesn't establish God's relationship with Israel. If you're thinking back to the discussion on Exodus 19, then you're on the right track. That's where God also calls His people to be missionaries.

In like manner, the focus of Exodus 24:3–8 is commissioning the Israelites to be Gospel-tellers. How so? There are only two other instances in the Old Testament where blood is applied to people. The first is when Aaron and his sons are ordained, and blood is placed upon their ears, thumbs, and big toes—then blood is sprinkled on them and their garments (Exodus 29:20–21; Leviticus 8:23–24, 30). The second time blood is applied to people appears in the cleansing of a leper (Leviticus 14:7, 14) to declare him clean (Leviticus 14:7, 9, 20).

In both instances, blood moves people into a different realm. It moves men from a common status into the priesthood and lepers from unclean to clean. In like manner, the blood ritual in Exodus 24 changes Israel's status from common to holy. The nation is now a holy nation—commissioned for its evangelistic task, thus comporting with Exodus 19:6, "You shall be to Me a kingdom of priests and a holy nation" (ESV).

Exodus 19:3–8 and 24:3–8, then, say the same thing—God saved Israel so the nation might spearhead His missionary movement in the world, so all people may gain access to Gospel gifts. Just as Israel's priests were set apart through liturgy in Leviticus 8, the people—as a royal priesthood—are consecrated through liturgical rites to serve God by serving the world.

The Israelites enthusiastically embrace their vocation, even as they echo Exodus 19:8 word for word. "All that the LORD has spoken we will do" (Exodus 24:7 ESV). The next time the people speak in the book, they say to Aaron, "Up, make us gods who shall go before us. As for this Moses, the man who brought us up out of the land of Egypt, we do not know what has become of him" (Exodus 32:1 ESV). That's what we call a short-lived commitment! Hosea 6:4 provides the best commentary: "Your love is like a morning cloud, like the dew that goes early away" (ESV).

God's Presence

Following a heavenly meal and the reaffirmation of Israel's vocation as missionaries, Moses goes farther up Sinai to experience God's presence (Exodus 24:12–18)—a major theme in the book. *Access to God's presence, though, is a double-edged sword.*

The Book of Exodus begins at a time of God's absence. The Israelites are living in slavery and intense suffering. Moses suddenly appears after forty years in the Midian desert and BAM—after ten plagues, God's presence delivers Israel. Restored nearness between God and His people—by setting apart Israel from other nations and dwelling in their midst—is Yahweh's goal (Exodus 19:5–6; 29:45–46).

However, in a dramatic turn of events, after constructing a golden calf to worship, chastened Israel weeps at the news that Yahweh will not go to the Promised Land with them (Exodus 33:4). Moses protests, "How shall it be known that I have found favor in Your sight, I and Your people? Is it not by Your going with us, so that we are distinct, I and Your people, from every other people on the face of the earth?" (Exodus 33:16 ESV).

To have Yahweh as God means to be with Him. Recall the fundamental covenant promise in the book: "I will be your God" (Exodus 6:7 ESV)—which is ultimately realized with divine presence filling the tabernacle (Exodus 40:34–38). By the end of Exodus, Yahweh resides with Israel. It's wonderful and good and life-giving.

There's another side to this coin, though. The Book of Exodus also teaches that if people come too close to God's presence, it may be a dreadful and deadly encounter. Consider these examples:

- Moses at the burning bush (Exodus 3:5–6)

- Yahweh's encounter with Moses in the night (Exodus 4:24–26)

- Yahweh's being "in the midst of the earth" during the plagues (Exodus 8:22 ESV)

- God's going "out in the midst of Egypt" in the tenth plague (Exodus 11:4–6 ESV)

- The mandated barricades around Sinai when Israel arrives (Exodus 19:12, 21–22)

- Yahweh's terror-arousing presence, which will drive out the Canaanites (Exodus 23:27–30)

- The prescribed consecration, clothing, and manner for the priests to draw near before Yahweh, lest they die (Exodus 28:42–43; 30:20–21)

- Yahweh's threat following the golden calf that if He were to go about amid His stiff-necked people for a moment, He would surely destroy them (Exodus 33:3, 5)

Add these verses together and what do we have? "It is a fearful thing to fall into the hands of the living God" (Hebrews 10:31 ESV). *Shed blood is our only hope.*

A LONG, DARK HALLWAY

God states that Israel will know (1) "I am Yahweh their God who brought them out from the land of Egypt" and (2) "in order to dwell in their midst" (Exodus 29:46). Both statements support a twofold division of Exodus. The initial narrative arc of rescue is followed by a second narrative arc with Yahweh dwelling with Israel in the tabernacle.

With Exodus 25, then, the book's rock-'em, sock-'em, gasp-and-gulp narrative comes to a screeching halt. We go from a death-defying story to description-filled architectural plans. This is a sudden jolt!

The second part of Exodus reminds me of a story.

"Daddy?" A little hand touched my forehead. I opened my eyes, which were fixed on the digital clock by my bed. It read 1:45—that would be *a.m.*

"What do you want, Jonathan?"

"I need to go to the bathroom."

Our home had just been remodeled and the bathroom was now down a long hallway. When you're four years old and wandering around the house at night, a new hallway looks five miles long with multiple side rooms where giants are waiting to jump out and eat little kids for late-night snacks. Jonathan had never been this way before.

Neither had Israel. God made a pledge to Moses to bring them into the Promised Land (Exodus 3:8). This hallway, however, looked five miles long with multiple side rooms where giants—Canaanites, Hittites, Amorites, Perizzites, Hivites, and Jebusites—were waiting to jump out and eat the Israelites for late-night snacks. And don't forget to add the mosquito (and various other bug) bites!

God knows long hallways aren't conquered by promising, "I'll be with you in spirit." Dark hallways need real presence. And real presence is what God delivers through His tabernacle. Heaven again comes down to earth!

GOD'S GIFT OF THE TABERNACLE

While God came down to call Moses from the burning bush (Exodus 3:8) and descended upon Sinai to give Moses the Ten Commandments (Exodus 19:18) because He wanted to live among Israel permanently, He told Moses, "Let them [the Israelites] make Me a sanctuary, that I may dwell in their midst" (Exodus 25:8 ESV). The tabernacle/sanctuary/tent of meeting—these are synonymous terms in the book—was patterned after God's heavenly house (Exodus 25:9, 40) and allowed Yahweh to take up enduring residence with His people.

The story in Exodus, therefore, moves from the Israelites building cities that glorify Pharaoh to the Israelites building a tabernacle that glorifies Yahweh. True, worship appears in Exodus 12–13 with several liturgical rites. A song is sung in Exodus 15:1–18. Moses and others eat and drink in God's presence in Exodus 24:9–12. However, the most obvious links to worship in Exodus take place when God commands Moses to build a tabernacle. The structure will end up being about thirty feet long, ten feet wide, and fifteen feet high. It will serve as a portable place where God will live among the people of Israel (Exodus 25:8; 29:45, 46).

Throughout Israel's forty-year travels in the wilderness, priests moved the tabernacle from place to place. Wherever it was erected, God's glory was in it (e.g., Numbers 14:10; 16:19, 42; 20:6). Asaph the psalmist calls it "the tent where [God] dwelt among mankind" (Psalm 78:60 ESV).

Out of the ninety-three occurrences of the word *holy* in Exodus, seventy-eight are concerned with the tabernacle—mostly in Exodus 25–40. *Holy* in Hebrew primarily means to be distinct, different, set apart. The Song of the Sea makes this clear: "Who is like You, O LORD, among the gods? Who is like You, majestic in *holiness,* awesome in glorious deeds, doing wonders?" (Exodus 15:11 ESV, emphasis added). This is Moses' message throughout the book—whether it's divine power demonstrated through plagues or the tabernacle's sequencing of fabrics and metals.

Yahweh is in a category all His own.

In two different sections of the book—Exodus 25–31 (the blueprint) and Exodus 35–39 (the building)—with painstaking detail, Moses describes items like beams, pegs, stands, curtains, and lampstands. He even includes recipes for incense and oil.

Details!

Had we been on the British coast in 1845, we would have seen two ships boarded by 138 of England's finest sailors. Their task? Chart the Northwest Passage around the Canadian Arctic to the Pacific Ocean. The captain, Sir John Franklin, hoped the journey would be the turning point in Arctic exploration. History shows it was. Not because of its success, but because of its utter failure. The ships never returned. Every crew member died. Those who later followed the expedition's path learned this all-important lesson: pay attention to the details.

The captain, Sir John Franklin, didn't. Though the voyage was projected to last three years, he only carried a twelve-day supply of coal for his auxiliary steam engines. What Franklin lacked in fuel, he made up for with entertainment. Each ship carried more than 1,200 books, china place settings, expensive wine goblets, and sterling silver flatware. Was the crew planning for an Arctic expedition or a Caribbean cruise?

God's plan in Exodus 25–31 includes details. Lots and lots of details! Moses writes about measurements, fabrics, colors, and precious stones. Little wonder that this section of Exodus can come across as dull, dry, tedious, and monotonous. We may read it only to end up thinking, "This is completely irrelevant."

Not so!

Most of us are used to biblical truth conveyed through Christ's parables and Paul's principles. In Exodus 25–31, God's message is instead embedded in liturgical rituals. For instance, from the outside of the tabernacle to its innermost shrine—the Most Holy Place—fabric types and metals move from the mundane to the more precious. As materials and workmanship grow more costly and involved, the objects they represent become more important.

Consider the metals. They move from bronze to silver pillar bases to pure gold connected to the tabernacle's furniture and vessels (e.g., Exodus 25:11, 17; 37:2, 6, 11). Yahweh appears above the Mercy Seat on the ark of the covenant (Exodus 25:22; 30:6, 36); hence, this is where the most sophisticated workmanship and costly metals are located. Inside the tabernacle, most of the furnishings and appointments were pure gold (e.g., Exodus 25:24–31).

What's the lesson? God's presence is the most valuable gift Israel will ever have—more precious than gold. Gold is the first item mentioned for the tabernacle (Exodus 25:3), and gold will be mentioned another forty-six times in detailing the tabernacle furnishings and priestly vestments.

The curtains also demonstrate Yahweh's value (Exodus 26:1–14). The outermost curtains were "fine goatskin leather" or "the hide of sea porpoise, or dolphin." The innermost curtain consisted of "blue, purple, and scarlet thread with skillfully embroidered cherubim" (Exodus 26:1). The veil separating the Holy Place from the Most Holy Place was hung from hooks made of gold that were attached to four wooden posts overlaid with gold.

Moses describes three types of embroidery work. In Hebrew, they are called *hoseb, roqem,* and *oreg. Hoseb*—the most precise—mixes threads and works with figures like the cherubim (e.g., Exodus 26:1, 31; 29:5; 31:4; 38:23; 39:3, 5, 8, 20). *Roqem* employs different threads but doesn't involve figures (e.g., Exodus 26:36; 28:39; 38:18, 23). *Oreg,* as we might expect, only employs one kind of thread (e.g., Exodus 28:32; 39:22, 27). The work described with *hoseb* includes the veil of the Most Holy Place as well as the tabernacle curtains. The tabernacle's outer veil doesn't include cherubim, hence its weaving is described using *roqem.*

Do you see how Moses reinforces the First Commandment—with amazing detail? Access to Yahweh's presence is Israel's most valuable gift. And the people understood this. When faced with losing God's companionship after the golden calf debacle, the Israelites lament that to have the Promised Land without Yahweh would be next to worthless. They call it a "disastrous word" (Exodus 33:4 ESV).

Mount Sinai and the Tabernacle

The description of Mount Sinai in Exodus 19 provides a preview of Israel's tabernacle. Both have three distinct areas—each with its own level of access. The top of Sinai, where only Moses was allowed to appear (Exodus 19:20), comports with the tabernacle's Most Holy Place—a place where the high priest entered once a year on the Day of Atonement (Leviticus 16). In Sinai's second area, along with Moses, a limited number of people were permitted; "Aaron, Nadab, and Abihu, and seventy of the elders of Israel" (Exodus 24:1 ESV). The tabernacle's Holy Place aligns with this zone. Both were off-limits to everyone except a select few. Additionally, the mountain's base, where an altar for burnt offerings was located (Exodus 24:4–5), is similar to the tabernacle's outer court (Exodus 27:9–19), which was accessible to all Israelites. Another feature of both places is that breaching their borders warranted death. Finally, just as Yahweh descended in a cloud on Mount Sinai (Exodus 19:9, 16; 24:15–16, 18), so, too, at the end of the book He responds to the tabernacle's completion in the same way (Exodus 40:34–35).

The tabernacle, therefore, was a "movable Mount Sinai." After all, the Hebrew verb meaning "dwell"—from which the Hebrew word derives for *tabernacle*—primarily denotes "to tent" or move from location to location.

The Tabernacle's Backstory

Tabernaclelike structures appeared in Egyptian wall paintings as early as 3000–2800 BC. Most of the tabernacle's technology, therefore, was older than the pyramids. From another perspective, though, the tabernacle is as old as several events in the Book of Genesis. Consider these associations between Noah and Moses:

- Both find favor in God's eyes (Genesis 6:8; Exodus 33:12–17).

- Noah and Moses complete their building project just as God directed them (Genesis 6:22; Exodus 39:42–43).

- On the first day of the new year, Noah removes the ark's covering and the Israelites erect and dedicate the tabernacle (Genesis 8:13; Exodus 40:2).

- Both structures announce a new beginning after catastrophic moral collapses (Genesis 6:1–5; Exodus 32).

Here are several more Genesis-Exodus links vis-à-vis the tabernacle and creation:

1. The Spirit hovers over creation (Genesis 1:2), while God gives Bezalel and other tabernacle workers the Spirit to complete their work (Exodus 31:3).

2. Just as Yahweh created a world in which he would dwell (e.g., Genesis 3:8), Israel's craftsmen re-create a place for Yahweh to dwell (Exodus 40:34).

3. The dedication of the tabernacle occurred on New Year's Day (Exodus 40:2, 17), thus corresponding to the first day of creation.

4. Yahweh's directions to Moses come in seven movements (Exodus 25–31) that correspond to seven acts of Moses (Exodus 40:17–33), and these sevens are parallel to the seven days of creation (Genesis 1:2–2:3).

5. Both Genesis 2:1–2 and Exodus 31:17 express concern over keeping the Sabbath.

6. The sequence in Genesis 1–3 is creation, fall, and re-creation. This is mirrored in the tabernacle's blueprint (Exodus 25–31), Israel's fall (Exodus 32), and the tabernacle's construction (Exodus 33–40).

7. When Moses describes the Israelites completing the tabernacle (Exodus 39:32), he employs the same word used earlier to announce God's completion of creation (Genesis 2:2).

8. An act of blessing occurs in both Genesis 2:3 and Exodus 39:43.

These connections make it clear. The tabernacle is a partial recapturing of Eden, likened to the garden Yahweh planted (Numbers 24:5–6). Note these similarities:

- Both are places where Yahweh walks among His people (Genesis 3:8; Leviticus 26:11–13; Deuteronomy 23:14).

- The menorah (Exodus 25:31–35) has treelike qualities, evoking the trees in the Garden of Eden (Genesis 2:16–17).

- The entrance of both Eden and the tabernacle was from the east (Genesis 3:24; Exodus 27:13).

- Eden is guarded by cherubim (Genesis 3:24), who also guard the ark (Exodus 25:10–22).

- Aaron's ordination is a process that—like creation—takes seven days (Exodus 29:31–37).

The tabernacle is phase one of God's plan to re-create the fallen world. It will reach its pinnacle in Jesus, who came to tabernacle among us (John 1:14). God's final and ultimate plan in Christ is to live among His people in Edenic perfection. "Behold, the dwelling place of God is with man. He will dwell with them, and they will be His people, and God Himself will be with them as their God" (Revelation 21:3 ESV).

ME AND WILE E.

As a child, I loved to watch *Looney Tunes*'s Road Runner cartoons. (I still do as an adult!) In almost every scene, Wile E. Coyote furiously chases the Road Runner. The bird suddenly stops. Wile E. tries to, but he can't, so he goes over the cliff. Then we see his saucer-sized eyes. Wile E. goes down. Straight down!

Like Wile E., we've gone over the cliff. Like Wile E., we've found ourselves in thin air. And, like Wile E., we've had that "oh-boy-this-is-gonna-hurt" look on our face.

Why do we end up in such a mess? The Bible calls it sin. Sin? It's the attitude that says, "I don't really, desperately, seriously need Jesus. Life is just fine with an occasional worship service, an occasional prayer, an occasional spiritual thought." With this nonchalant attitude, it's just a matter of time before we go down. Straight down. Then it hurts—a lot!

But falls don't faze Wile E.—at least not fatally. In the next scene, Wile E. Coyote is using Acme dynamite and chasing the Road Runner—again. We don't recover like that. We get stuck on a rocky canyon floor, wondering if we'll ever get up and get out. Then what?

God tenderly invites us to embrace access to His healing and forgiveness. Exodus 25–27 details where these gifts are located—the ark of the covenant, the bread of the Presence, the golden lampstand and its oil, and the altar of bronze. Old Testament Means of Grace overflow through these treasures—Gospel gifts foreshadowing God's ultimate promises in Christ Jesus.

EXODUS 25–27

It's significant that the ark of the covenant is the first order of business (Exodus 25:10–22)—especially in light of the fact that the ark isn't built until the tabernacle is completed (Exodus 37:1–9).

The ark is the ultimate place of God's presence. Moses makes this clear in Numbers 10: "And whenever the ark set out, Moses said, 'Arise, O LORD, and let Your enemies be scattered, and let those who hate You flee before You.' And when it rested, he said, 'Return, O LORD, to the ten thousand thousands of Israel'" (Numbers 10:35–36). The ark doesn't represent Yahweh. Neither does it symbolize His presence. Yahweh is "in, with, and under" the ark. He's enthroned between the ark's cherubim (1 Samuel 4:4; 2 Samuel 6:2; Psalms 80:1; 99:1). The ark is God's footstool (1 Chronicles 28:2) and Jerusalem His throne (Jeremiah 3:17).

The ark of the covenant was forty-five inches long, twenty-seven inches wide, and twenty-seven inches high—constructed from acacia wood and overlaid with pure gold. The golden cherubim over the ark were positioned with their faces looking down as divine glory was above them (Exodus 25:18–20). Golden rings on the side, through which poles were inserted, enabled priests to carry the ark without touching it, which could be deadly (see 2 Samuel 6:5–7).

THE GARDEN OF EDEN

A tent divided into two rooms lay at the heart of Israel's tabernacle. The first room was the Holy Place. When priests entered it, they saw the golden seven-branched menorah. It looked like a tree.

Looking around, priests would then see beautiful tapestry made up of angels. Angels? Along with the tree of life? *The Most Holy Place reflected the Garden of Eden.* The cloud of God's glory resided there, above the ark of the covenant. The Mercy Seat was on top of the ark of the covenant. Once a year, on the high feast of the Day of Atonement, the high priest would have access by placing animal blood on the top of the Mercy Seat.

Hebrew authors sometimes put their main point in the middle—a key idea for understanding the importance of the Most Holy Place. Moses wrote five books, placing Leviticus in the middle. Additionally, there are thirty-seven sections in Leviticus, with Leviticus 16 as the eighteenth section. What does that mean? Leviticus 16 is in the middle of the Pentateuch, making access to the Most Holy Place vis-à-vis blood on the Day of Atonement Moses' central and most important teaching. Access to the Garden of Eden was back in play!

But the Day of Atonement was partial. The Day of Atonement was preliminary. The Day of Atonement was predictive. It was just a shadow. Wouldn't it be great to have the substance? Well, here it is!

THE SUBSTANCE

When Jesus was baptized, heaven was opened, giving us access. "When [Jesus] came up out of the water, immediately He saw the heavens being *torn* open and the Spirit descending on Him like a dove" (Mark 1:10 ESV, emphasis added).

Mark uses the verb *torn* two times in his Gospel: when Christ is baptized and when Christ dies. "The curtain of the temple [60 feet in height, 30 feet in width and four inches thick] was *torn* in two, from top to bottom" (Mark 15:38). When Jesus shed His blood on the cross, the veil was torn. At long last—not just the high priest on the Day of Atonement but all believers have access!

That deep longing to reconnect with what we lost in the Garden of Eden? It won't be fulfilled when we party as hard as we can. It won't happen when we laugh as hard as we can. It won't happen when we work as hard as we can, make money as hard as we can, or live in a land of make-believe as hard as we can.

I invite you to come out of the shadows and live in reality. Jesus lets us off the hook for sin—that's forgiveness. Jesus also lets us into His presence—that's access. Jesus lets us into the Most Holy Place; into the Garden of Eden; into the loving arms of the Father; into the full power of the Holy Spirit, into the glory, the closeness, and fellowship with our Creator.

Are you under the gun at work? Now you have access. Do you have more to do than is humanly possible? Now you have access. Do your children make a piranha hour out of the dinner hour? Now you have access. Do people take more than they give? Do you have teenagers who won't listen? Students who won't try? Employees who won't work? Do you have hurts and hang-ups that cause untold hardship?

Hear the good news. You have access to the King of kings and the Lord of lords. *Jesus.* Death is defeated. The sacrifice complete. The veil torn. Paradise—*paradise*—restored forevermore!

You're not too old. You're not too sinful, too broken, or too messed up. And you're not too far gone. God welcomes you into His loving presence. I invite you to celebrate with David, "O Lord I love the habitation of Your house and the place where Your glory dwells" (Psalm 26:8 ESV).

CHAPTER 14

The Golden Calf: Exodus 32

They exchanged the glory of God for the image of an ox
that eats grass. They forgot God, their Savior, who had
done great things in Egypt. (Psalm 106:20–21 ESV)

You're still reading this book after the last chapter. Miracles still happen! I'm glad you're still with me. I was nervous after writing about the tabernacle—with its attention to so many details. I had this vision running through my mind of you reading chapter 13, going to your couch, turning up the television, devouring two bags of potato chips, drinking three cans of soda, and then yelling at no one in particular, "It don't matter no more. It just don't matter!" But you look good. You look really good! Are you ready for more?

STUCK IN SAND

It was the annual Lessing family vacation—version 2006. We were in Florida and couldn't wait to hit the beach. Then it happened. Just north of Daytona Beach, we saw the ocean. Everyone said, "Dad, take a left turn and let's hit the beach!" I did what any good dad would do. I took a left turn so we could hit the beach!

We hit the beach, alright, but we also hit some sand—some very deep sand. Everyone lurched forward. Four sets of eyes glared at me. A lesser man might have told everyone to get out and push the van back onto the pavement. Not me. No sirree! I would get us out the manly way. I hit the accelerator, full throttle. The van didn't budge. Neither did I. I hit the accelerator again, confident that we'd get out.

The result? We ended up going deeper and deeper in the sand. My children blurted out, "Dad, what were you thinking?" That was the problem. I wasn't. We were stuck with no way out.

Aaron knows. Aaron, Moses' older brother, knows what it feels like to be stuck in sand. He took a wrong turn. Then he got stuck. Then Aaron hit the accelerator and ended up digging himself and the Israelites into a huge hole.

Aaron—Israel's first high priest—unravels everything Yahweh and Moses accomplish in Exodus 24. For example, Exodus 24:4–5 describes Moses rising "early" to offer "burnt offerings" and "peace offerings" (ESV). Exodus 32:6 states, "They rose up early the next day and offered burnt offerings and brought peace offerings" (ESV). Additionally, Moses, Aaron, Nadab, Abihu, and the seventy elders participated in a covenant meal (Exodus 24:11). In like manner, Exodus 32:6 continues with words describing another meal: "the people sat down to eat and drink and rose up to play" (ESV). The wheels fall off when feasting leads to "playing." The term suggests sexual activity in Genesis 26:8 and 39:14 and 17. Paul confirms what happened at Aaron's feast of the golden calf. The Israelites indulged in sexual immorality (1 Corinthians 10:7–8).

BREAKING THE SIXTH COMMANDMENT

Like it or not, in a crisis the IRS knows exactly what to do. Their handbook states, "During a state of national emergency, the essential functions of the IRS will be as follows: assessing, collecting, and recording taxes." While everyone panics, the IRS knows exactly what to do. Get our money!

When faced with the huge crisis of not having Moses, Aaron and the Israelites have no idea what to do—so they build a golden calf and worship it. Their celebration leads many to break the Sixth Commandment, "You shall not commit adultery" (Exodus 20:14 ESV). Oh no! What a humongous hole!

Someone slides a room key in our direction. Someone shows up on Facebook and just wants to talk. Someone offers a listening ear, a gentle touch, or more. Justifications and rationalizations pop up like dandelions on a warm day in late May. "No one will know. I won't get caught. What's the big deal?"

Let me say this as clearly as possible. Don't hit the accelerator! If you're stuck in an emotional, financial, or relational hole, don't make matters worse by doing something you'll regret for the rest of your life. Here's what I suggest. Make a list of all the people you would hurt by doing something immoral. One bad decision is a poor exchange for a lifetime of lost legacy.

The "great" sin/wickedness is a term found in Genesis 20:9 and 39:9 (ESV). It refers to sexual immorality. Little surprise that—since Moses authored Genesis, the backstory to Exodus—he employs this term in Exodus 32:21, 30, and 31 to refer to adultery.

Worshiping the golden calf is also a great sin because of who committed it—Aaron, the high priest, and the Israelites, God's chosen people. It's also a great sin because of where they committed it—on Mount Sinai, God's holy mountain. Finally, it's a great sin because of when the Israelites committed it—right after God delivered them from Egypt with a mighty hand and outstretched arm.

HOW LONG?

By giving Israel enough manna for one day, God teaches His people to live one day at a time (Exodus 16). Then Yahweh warns the Israelites not to expect to conquer their Canaanite enemies in a day. "Little by little I will drive them out from before you" (Exodus 23:30 ESV). Did the Israelites heed this advice? Did they learn to be patient? "When the people saw that Moses delayed to come down from the mountain, the people gathered themselves together to Aaron and said to him, 'Up, make us gods who shall *lead* us. As for this Moses, the man who brought us up out of the land of Egypt, we do not know what has become of him'" (Exodus 32:1).

The last time God's people spoke in unison they said, "All that the LORD has spoken we will do, and we will be obedient" (Exodus 24:7

ESV). What a tectonic shift! Moses had been on the top of Mount Sinai forty days and forty nights. People were getting impatient. "How long?"

We know the feeling. We see how long it takes to get through school. We see how long it takes to build a marriage. We see how long it takes to raise children. We see how long it takes to save money. We don't like a God who makes us wait. We want a god who can make us happy—now!

Without batting an eye, Aaron concedes and sells the farm. "'Take off the rings of gold that are in the ears of your wives, your sons, and your daughters, and bring them to me.' So all the people took the rings of gold that were in their ears and brought them to Aaron. Then he received the gold from their hand and fashioned it with a graving tool and made a golden calf" (Exodus 32:2–4 ESV). Aaron offers a god who can satisfy right now.

The word in Exodus 32:1 reveals the core issue: *lead*. The expression is never used of Yahweh or Moses. *Lead* is reserved for one person in the Book of Exodus—the Angel of the Lord, the preincarnate Christ (see Exodus 3:2; 14:19; 23:23; 32:34). Yahweh isn't completely sidelined; at least that's how the Israelites understand the situation.

One of the ironies in the Book of Exodus is that, just when the Israelites wanted tangible evidence that Yahweh was with them (the Angel of the Lord), God was instructing Moses on how to make that happen through the tabernacle. Strengthening this interpretation is that both were made from gold—the calf completely, the tabernacle in part. The Israelites aren't totally rejecting Yahweh. They are, however, rejecting His ordained means of worship—the tabernacle. This clarifies why Moses places the golden calf debacle in the middle of the tabernacle's blueprints (Exodus 25–31) and construction (Exodus 35–40). *Will the Israelites worship Yahweh according to their desires or His?* Let's take a closer look at these two ways of worship.

THE TABERNACLE	THE GOLDEN CALF
Yahweh's initiative	Israel's initiative
People freely give to its construction	Aaron demands gold
Detailed preparations	No planning
Lengthy building process	Lightning-fast assembly
Guard Yahweh's holiness	Instant accessibility for all
Yahweh is the invisible God	The calf is a visible god
Yahweh is personal	The calf is an impersonal object

Moses couldn't have construed the differences between the two more sharply.

The Israelites aren't succumbing to the kind of idolatry we see in other parts of the Old Testament. The people want to see God's Messenger—a noble desire. John helps us. "Every spirit that confesses that Jesus Christ has come in the flesh is from God" (1 John 4:2 ESV). Yahweh's Messenger, the Second Person of the Trinity, comes in the flesh of a Man, not in glittering gold. "They exchanged the glory of God for the image of an ox that eats grass" (Psalm 106:20 ESV).

In Exodus 28–30, God gives instructions regarding the ordination and central role of the high priest. In chapter 32, however, Aaron—Israel's first high priest—allows other gods in Yahweh's presence (cf. Exodus 20:3). Before Moses can get the tabernacle's design to Israel, Aaron has already completed a building project of his own—the golden calf. He takes a wrong turn, gets stuck, hits the accelerator, and digs himself into a gigantic hole.

"Aaron saw how excited the people were, so he built an altar in front of the calf. Then he announced, 'Tomorrow will be a festival to the LORD!'" (Exodus 32:5). How often do we exchange the real God for a fake god and then claim that the fake god is the real God? Answer? Often! What are the top fake gods in America? Money, sports, and jobs. They promise everything. In the end, money, sports, and jobs deliver nothing.

IDOLATRY

We're image-bearing creatures. God made us to reflect Him. That's what Moses teaches. "God created man in His own image, in the image of God He created him; male and female He created them" (Genesis 1:27 ESV). Adam and Eve became the first idolaters because they shifted their loyalty from God to the serpent whose deceitful character our first parents came to represent. They started lying and blaming immediately after the fall (Genesis 3:10–13).

Throughout the Old Testament, the Israelites who worship idols receive a curse by becoming as spiritually inanimate, empty, blind, and deaf as the idol of their devotion (Psalms 115:4–8; 135:15–18). Yahweh says to idolatrous people, "You like idols? Now you're going to become like your idol, and that's your judgment." This sounds a lot like God's rationale when He hardened Pharaoh's heart, doesn't it? "Pharaoh, you like your hard heart? My judgment is to confirm you in your stubborn pride."

If we don't emulate our Creator, we commit ourselves to some part of creation—then we reflect it. For instance, if I fully commit myself to things (boats, houses, cars, etc.), then I become impersonal. Things don't have personalities and, sooner or later, neither will I. That's why God warns us that we become what we worship.

Moses describes this verdict in Exodus 32:8–9. The Israelites "turned aside quickly out of the way" and became "stiff-necked" (ESV). God's people became like the god they worshiped. Like cattle, they ran wild and were difficult to rein in.

Truth be told, Israel's dominant trait throughout the golden calf fiasco and its aftermath is that they are "stiff-necked"—a designation that likens God's people to Pharaoh himself in his hardness (Exodus 7:3; 13:15). Not once but three times Yahweh asserts that the Israelites are "stiff-necked" (Exodus 32:9; 33:3, 5).

Exodus 21:24–25 gets to the heart of God's judgment against His people's sin. An "eye for eye, tooth for tooth, hand for hand, foot for foot, burn for burn, wound for wound, stripe for stripe" (ESV). Now it's a calf for a calf. The Israelites have become animals. Alas!

God's verdict—giving people over to what they worship—is a hallmark of Paul's argument concerning idolatry. In Romans 1:24, 26, and 28, the apostle affirms that God gives sinners over to their sin. This leads to the breakdown of every human relationship through sexual impurity (Romans 1:24), lesbianism (Romans 1:26), homosexuality (Romans 1:27), and disobedience toward parents (Romans 1:30). "They were filled with all manner of unrighteousness, evil, covetousness, malice. They are full of envy, murder, strife, deceit, maliciousness. They are gossips" (Romans 1:29 ESV).

Idolatry exacts the highest price. *We lose everything.*

Normally, our idol isn't as crass as a golden calf. It might be some God-given gift that we use as a substitute for Jesus. Our idol may be a job, nation, education, team, or hobby. The list is endless. Why do idols have such power? Satan is the spiritual reality behind every addiction, every compulsion, and every obsession (1 Corinthians 10:20).

When we become impatient—just like the Israelites in Exodus 32—we look to things and people for safety and salvation. We trust their promises. We make sacrifices that they demand. False gods and pseudo-saviors, though, never fail to fail.

This explains God's jealousy. "I the LORD your God am a jealous God" (Exodus 20:5 ESV). God is jealous—but not in the sense that He envies or is suspicious. Rather, in the sense that He will not allow Himself to be replaced by any rival. "You shall worship no other god, for the LORD, whose name is Jealous, is a jealous God" (Exodus 34:14 ESV). His love springs from a deep well of emotion. Yahweh feels for Israel—and for us—passionately.

"Little children, keep yourselves from idols" (1 John 5:21 ESV).

Exodus 20:2–6 and the Golden Calf

Exodus 20:2–6 plays a key role in the unfolding of the golden calf episode. For instance, in Exodus 20:2, God proclaims: "I am Yahweh your God who brought you out from the land of Egypt." In the golden calf scene, this phrase is repeated five times—often horribly parodied. The people say of the newly fashioned calf idol: "These are your gods, O Israel, who brought you up out of the land of Egypt!" (Exodus 32:4 ESV). The expression "who you brought out of the land of Egypt" is twice repeated in the ensuing dialogue between God and Moses (Exodus 32:7, 11). Yahweh then cites the people's idolatrous claim verbatim: "They have . . . said, 'These are your gods, O Israel, who brought you up out of the land of Egypt!'" (Exodus 32:8 ESV).

Moreover, the accusation that the people made or made for themselves an idol (expressly forbidden in Exodus 20:4–6) is repeated in Exodus 32:1, 4, 8, 20–23, 31, and 35. Yahweh also adds, "They have bowed down to it" (Exodus 32:8), recalling the prohibition, "You shall not bow down to them" (Exodus 20:5 ESV). Further, Yahweh's self-description in Exodus 20:5 as "a jealous God" (ESV)—a concept often associated both with anger and with fire—is reflected in His anger burning against the people (Exodus 32:10).

What shall we make of this network of words and phrases? Israel's rebellion with the calf in Exodus 32 is a counterfeit, perversion, and repudiation of Yahweh's entire program set forth in Exodus 20–31, all of which itself derives from Yahweh's name and character as proclaimed in Exodus 20:2–6.

Beauty to Ashes

While Moses is on Mount Sinai, thinking things are just fine—truth be told—they're getting more out of hand by the minute. After forty days and nights on the mountain, Moses finally comes down. What he sees isn't pretty. Not even close.

In place of Israel's unique identity as "My [Yahweh's] people" (e.g., Exodus 3:7, 10; 6:7), Yahweh disowns them as "your [Moses'] people" and "this people" (Exodus 32:7, 9). Instead of a distinct standing among the nations (Exodus 19:5–6), Yahweh will make them an object of reproach (Exodus 32:12). In lieu of giving Israel a long life in the land (Exodus 6:8; 20:12) and planting the nation on His own mountain (Exodus 15:17), Yahweh plans "to kill them in the mountains and to consume them from the face of the earth" (Exodus 32:12 ESV). Instead of an enduring covenant between Yahweh and Israel, the tablets of the testimony are shattered at the foot of the mountain (Exodus 32:19). In place of a people miraculously sustained with water from the rock (Exodus 17:6), the Israelites are forced to drink the charred and pulverized golden calf mixed with water (Exodus 32:20). In lieu of Yahweh multiplying them like stars (Exodus 32:13) and sparing them from diseases (Exodus 15:26), three thousand are struck down by the sword and Yahweh afflicts His people with a plague (Exodus 32:35). And in place of the promise that He will dwell with Israel (Exodus 3:12; 29:45–46), Yahweh declares that He will not and cannot live in their midst (Exodus 33:3–5).

Everything's gone from beauty to ashes.

If I was Moses, I'd wash my hands of the whole mess. But Moses won't do that. Moses couldn't do that.

MOSES' PRAYER

In Exodus 32:10, Yahweh vows He will destroy Israel. By Exodus 34:10, the relationship is restored. What happened? Moses prayed. Moses prayed like a father pleading for his children. We need some context.

The Israelites demonstrate disdain for their leader, saying, "As for this Moses" (Exodus 32:1 ESV). Yahweh returns the favor when He talks to Moses and refers to the Israelites not as "My people" (e.g., Exodus 3:7 ESV) but instead He calls them "your people" (Exodus 32:7 ESV) and "this people" (Exodus 32:9 ESV). The Israelites abandon Moses, then Yahweh. Yahweh, in turn, abandons Israel. It's up to Moses to bring the two back together. Instead of taking God up on His offer to become a new Abraham (Exodus 32:10), Moses steps into the breach to become a mighty mediator.

Moses' first argument is that God's relationship with Israel is public; hence, to disown His people would bring public shame, dishonor Yahweh, and render His missionary plans for the world null and void. It's as though Moses asks, "What will the neighbors think?" After all, Yahweh brought Israel out of Egypt so that the nations might know that He alone is God (e.g., Exodus 9:16; 14:4, 18).

Next, Moses appeals to God's promises to the patriarchs. Moses' strategy takes Yahweh (and us) back to Genesis 12:2–3—God's plan to bless all the families of the earth through Abraham, Isaac, and Israel. Moses isn't defending Israel. He isn't minimizing the people's sin. He's calling upon God to be faithful to the patriarchal covenant.

Moses then makes His most daring move. He commands Yahweh to relent. Yahweh wastes no time. "The LORD relented from the disaster that He had spoken of bringing on His people" (Exodus 32:14 ESV).

Sin is greater than we think. Grace is more amazing than we can conceive. And Moses is more successful than we could ever imagine. "Therefore, He said He would destroy them—had not Moses, His chosen one, stood in the breach before Him, to turn away His wrath from destroying them" (Psalm 106:23 ESV).

CLAIM THE COVENANT

What does Moses teach us? When things look totally hopeless, claim the covenant—God's covenant with Abraham, Isaac, and Israel. This is an everlasting covenant sealed in blood (see Genesis 15:7–21). Sin can't break it. Idolatry can't nullify it. Death can't defeat it. And a huge hole in the sand can't destroy it.

God fulfills His covenant with the patriarchs in the death of Jesus. Christ's shed blood shows us that God is always loving. God is always kind. God is always forgiving. God is always abounding in grace and mercy.

We have all taken wrong turns. We have all built golden calves. We have all worshiped other gods. We have all known the hell of the hole. What can we do? We can do what Moses did. Claim the covenant.

Claim Christ's new covenant promises delivered to us in His cleansing, powerful, and renewing blood.

GOD RELENTED

Did God really relent after Moses prayed? Indeed! Let's look at this by considering the Fourth Petition of the Lord's Prayer, "Give us this day our daily bread" (Matthew 6:11 ESV). The other six petitions of the Lord's Prayer invite us to pray for the hallowing of God's name, the advancement of His kingdom, the doing of His will, the sharing of forgiveness, protection from temptation, and deliverance from the evil one. Our Father in heaven consistently and generously responds to these prayers. When it comes to these petitions, God's mind is made up.

There are times, however, when we find ourselves wrestling in the sleeplessness of the night with issues that fall under the Fourth Petition. Martin Luther defines them in the Small Catechism as an upright spouse and children, food, drink, money, good weather, peace, health, and the like. It's in this realm that we find ourselves wondering, will God relent concerning my cancer, my unemployment, my financial mess? Or is God unchanging in such a way that these Fourth Petition prayers are nothing more than boomerangs that only form and shape me? Is it true that prayer doesn't change God—prayer only changes the one who prays?

God changes His course of direction at some of the key junctures in the Old Testament: the flood story (Genesis 6:6), here in the golden calf episode (Exodus 32:12, 14), and when Israel's monarchy is instituted (1 Samuel 15:11, 29, 35). Divine change is even incorporated into Israel's creedal statements (Joel 2:13; Jonah 4:2).

When we pray Fourth Petition prayers, God may relent. We're not in the hands of an unfeeling, ironclad deity. God's willingness to modify an earlier decision demonstrates His priority of grace. To be affected and interact genuinely doesn't mean some imperfection in God. In fact, it's a sign of stubbornness and sinful pride when someone is unwilling to listen and respond to new information.

To clarify. In certain situations, God may intervene and change events. However, neither His attributes nor His plan to save the world will ever change. Concerning these, we have this promise: "Jesus Christ is the same yesterday and today and forever" (Hebrews 13:8 ESV).

Should I ask God for my daughter to be healed, a drought to end, or an employer to increase my salary? Yes! God loves us so much that we can confidently ask Him, in the name of Jesus, to relent. God may reverse a sickness, an infertile womb, or a fractured relationship.

This is how Paul prayed. Three times he begged the Lord to remove the thorn in his flesh (2 Corinthians 12:7–10). Jesus responded, "My grace is sufficient for you, for My power is made perfect in weakness" (2 Corinthians 12:9 ESV).

Let me put it this way. When it comes to Fourth Petition prayers, God may say, "Grow." That's His answer to Paul's thorn in the flesh. "I'm not going to change your situation. Paul, I'm going to change you. Grow!" At other times, God answers, "No." The request is so far removed from God's will that He shuts and locks the door. And sometimes God may say, "Go." Just like He did for Moses!

Because God may not relent when we pray Fourth Petition prayers, we always include these words: "Yet not what I will, but what You will" (Mark 14:36 ESV). The words of this hymn say it best:

> Come, my soul, with ev'ry care,
>
> Jesus loves to answer prayer;
>
> He Himself has bid thee pray,
>
> Therefore will not turn away.
>
> Thou art coming to a King,
>
> Large petitions with thee bring;
>
> For His grace and pow'r are such
>
> None can ever ask too much. (*LSB* 779:1–2)

EXCUSES

When I used to hit my big sister—a very long time ago!—I wouldn't tell my dad that it was because of sin in my heart. No. I raised my voice to defend my actions. "Luann was picking on me!" When I was a teenager and came home long past my curfew, I wouldn't tell my mom I was only thinking of myself. No. I raised my voice and blamed my friends. "They lost track of time!" When I got impatient with my three children while they were growing up, I wouldn't admit that they were intruding on my time and that I was being selfish. No way. I raised my voice and pointed out that they had better get busy entertaining themselves—or else!

I know about lame excuses. So does Aaron. When Moses points out his part in the golden calf episode, Aaron says, "I said to them, 'Let any who have gold take it off.' So they gave it to me, and I threw it into the fire, and out came this calf" (Exodus 32:24 ESV). Moses doesn't dignify this with a response. Why? It's lame!

Here are some more lame excuses: "She talked me into it." "I was so busy that I forgot." "I guess I didn't hear you correctly." "You have no idea how difficult you are to live with." "Other people do it all the time." "I didn't have any choice." "If only my parents had been better role models." "I was planning on giving it back."

Want a few more? "I'm not on a quest for power; I'm simply a great leader." "It wasn't a lie. It was just a different perspective on what happened." "I wasn't being proud. I was simply recounting the facts."

Have you noticed that dogs are great at confessing sin? Cats? Not so much! The moment you walk into the house, if a dog has sinned, his eyes will squint and dart one way, then the other. His ears will be flat. His head will be lowered. His tail will be between his legs. When you discover the actual crime—a mistake on the rug, a broken what-not, a chewed shoe—it only takes one phrase to crush your dog's faint optimism. In a low, I'm-the-master-of-the-world voice, you intone, "Oh, how could you?" Complete canine collapse ensues. He throws himself on your mercy.

Dogs confess. Cats? Never bet on it!

Unfortunately, we're more like cats than dogs. We have the uncanny ability to shift the blame, ignore the consequences, shirk all responsibility.

It's so much better to come down from our high horse. It's so much better to stop defending and justifying. Can you say this with me? "I, a poor, miserable sinner, confess unto You all my sins and iniquities" (*LSB* p. 184). Can you hear Jesus say this? "You are fully, freely, and forever forgiven—washed pure white in My cleansing blood."

AARON'S SCAPEGOAT

Aaron not only gives a lame excuse but he also blames the Israelites. They become his scapegoat. "Moses said to Aaron, 'What did this people do to you that you have brought such a great sin upon them?' And Aaron said, 'Let not the anger of my lord burn hot. You know the people, that they are set on evil'" (Exodus 32:21–22 ESV). Aaron's alibi? "It's all *their* fault!"

In 1987, a man named Martin Handford began writing a series of children's books called *Where's Waldo?* Waldo is in every scene in every Handford book—hidden from plain view. The fun comes in trying to find Waldo with his striped shirt and cool-looking glasses.

You're probably not looking for Waldo today. But you could be looking for someone else. I'm willing to bet the farm that sometimes you've found yourself desperately looking for whom? A scapegoat. A scapegoat is a person we blame for all our pain and for all our problems.

Parents can become our scapegoat. "My parents weren't perfect!" I've got news for you. There are no perfect parents. Peers can become our scapegoat. "Well, my peers aren't perfect!" I've got more news for you. There are no perfect peers. Partners can become our scapegoat.

"Well, my partner isn't perfect!" I've got even more news for you. There are no perfect partners.

But we still insist, "They're guilty! They're all guilty as charged!" That's why we twist their words, interrupt their sentences, and point our accusing fingers. It's easy to blame and berate parents, pastors, peers, professors, and partners—sometimes we even blame our precious little pets!

Isn't it time to find the right scapegoat? Someone who will lovingly carry our pain and our problems? Isn't it time to find a scapegoat who will take it all away? Moses describes Him in Leviticus 16:20–22. It's one of the rituals that took place on Israel's Day of Atonement—God's gift of a scapegoat.

Azazel—the Hebrew term for "scapegoat"—is a compound word consisting of the noun "goat" and the verb "go away." Azazel is the "go-away goat." He's condemned. The guilty go free. Azazel bears the curse. The cursed bear the blessing. Azazel dies in the desert. The sinful live in the Promised Land. Azazel is covered with shame. The shamed are covered in mercy. Psalm 103:12 beautifully expresses the idea: "As far as the east is from the west, so far does He remove our transgressions from us" (ESV). How far is the east from the west? That's how far God removes our wickedness, rebellion, and sin.

On the Day of Atonement, as a man led Azazel to a desolate and barren land, the Israelites cheered and shouted with joy. They celebrated as the sin-bearing goat was released—never to be seen again. What a happy day when God's people watched the silhouette of the scapegoat disappear over the horizon, etching indelibly upon their hearts a profound insight into the nature of their loving God. Azazel—the "go-away goat"—takes every sin away.

Paul writes, "This ritual is only a shadow of the reality yet to come. And Christ Himself is that reality" (Colossians 2:17). The scapegoat ritual is just a shadow. Wouldn't it be great to have the reality? That would be Jesus.

The appointed man takes the scapegoat in Leviticus 16:22 to "a land *cut off*." Isaiah 53:8 says that Jesus is "*cut off* from the land of the living." That's why He cries out, "My God, My God, why have You forsaken Me?" (Matthew 27:46 ESV). Christ was cut off. We will never be cut off from God's loving presence—ever!

MOSES' FOLLOW-UP

Moses wastes no time. He destroys the calf, calls Aaron on the carpet, and gives the Israelites a choice, "Who is on the LORD's side?" (Exodus 32:26 ESV).

Centuries later, when confronting the false god Baal on Mount Carmel, the prophet Elijah borrows Moses' strategy. "If the LORD is God, follow Him; but if Baal, then follow him" (1 Kings 18:21 ESV). In both cases, only a remnant remained faithful. For Moses, it was the tribe of Levi who then went through the camp and enacted divine judgment—about three thousand people were killed (Exodus 32:26–28). For Elijah, the remnant was the seven thousand Israelites who refused to bow down to Baal (1 Kings 19:18). In our day, the faithful remnant are those who "press on toward the goal for the prize of the upward call of God in Christ Jesus" (Philippians 3:14 ESV).

CHAPTER 15

In with the New: Exodus 33–40

Restore us, O God; let Your face shine,
that we may be saved!
(Psalm 80:3 ESV)

Sam's Club leads me into temptation—every time. I know I don't need one hundred pounds of Captain Crunch cereal. But look at the price! What a deal! I know I don't need a five-gallon jar of jalapeño peppers. But look at the price! What a deal! Two years later, the jalapeños in my refrigerator have turned purple. But look at the price!

Trips to Sam's Club always mean I need to clean out my refrigerator. Out with the old. In with the new!

In Exodus 33–40, Moses describes Israel's great fall as well as God's great faithfulness. These chapters are a lot like refrigerator or spring cleaning. It's out with the old (guilt over the golden calf disaster) and in with the new (God's gift of forgiveness).

WILL GOD GO WITH ISRAEL?

Exodus 33 begins with *most* of God's promises intact—the Promised Land with assured victory over the land's inhabitants and the Messenger's guidance along the way. What's lacking—and what crushes the Israelites—is that Yahweh's tabernacling presence will not go with them (Exodus 33:3, 5). Why? He would destroy them. This would not be good—either for God or for Israel!

Because Yahweh reneges on His promise to dwell in Israel's midst via the tabernacle, Exodus 33 begins with these words: "The LORD said to Moses, 'Depart; go up from here, you and the people'" (Exodus 33:1 ESV). While Yahweh pledges safe passage into the land that will still flow with milk and honey, He tells Moses that He will no longer accompany them—out of mercy, lest He destroy Israel. The Israelites take this as a "disastrous word" (Exodus 33:4 ESV). God's decision not to accompany Israel into the Promised Land isn't just a minor adjustment to the plan. *It's the end of everything.*

In a moment of stark realization, the people come to their senses. Without God's presence, life will be in vain. Safety and abundance are not enough in the Promised Land. Nothing is complete without divine companionship. "Whom have I in heaven but You? And there is nothing on earth that I desire besides You" (Psalm 73:25 ESV).

Yet God leaves the door open to change His decision when He says, "*if* for a single moment I should go up among you" (Exodus 33:5). Did you catch that? Judgment is not set in stone. A glimmer of morning light appears on the eastern horizon.

Exodus 33:7–11, then, looks back on "the good ol' days"—when the Yahweh-Moses-Israel triad functioned harmoniously. After the golden calf, God hopes these relationships can be restored. That's how things eventually unfold, but for the rest of Exodus 33, Israel is betwixt and between, not knowing their future.

MOSES PRAYS AGAIN

Moses—bold Moses—dialogues with God again in Exodus 33:12–23. Surprisingly, in Exodus 33:13, he refers to Israel as a "nation." The only other place in the book where this word applies to Israel is in Exodus 19:6 where Yahweh calls Israel "a holy nation" (ESV). Just as he did in Exodus 32:11–13, Moses again appeals to God's plan to use Israel as His missionary to restore the world. God's answer is clear: "This very thing that you have spoken I will do" (Exodus 33:17 ESV). Moses' request is granted. *The mission will proceed as planned.*

Emboldened, Moses makes another request. "Please show me Your glory" (Exodus 33:18). He wants Yahweh to promise that He will live among His stiff-necked and idolatrous people. God grants Moses' prayer as well and the answer becomes one of the key texts in the entire Bible (Exodus 34:5–7).

"YAHWEH, YAHWEH"

It looks like Exodus 32–33 presents only two options. Option one: If God stays with Israel, He will destroy the nation. Option two: If God distances Himself, the Israelites will live in despair. Thank God, He offers a third option—divine forgiveness.

Moses writes, "Then Yahweh came down in a cloud and stood there with Moses. He called out His name, Yahweh" (Exodus 34:5). Earlier, divine glory appeared in a cloud (Exodus 16:10) as well as in a cloud and fire (Exodus 24:16–17). This time, God's glory in a cloud will reveal His name.

What does God do when He defines His name after the golden calf? Scold Israel again? Shame them? Berate them? Reject them? Condemn them? No! God comes in mercy. In Exodus 34:6, He cries out, "Yahweh! Yahweh!" This is the first and the last time God repeats His name in the Old Testament. In doing so, He gives Israel a greater revelation, a fuller answer to these two questions, "What is Your name?" (Exodus 3:13) and "Who is Yahweh?" (Exodus 5:2).

Yes, the Israelites are a stiff-necked people. Yes, they deserve the same fate as Pharaoh. But Yahweh is Yahweh. He doesn't only condemn sin; even more, He mercifully forgives rebel sinners. "Mercy triumphs over judgment" (James 2:13 ESV). Yahweh relents from His initial decree to destroy (Exodus 32:10–14). He also decides to abide with Israel and go with them to the Promised Land vis-à-vis the tabernacle.

How can Israel be so sure?

ISRAEL'S CREED

In the wake of the golden calf apostasy, it's significant that in Exodus 34 the Israelites retreat from the stage. Yahweh and Moses remain. Yahweh's fullest revelation of His name and nature is proclaimed to this single mediator, and Yahweh's renewal of His covenant is declared and enacted in the presence of Moses alone (Exodus 34:10, 27).

Here's *the* revelation of God in the Old Testament:

> And He called out, "Yahweh, Yahweh, the God of compassion and grace, slow to anger and abounding in covenant loyalty and faithfulness. Keeping covenant loyalty to thousands and forgiving iniquity and rebellion and sin. Yet He will surely not acquit the guilty, visiting the iniquity of the fathers upon the sons and upon the sons of sons up to the third and fourth generation." (Exodus 34:6–7)

Israel's neighbors in Canaan, Mesopotamia, and Egypt didn't understand their gods and goddesses this way. Not even close! Their mythologies describe deities who are violent, inaccessible, dominating, and capricious. Mercy and forgiveness are unique to Yahweh, the God of Israel, the Maker of heaven and earth.

The words in Exodus 34:6–7 are so profound that they appear again, with slight variations, in fifteen other passages (Deuteronomy 4:31; Psalm 78:38; 86:5, 15; 103:8; 111:4; 112:4; 116:5; 145:8; Joel 2:13; Jonah 4:2; Nehemiah 9:17, 31; 2 Chronicles 30:9). Yahweh's grace-filled qualities are mentioned first because they are from eternity and last into eternity. His judgment upon sin follows. It appears in time and will end on the Last Day. There exists in Yahweh a tension between tender mercy and stern moral retribution. Out of the two, though, He's inclined towards showing steadfast love. Exodus 34:6–7 employs five statements to make this assertion. Let's look at them.

Compassionate is the attribute stated. This word denotes a deep-seated pity for people in need. It's a characteristic that can be compared with the concern of a father for his child (Psalm 103:13) or a mother for her son (Isaiah 49:15). The word is also closely related to a Hebrew word for a mother's womb. Understood this way, divine compassion expresses the emotional connection a mother has for a child in her womb. *This is how God feels about you.*

Next is the word *gracious.* It means favor, benevolence, and kindness. Yahweh forgives Israel's sin and renews covenant promises because He is—in His heart—gracious. In the Old Testament, this adjective only modifies Yahweh, making Him the fountain and source of all grace. Here is a telling illustration: "If ever you take your neighbor's cloak as a pledge, return it to him by sunset, because his cloak is the only covering he has for his body. What else will he sleep in? When he cries out to Me, I will hear, for I am *gracious*" (Exodus 22:26–27). Yahweh hears the cry of someone who is cold because his only coat has been taken from him as a pledge against his debt. God is moved by simple human need.

Third, Yahweh is also "slow to anger." That's so not me—especially when I'm in a hurry at the grocery store. "My!" I gasp when I see long lines at checkout counters. "There are people to see and places to go. I don't have time to stand in a *grocery* line."

Taking a closer look, I see that all the lines are long—except one. I dart over there, only to find someone with what appears to be hundreds of items and—oh, no—a cartload of coupons! Coupons that need to be cross-checked by a cashier-in-training. I begin humming a hymn, "Stricken, Smitten, and Afflicted" (*LSB* 451). Then, looking up, I see that the cash register has gone haywire. An assistant manager rushes to the rescue. "Come on!" I mutter as ten people turn their heads toward me. I quickly realize that what I thought was a whisper was more like a shout. Twenty minutes later, I finally get to buy my measly milk and cottage cheese—both of which, by this time, have gone sour.

"Slow to anger?" Not even close!

Unless you're Yahweh. If He was quick to anger, His grace wouldn't last a second in my life. If God shot rockets of wrath every time I sinned,

I would have been blown to smithereens a bazillion times. But God shouts from Sinai, "I am *slow* to anger!"

Fourth, God is also "abounding in steadfast love." This phrase has the only word used more than once in Exodus 34:6–7. It's also the only word modified by an adjective—*abounding*. The Hebrew word *hesed* is often translated "steadfast love," "compassionate commitment," or "covenant loyalty." While Exodus 20:6 promises *hesed* to those who love Yahweh and keep His commandments, Exodus 34:6 makes it clear that *hesed* comes to Israel apart from obedience. Yahweh arrived at this decision after the golden calf incident. *If the relationship was going to continue, it was going to be up to Yahweh, not Israel.*

In Romans 15:5, Paul employs the expression "the God of endurance" (ESV). This is so strange to me. If Paul is anything, Paul is the apostle of human endurance—challenging us to buck up, toughen up, hang in there, and run the race with grit and determination.

Our endurance, however, pales in comparison to God's. Our hope can't be in our endurance. It must rest in God's. His love endures for us, come what may. That's *hesed*.

Twenty-six times, Psalm 136 celebrates that divine *hesed* endures forever. We've all listened to people repeat themselves; it gets old. Not this word. Not this gift. Not this psalm. Not ever. God's *hesed* is never ill-timed; it never disappoints, and it never fails. And God's *hesed* is form-fitted for you—your pain, your temptations, your tests, your trials, your heart-crushing disappointments.

"Abounding" announces that God's *hesed* isn't limited. God is like the federal government. Whenever there's a need, God just prints off more *hesed*. There is a difference, though. God has an infinite treasury of steadfast love to cover all the currency He prints. His infinite resources of steadfast love will never run out! God go in debt? God go bankrupt? Never!

Finally, in Exodus 34:7 is God's action of "forgiving iniquity and transgression and sin" (ESV). There are only three Hebrew words for sin and God uses all three right here. What's He up to? Yahweh announces that He forgives every type of sin.

Moses then pleads with God—affirming that Israel "*is* a stiff-necked people" (Exodus 34:9 ESV, emphasis added). Not "was." Not "used to be." And Moses doesn't promise Israel will begin a regimen to increase their devotion to God. Moses calls it as he sees it. Israel *is* stiff-necked. God's people, ourselves included, never graduate from their need for grace.

MARVELOUS AND AWESOME

In Exodus 34:10, God says, "Behold, I am making a covenant. Before all your people I will do *marvels,* such as have not been created in all the earth or in any nation. And all the people among whom you are shall see the work of the LORD, for it is an *awesome* thing that I will do with you" (ESV, emphasis added). Yahweh is about to do and create such wonders greater than all His wonders in the book thus far—in Egypt (Exodus 3:20) and at the Red Sea (Exodus 15:11). The new and ultimate wonder is that Yahweh makes a promise with a stiff-necked people—a promise made possible solely by His merciful character and His forgiveness of Israel's iniquity, rebellion, and sin.

The word *created* in Exodus 34:10 (ESV) derives the same Hebrew word that appears in Genesis 1:1. By renewing His covenant with Israel, God is re-creating them. Forgiveness for these idolatrous people is so spectacular, Yahweh also employs the exuberant words "marvels" and "awesome" (ESV).

Divine pardon is so new and remarkable that, after the golden calf flap, the great event of the exodus deliverance—for a moment—almost seems forgotten. No reference is made to this hard-won renown. It's not cast aside. It's overshadowed. For moving forward, the renown of Yahweh will lie most chiefly in something else. What could that be? He is the God who forgives.

THE PRIORITY OF GOD'S FORGIVENESS

In contrast to Pharaoh, whose name is never mentioned in Exodus, thus making evil impersonal, Yahweh can be known and so can His chief gift—forgiveness.

Forgiveness is so prevalent in the Bible that it almost becomes cliché. "To err is human, to forgive, divine." Up to this point in Genesis and Exodus, however, God hasn't explicitly forgiven anyone. Abraham bargained that God might forgive Sodom for the sake of fifty righteous persons (Genesis 18:24) and God concurred that hypothetically, He might do so (Genesis 18:26). But there weren't even ten righteous people, so God didn't forgive. Instead, the cities were destroyed. And Pharaoh—who was temporarily humbled and so confessed his sin against Yahweh and Moses—begged Moses to forgive him (Exodus 10:16–17). Yet Pharaoh's humility was short-lived. There was no forgiveness.

At Sinai, God promised to send His Messenger before Israel to guard them on their way, but He also warned them not to be rebellious because the Messenger that bears Yahweh's name will not forgive their rebellion (Exodus 23:20–21). Only when He realizes Israel's towering need for forgiveness because of their "great sin" (Exodus 32:21, 30–31 ESV) does Yahweh for the first time in Genesis-Exodus forgive "iniquity and transgression and sin" (Exodus 34:7 ESV).

This helps us understand the tension within Exodus 34:6–7. For God's mission to move forward, He must extend forgiveness and grace to Israel while, at the same time, not clear the guilty. This is what we see in the aftermath of the golden calf—God both forgives and punishes to maintain His honor *and* His missional purposes among the nations.

God's mercy and forgiveness take priority—not His anger and punishment. This is demonstrated by placing Gospel characteristics first in Exodus 34:6–7. Also note the preponderance of mercy, loving kindness, and forgiveness when compared to the warning of judgment—which comes at the end of Exodus 34:7. Later in the chapter, Moses goes on to appeal to divine grace for this "stiff-necked people" (v. 9) and God responds affirmatively. He reestablishes a new covenant with Israel, directing the tabernacle's building as well as the consecration of the priests. At the end of the book, Yahweh comes to dwell in a glory-cloud and fire in this tabernacle.

If Yahweh delights in forgiving wickedness, rebellion, and sin, where does He put all of it?

THE LAMB OF GOD

On Good Friday, Jesus forgives all sin of all people of all time, and places it where? Upon Himself—all wickedness, all rebellion, all sin. Jesus is Yahweh in the flesh, "the God of compassion and grace, slow to anger and abounding in covenant loyalty and faithfulness" (Exodus 34:6–7). Jesus teaches this love. Jesus lives this love. Jesus demonstrates this love by shedding His blood on the cross for you. "Behold, the Lamb of God who takes away the sin of the world!" (John 1:29 ESV). Palm Sunday announces it. Good Friday shows it. And Easter Sunday celebrates it!

When I was a child, it was my heart's desire to play hide-and-go-seek with the big kids on the block. They asked if I knew how to end the game. I said, "Sure, every kid in America knows the words that end hide-and-go-seek. They're 'Ollie, Ollie ox in free.'" No. That's incorrect. Originally, the words were, "All and all and all are free."

Moses understood this. That's why after encountering the meaning of God's name, he throws himself to the ground and worships (Exodus 34:8).

I invite you to follow Moses. Trust that God is who He says He is. Repeat "Yahweh, Yahweh" until it drowns out the voices of fear and shame, guilt and blame. Throw yourself before Him. "All and all and all are free!"

Our past is behind us. God's grace is before us. A new beginning awaits that includes living generously.

ISRAEL'S GENEROSITY

Here's a letter no pastor ever wants to receive: "Dear Pastor. In reply to our church's annual stewardship program, my wife and I regret to inform you that, due to federal laws, state laws, county laws, corporation laws, mothers-in-law, and outlaws, we're compelled to pay a business tax, amusement tax, school tax, gas tax, light tax, water tax, sales tax—even our brains are taxed. For our own safety, we're required to carry life insurance, property insurance, liability insurance, accident insurance, tornado insurance, burglar insurance, business insurance, unemployment insurance, and fire insurance. Truth be told, we've been informed, summoned, commanded, and compelled to provide an inexhaustible supply of money for every known need, desire, charity, and hope under the sun. Therefore, we cannot and we will not financially support our church. Have a nice day, Pastor."

Is this how Israel responds to the revelation of Yahweh's name? What do you think?

Exodus 35:21–29 accents Israel's sheer delight to give God offerings for the tabernacle. People bring their gifts gladly—not under compulsion like when Aaron commanded gold to build the calf (Exodus 32:2). In fact, after the golden calf episode and God's absolution, the Israelites need to be commanded to stop giving (Exodus 36:3–7). Imagine your pastor announcing after this Sunday's offering, "Folks, we have way too much money. For the foreseeable future, please refrain from giving financial gifts to our church. Thank you and please stand for the prayers."

Looking at this section of Exodus more broadly, from Exodus 35:1 to 40:38, eighteen times Moses does exactly what God commanded. Moses' obedience and Israel's generosity came from their heart—a theme repeated in Exodus 35:5, 21–22, 29; and 36:2. The golden calf flagrant disobedience yields to robust and wholehearted living—driven by Yahweh's abounding grace.

PROBLEMS IN CORINTH

God's people in Corinth apparently didn't know about Exodus 35–40. They had told Paul, in so many words, "We cannot and we will not financially support our church. Have a nice day, Pastor." What did the apostle do? Like Moses, Paul trusted God's forgiveness to motivate people financially.

In 2 Corinthians 8–9, Paul doesn't bark out orders or give commands. Instead, the apostle relies on the Gospel—following Moses—to change the Corinthians' hearts and giving habits. Consider these Gospel words in 2 Corinthians 8–9: "grace" (2 Corinthians 8:1, 4, 6, 7, 9; 9:14); "fellowship" (2 Corinthians 8:4; 9:13); "love" (2 Corinthians 8:7, 24; 9:7); and "gift" (2 Corinthians 8:12, 20; 9:5 [two times], 15). Paul never mentions money. Not even once. However, the apostle does highlight the Macedonians' generosity, who were "begging us earnestly for the favor of taking part in the relief of the saints" (2 Corinthians 8:4 ESV). The Macedonians took a page out of Israel's response to divine forgiveness.

Two Kinds of Givers

Corinth was on the Corinthian isthmus, which joined mainland Greece with the Peloponnesus—a peninsula forming the southern part of Greece. The strategic location made Corinth the crossroads of the ancient world. Trade between east and west, north and south passed through the city. Consequently, Corinth became exceedingly rich. This made for at least two kinds of people.

Great national wealth tempts some not to earn money at all. These people say, "I want stuff. I need stuff. But I'm not going to take work seriously. I'm not going to take personal responsibility for earning money. I'm going to have an entitlement mentality. The world owes me. The government owes me. My parents owe me. I'm going to stay on a couch and expect money to come my way." The Bible says there's a direct relationship between the couch and catastrophe, between sloth and self-disintegration, between the refusal to earn money and the loss of self-respect.

On the other end of the spectrum are those addicted to money. If this is you, then you started out working diligently—but that wasn't enough. You wanted more. You needed more. Now you work not just for dignity—you work to feel like deity. After all, when people earn a lot of money, it allows them to feel like a god. You can buy what you want, go where you want, avoid what you want, vacation where you want, and live where you want. It's addictive stuff. So you roll up your sleeve and shoot up every morning because the goal in life is singular: wine, dine, then fully recline. What's the problem with this approach to money?

ON LOAN OR DO WE OWN?

One day you say, "Reed, my wife and I will be vacationing in Florida for a year, so we're going to let you use our lake house." I use your lake house for a year—enjoying it immensely. You call up and say, "We're having such a good time, we're going to stay in Florida. Use our lake house for another year." My heart skips for joy! After another year you call and say, "We're ready to move back in." I say, "What do you mean? You can't move in here. This is my house. Possession is nine-tenths of the law!"

You say, "That's crazy!" Yes, it is. Do you want to know where my faulty thinking came from? What I thought I owned was really on loan.

What's at the root of our addiction to money? We think that because God gives us something for an extended period, it's all ours. Not true! God has a different financial model. *What we think we own is really on loan.*

A few years ago, I was teaching in Kenya. One evening I went to an ATM machine to withdraw some money. It gave me the option to check my balance, so I punched the button. The machine gave me the balance of $360,000. Startled, I wondered, "Where did all this money come from?" Then I thought, "Maybe I should leave the country more often!" I even checked the account number to see if the ATM had linked me to the wrong account. After seeing that it was indeed my account, I finally realized the machine was giving me my balance not in terms of American dollars but in terms of Kenyan shillings. At the time, the exchange rate of shillings to dollars was about 90 to 1. This made the balance of my account $4,000, not $360,000.

Because of Jesus, your balance is astronomical. And it's not a computing error. You have all the wealth and riches of the Gospel! "For you know the grace of our Lord Jesus Christ, that though He was rich, yet for your sake He became poor, so that you through His poverty might become rich" (2 Corinthians 8:9 ESV).

That's why the Macedonians gave to Paul's appeal willingly. They also gave joyfully. "Out of the most severe trial, their overflowing joy and their *extreme poverty* welled up in rich generosity. For I testify that they gave as much as they were able, and even beyond their ability. Entirely on their own, they *urgently pleaded* with us for the privilege of sharing in this service to the saints" (2 Corinthians 8:2–4). The expression *extreme poverty* means "bankrupt," "down-to-the-last-dime," or "hitting rock-bottom." The Macedonians, though, didn't let their financial needs short-circuit their generosity to those in need.

They even "urgently pleaded" to Paul for the opportunity to give money. Normally we think of the pastor as begging the would-be givers. Here, it's the givers—Macedonians who could least afford it—begging the pastor for the opportunity to give.

The riches of the Gospel change people so that they give willingly and joyfully and sacrificially. They think of money on loan instead of owned.

MONEY AND MANURE

Money is like manure. We can either spread it around and help things grow—like fertilizer—or we can pile it up so it becomes putrid and foul-smelling to the Lord. What did the Corinthians finally do?

The oldest Christian document after the New Testament is called 1 Clement. In this letter, a church leader named Clement wrote to—

of all people—the Corinthians. Did Clement say anything about their stewardship? Their offerings? Their generosity? Clement remarked that Christians in Corinth were known for "giving more gladly than receiving" (1 Clement 2:1).

What a triumph! Grace (a word Paul uses twelve times in his Greek version of 2 Corinthians 8–9) empowered the Corinthians. God's extravagant grace in Jesus Christ empowers us to also be known for *"Giving more gladly than receiving."*

An elderly lady was stopped for speeding. She was going seventy in a forty-mile-per-hour zone. The policeman asked her, "Why were you going so fast, ma'am?"

She said, "Sir, the sign back there said seventy."

"No ma'am," he replied. "That wasn't the speed limit sign. That was the highway number sign. This is Highway 70."

"Oh, my goodness!" she exclaimed. "I'm so glad you didn't see me on Highway 129!"

Numbers are important. Ask a highway patrolman, a mortgage banker, or a math teacher. Numbers are important. So are the numbers we write on checks to our church. Let's let generosity prevail.

PRESENT, YET VEILED

Have you noticed that Yahweh is both present and yet veiled throughout the Book of Exodus? When leading Israel out of Egypt and through the wilderness, Yahweh is with Israel—through a pillar of cloud by day and fire by night (Exodus 13:21–22). At the Red Sea, "Yahweh, in the pillar of fire and cloud, looked down upon the Egyptians" (Exodus 14:24–25). At Sinai, He appears visibly to meet with the people, yet comes hidden "in a thick cloud" (Exodus 19:9 ESV). After the blood covenant ceremony at Sinai, Moses, Aaron, Nadab, Abihu, and the seventy elders "saw the God of Israel" although they're only allowed to gaze upon His feet standing on pavement (Exodus 24:10 ESV). Moses has the exceptional experience of speaking to God "face to face, as a man speaks to his friend" (Exodus 33:11 ESV). Yet even Moses must be shielded from seeing God's face directly (Exodus 33:20–23).

Will things be different at the end of Exodus when Yahweh leaves His lofty abode on Sinai and descends into the tabernacle to live with Israel? No. Yahweh again hides His presence behind both a veil (Exodus 26:31–33; 40:2–3) and a cloud (Exodus 40:34–38). At the tabernacle's dedication, not even Moses can enter it due to the cloud (Exodus 40:35). Thus, while fire, cloud, and veil are attached to Yahweh's coming near and revealing His glory to Israel, they paradoxically stress His continuing inaccessibility and hiddenness.

A GREATER GLORY

God's glory is both an ongoing motif in the Book of Exodus as well as a theme highlighted in Hebrews 1:3. "[The Son] is the radiance of the glory of God and the exact imprint of His nature" (ESV). We don't have Israel's fire, cloud, and veil. We have God's Son—Jesus. God's means of revelation are great in Exodus, but they come nowhere close to "the exact imprint of God's nature."

If a fire, cloud, and veil covered God's full presence, what covers Jesus—the Second Person of the Trinity? Flesh and blood. A human body covers Jesus. "Veiled in flesh the Godhead see, Hail the incarnate Deity!" (*LSB* 380:2). Charles Wesley made these words famous in his Christmas hymn, "Hark! The Herald Angels Sing."

The Greek word translated in Hebrews 1:3 "exact imprint" is *character*. *Character* in first-century Greek meant a perfect image produced by a stamp. The Father's perfect image is stamped on Jesus. The Savior puts it this way, "Whoever has seen Me has seen the Father" (John 14:9 ESV). That's what makes Christ's glory greater than God's glory shown to Israel. We have Jesus—the Word made flesh!

MOSES CAN'T GO IN—YET

The Book of Exodus ends with the tabernacle completed and the divine glory-cloud covering the tent of meeting. Everything seems to be in place. There's one problem, though. And it's huge. Moses can't enter God's presence (Exodus 40:35). This dilemma is accented again in Leviticus 1:1, "Yahweh called Moses and spoke to him *from* the tent of meeting." The matter is resolved by Numbers 1:1, which states, "Yahweh spoke to Moses in the wilderness of Sinai, *in* the tent of meeting."

What changed?

Leviticus 1–7 describes divinely ordained sacrifices while Leviticus 8 narrates God's gift of the priesthood and Aaron's ordination. After Leviticus 8, Moses—along with Aaron—has access to God's presence. "Moses and Aaron went into the tent of meeting, and when they came out they blessed the people" (Leviticus 9:23 ESV).

OH, THE PLACES YOU'LL GO!

Those of us who love to travel feel our hearts skip with great joy when someone says, "Pack your bags!" In no time at all, we're packed and ready for adventure. Where will it be this time? Toledo? Tennessee? Timbuktu? Do I need my passport? My compass? My canteen? Then, in a flash, we're off—in the car, on a train, or flying in a 747 jet plane.

That's how Moses ends the Book of Exodus. He orders the Israelites to gather their goods, saddle up their horses, and get ready to ride.

Yahweh's speech in Exodus 34:6–7 results in Moses bowing low in reverent worship and humbly petitioning for Israel's forgiveness. Divine absolution results in obedient Israelites who gladly bring offerings and participate in the construction of Yahweh's tabernacle—a place of worship and atonement. In its closing scene, the Book of Exodus ends with the glory of Yahweh tabernacling in the midst of His people, and with "all the house of Israel" (Exodus 40:38 ESV) gazing upon Yahweh's fire and cloud in all their journeys.

Did you catch that? The book ends with the word *journeys*. It's travel time!

While the Book of Exodus opens looking back—"These are the names of the sons of Israel who came to Egypt with Jacob, each with his household" (Exodus 1:1 ESV)—it closes looking forward, "For the cloud of Yahweh was upon the tabernacle by day, and fire was in it by night, in the sight of the whole house of Israel, in all their journeys" (Exodus 40:38). The twelve households of Jacob's sons (Exodus 1:1–5), heirs of the covenant promises and blessing of the patriarchs, have become the singular "house of Israel" (Exodus 40:38 ESV). Yahweh will lead them to the land of promise and dwell there with His people throughout their generations.

Today

God still says, "Pack your bags!" God still commands, "Get ready to travel ardently and resolutely to the promised land."

Today.

But we're inclined to travel down another avenue called "Someday." I did, when my three children were in elementary school. My self-talk went like this:

"Someday, when my children are grown, things are going to be much better. The garage won't be full of bikes and trikes and broken kites. I'll be able to park my car in the garage, get out, and not stumble over tennis balls, basketballs, baseballs, footballs, and soccer balls. Someday."

"Someday, when my children are grown, the sink won't be full of sticky dishes. The garbage disposal won't be clogged with rubber bands and spoons. The refrigerator won't be stuffed with empty jelly jars and nine different kinds of fruit juice."

"Someday, when my children are grown, the car windows will be free of fingerprints, tongue licks, footprints, and dog tracks. [Nobody knows how dog tracks got on the car windows. The investigation is still ongoing!] Someday, when the kids are grown, the back seat of the van won't be declared a national disaster area and I won't sit on crayons ever again. *Someday.*"

What a miserable way to live.

Don't leave Egypt and begin heading to the Promised Land *someday.*

God rescued Israel from the clutches of Pharaoh, from the waters of the Red Sea, from thirst and hunger in the wilderness, from Aaron's golden calf, and from overwhelming guilt and remorse. He did it because He's Yahweh—the gracious and compassionate God. Then He came down into the tabernacle to lead His people to a land flowing with milk and honey. This is *our* story. This is *our* song, so we praise our Savior, all the day long.

But how?

Saddle up, buckle up, pack up, and get moving into God's promises.

Today.